MEDIA MANAGEMENT

Bogusław Nierenberg

MEDIA MANAGEMENT

A COMPARATIVE ANALYSIS
OF EUROPEAN AND AMERICAN SYSTEMS

JAGIELLONIAN UNIVERSITY PRESS

Publication subsided by the Faculty of Management and Social Communication of the Jagiellonian University and the Faculty of Media and Advertisement Management of the Insitute of Culture of the Jagiellonian University

Reviewer
prof. dr hab. Beata Glinka

Translation
Michelle Atallah

Cover design
Agnieszka Winciorek

ISBN 978-83-233-3990-8
ISBN 978-83-233-9391-7 (e-book)

www.wuj.pl

Jagiellonian University Press
Editorial Offices: Michałowskiego 9/2, 31-126 Kraków
Phone: +48 12 663 23 81, +48 12 663 23 82, Fax: +48 12 663 23 83
Distribution: Phone: +48 12 631 01 97, Fax: +48 12 631 01 98
Cell Phone: + 48 506006 674, e-mail: sprzedaz@wuj.pl
Bank: PEKAO SA, IBAN PL 80 1240 4722 1111 0000 4856 3325

For my wife and sons

Contents

Part 3

Introduction

It seems obvious and trivial to state that the basic determinant of the contemporary world is its mediality. Meanwhile, the platitude of some phenomenon is, in no way, synonymous with its common understanding. Mediality does not stand for the knowledge of its governing rights either. It appears that the case is similar with media management. Europe, including Poland, differs in this respect from the United States. One of the weaknesses of the Polish economic and social situation, for example, results from the inability to govern. In Poland it is the doctor who manages a hospital and the actor who is in charge of the theater. Obviously, it could be both the doctor and the actor, provided that they possess the relevant competency in scope of management. For management is not arcane knowledge. It can be learned. Media management can be learned as well.

The aim of this monograph is to compare scientific output in the scope of media management; focusing on the United States as well as on European countries, primarily Poland, and sharing the results of the research which I have been conducting for many years. From my point of view, in order to understand the essence of contemporary media management, there are two statements by Peter Drucker which are crucial to consider. First: "information shall always be a basic resource of the 21st century, and, the second: the more common the information, the more valuable." In so far as the first maxim seems to be quite commonly accepted, although the consequences of such a statement are not always brought to one's attention, the latter demolishes the foundations of traditional economic knowledge. In classic economics, it is assumed that the rarer good, the more precious it is and vice versa. The universal availability of a given good lowers its price. However, research by P. Drucker contradicts this thesis. In this book I have attempted to clarify this apparent contradiction by media dualism described in 1989 by Robert Picard and my own formula of "media buttons (informational)" which made it possible to comprehend the paradox captured by P. Drucker's findings. An explanation of these problems is included in Chapters 2 and 3.

In this thesis, I have assumed systemic methodology for the purpose of describing phenomena related to media management. According to systemic methodology, the phenomena under investigation should be perceived as a unity indirectly or directly, because – as it seems – this kind of perception of reality makes it possible to express the essence of a given question, not only its structure. Russell Ackoff [1974: 68] claimed that systemic behaviors are shaped both by the environment and are created by it as well. Improvement of the environment along with an increase of the influence on systems which it includes, requires each system to account for everything that enables to improve both the environment and themselves.

While describing the investigated phenomena I was careful not to lose sight of three key questions, essential for their systemic comprehension: 1. Why do I see what I see? 2. Why are things the way they are? 3. Why do things tend to change? These seemingly trivial questions not only describe the structure of the investigated problem, but also make it possible to inquire into the essence of the problem. Unfortunately, many researchers call the structure description a system which appears to be a methodological overuse. A positive instance in this scope is provided by a monograph by Daniel Halin and Paolo Mancini, entitled "Comparing Media. Three Models of Media and Politics." Its authors did not merely limit themselves to depicting investigated structures but attempted to delve deeper into the essence of the described phenomena. They asked questions that were substantial from the systemic methodology point of view, reached deep into the traditions of given systems in order to understand their sense and discover correlations between the described objects. Systemic research is strenuous and arduous, yet it enables us to reach the very core of the investigated phenomena and formulate conclusions concerning their essence.

In this monograph I offer clear definitions regarding the described problems in the European grounds, focusing on the Polish problems in particular. The notion of "media management" that has been adopted from the English language has two meanings according to commonly accepted assumptions: 1. "media management"; 2. "management in the media". In the case of the first meaning, it concerns not only all levels of management (mega, mezzo and micro), but also ways of influencing media activities (media organizations) by means of various normalizations (e.g. legal), or regulators of media markets, but also public or commercial media use for other purposes (e.g. in advertising and social campaigns which in general take place by means of different media). However, when discussing the second meaning under the term of "management in the media" one should understand all decisive processes concerning media organizations themselves. These might include activities examined both in functional conceptualization (referring to specific actions that contribute to management), procedural (referring to planning and monitoring of the process itself) or structural (concerning the construction of the very organization). Consultations carried out among scholars connected with this

research area are more conducive to refer to the notion of "media management" as a wider notion in comparison to "management in the media", being of
a more narrow meaning. The notion of "management in the media" is already
included in "media management." The very establishment of such notions as
"human resource management," "quality management," "knowledge management," etc. is without significance in the Polish language.

While describing the examined phenomena, I was trying not to lose sight
of three of them for the systemic "quality management," "knowledge management," etc. and it is in this perception of the notion of "media management"
that has been the subject of analysis and scientific review in this monograph.

Chapter 1 outlines the origins of management science along with detailed
science, including media – as a developing sub-discipline which seems to be of
growing importance due to the scope of the described phenomenon, namely
the media in the contemporary world. The humanistic conceptualization of
management sciences has also been indicated, adding up to the Polish specification of classifying scientific disciplines.

Chapter 2 is devoted to systemic methodology which, in the author's opinion, offers useful research tools for the purpose of describing media management. This chapter describes various systemic concepts as well as media systems. The fundamental publications in this field, such as, *Four Theories of the
Press* by Fred Siebert, Theodore Peterson and Wilbur Schramm or the already
mentioned *Comparing Media Systems: Three Models of Media and Management* by Daniel Hallin and Paolo Mancini were cited. References were also
made to the achievements of Polish researchers on this subject. Within this
regard, an analysis of media systems until now unexamined was offered in the
conceptualization proposed by D. Hallin and P. Mancini, including the Polish
media system. The concept of a Triangle of Media Powers has also been mentioned [Nierenberg 2007].

In Chapter 3, key for the considerations included in this monograph, theoretical concepts related to media management were indicated and on this
basis a new conceptualization of this process was offered, taking into consideration the paradox of P. Drucker's findings which suggested that the more
common the information, the more valuable it becomes. According to classical analysis such a statement of position would be a contradiction of basic
economic laws, according to which the rarer a good, the more precious it
is. An examination of this paradox is included in this chapter, based on the
accomplishments of R. Picard, one of the most distinguished economics researchers in the world. Picard points at the dual nature of media enterprises,
and based on his own research concerning media markets and their various
aspects in the context of media management, including the Triangle of Media
powers concept. Moreover, this chapter indicates that information is possible

or even has to be managed. An overview of the theoretical concepts of media management, including the systemic approach has become the basis of this ascertainment.

This part of the thesis indicates that when it comes to contemporary legal status, Polish public media management needs to use two purposes: commercial and public interest, as this media has yielded a form of commercial law companies which are inherently profit-oriented. On the other hand, Polish public media are now subject to the Broadcasting Act which describes public interest (mission), and the executor of which is the National Broadcasting Council (KRRiT – Polish regulator of electronic media market). Moreover, this chapter points to consequences of such a legal status for the way of managing public media in Poland.

Chapter 4 studies systemic and economic aspects of information which for many years were the domain of IT specialists. Occasionally, this information has been of interest to economists, sociologists, conduct experts and political scientists. Meanwhile, Daniel Bell or P. Drucker indicates this information as a primary resource of the present times. This fact has given rise to uncommon economic and social consequences. It has been of tremendous importance for media markets, e.g. the fact that information as a resource has become the basis of network-type organizations.

Chapter 5 describes the economic aspects of media management. Denis McQuail referred to media as a "business like no other". In order to help our reader understand the concerns examined in this chapter, research by R. Picard and others indicating the dualism of media organizations has been included. This research indicates that media enterprises deliver not only media content but are also capable of drawing one's attention – an extremely valuable resource in the contemporary world. In effect, media organizations offer their products in two markets at a time: the market of media services and the market of advertising.

Furthermore, Chapter 5 sheds light on various types of media markets, ways of managing the media organization finances, as well as new economic phenomena appearing in media markets by means of digitization and the new media. For example, Chris Anderson's *Long Tail Economics* concept. The issue of financing public media, a problem that seems to extend beyond Poland was discussed as well.

Chapter 6 is devoted to describing advertisement management. Advertisements are an inseparable element of the media market, constituting the basis of revenue for many media organizations. The origins of advertising have been pointed out as an essential element of the market communication process. The development of advertising is briefly described along with its most essential aims and functions. Also, mechanisms governing the activity of advertising agencies together with ways of building advertising campaigns are described in this chapter. Following the lead of two specific advertising campaigns, the factors influencing either success or failure of these campaigns were analyzed. Moreover, the manners of studying how advertising is perceived by the recipient was also indicated. The size of the auditorium of individual media – whether of the old or the new type – is a key element, preordaining the placing of advertising budgets in a particular medium. It is indicated that the most efficient method of testing in the case of advertising campaigns probably involves investigating them by means of a mini-market. There are three mini-markets of this type in the world, two in the USA and one in Europe. The author of this monograph investigated such a unit in the city of Haßloch, Germany.

Chapter 7 contains a description of human resource management in media organizations. It focuses on two essential professional groups: managers (media pilots) and journalists. For many decades journalism served as a kind of social mission, while nowadays it is simply becoming a media profession. This process was described, among others by Ryszard Kapuściński, a notable Polish journalist who pointed out that the mission of the journalistic profession terminated the moment business people understood that information is a commodity that yields profit. It seems that R. Kapuściński was one of the last "journalists" in the classical understanding of this profession. In the contemporary world, one notices growing demand for "media-workers," with decreasing demand for journalists. In order to enhance the findings presented in this chapter, a case study is cited. With reference to media pilots one used examples of Greg Dyke (the former CEO of British the BBC) and of Kamil Durczok (the editor-in-chief of the news program of the *Fakty* on the Polish station TVN).

Strategies of media enterprises and value creation are discussed in Chapter 8. Here, the basics of value chain creation in media organizations are pointed out along with basic determinants which should be taken into consideration while creating the strategy of media organizations, i.a.: globalization of media markets; change in the structure of media industry; informational revolution as well as growing customer demands. These determinants are connected with two essential phenomena: digitization and convergence. Thanks to these phenomena we have been witnessing a communication revolution the after-effects of which are difficult to predict. We may only presume some trends; however, it is hard to predict the final shape of these processes. In this chapter the formation of the value chain as well as elements which comprise this value are described. An essential element here is the identification of the needs of particular "stakeholders."

Chapter 9 addresses borders of media freedom. Deontological codes are recalled, and cases when good manners get infringed upon are discussed, which,

for accused people or institutions often have the dimension of personal tragedies. It is highly astounding that in Poland so little time is devoted to the educational process of future journalists and the ethical foundations of this profession. The chapter also deals with the phenomenon of media "bootlegging".
The young generation in particular (of course this cannot be generalized to all
young people) does not see anything unethical in usurping the effects of someone else's talent or intellectual work if it takes place over the Internet. Moreover,
in this chapter, I point out how big the challenge for media managers is and
will be in striving to match the ethical requirements as in the world of modern
media, the limits of good manners and taste are being crossed far too often. This
seems to result mainly from the pursuit of profit. A highly characteristic example
can be drawn from the movie "The Paper". Its protagonist, Tony Hackett (star-
ring Michael Keaton), a reporter of a city division of the New York daily "The
Sun" is striving to explain the murder in which two young African-Americans
are the main suspects. Hackett doubts their guilt. In one scene he asks his boss:
– "What if they're innocent" "Taint them today, make them look good on Satur-
day. Everybody's happy." – replies the chief editor (portrayed by Glenn Close).
The reasons for such a statement are to be found not only in the pursuit after
profit but also in the feebleness of academies that educate journalists.

In Chapter 10, the close of this monograph, potential trends and directions of media industry development, as well as challenges waiting for those
who will be managing media organizations within the following years, are discussed. Every anticipation is burdened with some potential pitfall; however,
in a situation of the dynamic development of the media industry in such turbulent surroundings, this pitfall might be so big that in a several the prognos-
ticator may be subject to ridicule. It may end up like the case of the French
Academy of Sciences, which at the end of the 19th century predicted that Paris
was going to become completely impassable within several years. And it is
not even due to a large number of hackneys but to a huge amount of horse
heap with nobody to dispose of it. Who would have predicted at that time that
a slow, noisy car was going to displace elegant hackneys? Perhaps it is already
knocking at the door or even already exists. The equivalent of this may be
an invention which deprives many contemporary media-related deliberations
of rationality. Therefore, having made such a stipulation I believe that within
the coming years, media functioning and, what follows, their management are
still going to be determined by: digitization and convergence, globalization,
the new media, virtual networking sites, rivalry of network organizations with
hierarchal-type organizations and phenomena. The adverse effects of which
can be already noticed nowadays: technological and informational exclusion.

It appears that within the following years, media management shall become
an essential sub-discipline of management sciences. It is probably going to be

the result of processes which have undergone identification in this monograph and which shall determine (or have already determined) the course of events. By means of the media, a communication revolution is taking place, consequences of which are difficult to imagine. For the first time in world history – as remarked by M. Castells [1996: 36] – media organizations are gaining dominance over hierarchal-type organizations. Undoubtedly, media management shall be determined by information properties, the basic resource controlled by the media. Another unknown is the fate of public media which in Europe (including Poland) should be one of the pillars of civic society but has become in many countries (including Poland as well) a political prey (party which wins election takes over influences in public media). However, the continually strong position of public electronic media in Europe is one of basic determinants which distinguishes European and American markets.

This monograph was created on the basis of the monograph "Media Management. Systemic Approach" published in 2011 by Jagiellonian University Press. Dear reader, the monograph you are currently reading, was primarily meant to be updated. However, in the course of works so many issues underwent changes that the change in the title of the book was inevitable, as in its present shape it serves as a comparative analysis of American and European (mainly Polish) systems of media management. Therefore, I would like to thank my colleagues as well as all researchers whose remarks have contributed to the final shape of this monograph. Most of all, however, I wish to thank Professor Bożena Mierzejewska for her invaluable help while giving the book its final shape.

Bogusław Nierenberg

Management is about human beings. Its task is to make people capable of joint performance, to make their strengths effective and their weaknesses irrelevant.

This is what organization is all about, and it is the reason that management is the critical, determining factor.

Peter F. Drucker

Part 1

Chapter 1. Origins of Management Sciences

Management as a subject of scientific interest dates back to the end of the 19th century. However, this does not mean that it was only then when humanity learned how to manage. The very idea of managerial processes is as old as civilization itself. Management, as a specific set of actions leading to a particular aim, was not of special interest because on the one hand, it used to be perceived as something natural, a thing that does not require any clarification, and on the other, it was not until the end of the 19th century that humanity was faced with the problem of the lack of possibility for further development. Humanity vividly resembled a statement made by Marshall McLuhan: "Fish don't know water exists till beached [McLuhan 2001: 57]." This statement refers to communication processes, but what is most striking about this statement is McLuhan's accuracy regarding the previous handling of managerial processes.

1.1. Management from a historical perspective

Each civilization requires the use of processes currently referred to as management. It seems that until the beginning of the 20th century, the set of actions that comprised management were not defined by the use of this term. Previously, it was the sentiment of McLuhan's simile that was applied in reference to such cases. At the same time one may say that humanity, in this respect, resembled Mr. Jourdain by Molier, a person unaware that he has been speaking only in prose all his life [Molier 1951: 29]. Indeed, in order to raise any edifice or undertake any enterprise, it would be essential to plan it above all, organize and manage, and finally to control whether the enterprise has been carried out according to the undertaken plan. In a word, one must perform actions which, according to one of the definitions, are referred to as functions of management [Griffin 1999: 37]. One has to agree with these researchers who demonstrate that the phenomenon of organization and the management process are a few thousand years older than the reflection upon them [Griffin 1999: 37].

Due to its complex nature, management has been defined and understood differently by various social groups, including managers themselves. Peter Pringle and Michael Starr draw attention to the fact that management is not a strange thing, as it is derived from an immense diversity of roles and responsibilities held by managers in an organization [Pringle, Starr 2006: 19–21]. The definition of diversification may be created by researchers of management processes themselves. Peter Schoderbek, Richard Cosier and John Aplin, in a general way, indicate that management is a "process of achieving organizational aims [Pringle, Jennings, Longenecker 1988: 8]." By contrast, Charles Pringle, Daniel Jennings and Justin Longenecker point out that "management is a process of obtaining and connecting human, financial, information and commodity resources to obtain primary objectives connected with manufacturing particular products or services which are required by particular social groups [Schoderbek, Cosier, Aplin 1988: 8]." Other researchers suggest that management should be defined by functions related to managers' actions. As an example, some of the actions are classified by Howard as: managing, coordinating and influencing the function of an organization in a way which makes it possible to obtain expected results and increase productivity [Carlisle 1987: 10]. Wayne Mondy, Robert Holmes and Edwin Flippo extend these functions and emphasize the importance of the human factor. In their opinion, "management can be defined as a process of planning, organizing, influencing and controlling in order to achieve organizational goals by means of coordinated use of human and matter-of-fact resources [Mondy, Holmes, Flippo 1983: 6]." Along with this definition is another proposed by Ricky Griffin, according to whom management is a "set of actions (including planning and decision-making, organizing and leadership, i.e. managing people and controlling) directed at organization resources (human, financial, substantive and informational) and performed with a view to achieving goals of given organization in an efficient and effective way [Griffin 1999: 38]."

From a historical point of view it can be ascertained that it was 6000 BC when groups of human beings got involved in the implementation of gigantic enterprises. Construction of Egyptian pyramids, leading the Jews from Egyptian captivity, construction of Roman roads and aqueducts or the Great Wall of China required people capable of managing in a very efficient way. R. Griffin indicates that management processes have been shaped under the influence of three major forces [Griffin 1999: 68–69]:

- social
- economic
- political.

By social forces we mean norms and values that are characteristic for a given culture. For a long period in history, organizational managers treated their workers with disdain; it was the norm. Aristotle, one of the greatest philosophical minds, perceived slavery as a normal condition. Norms and values undergo changes parallel with the passage of time. Cornelius Vanderbilt treated workers employed at his plants with contempt. He resolved strikes using verbal methods and did not care about public opinion ("Public opinion? To hell with public opinion"). Today, making little of public opinion would be deadly for any organization. This primitive understanding of social forces has evolved over the years into an understanding of complex dependencies that take place in organizations such as leadership, motivation, human resources management [Griffin 1999: 68–69]. A notion of organizational culture was created as well. Geert Hofstede defined culture as collective programming of the mind that distinguishes one social group from others [Hofstede, Hofstede 2007: 16–19].

Economic forces constitute another factor that influences the management shaping process as seen from a historical approach. They were connected with given economic systems and development trends. Under the influence of economic muscle, various fields of management developed, including environment analysis, strategic planning and organization designing [Donaldson 1988: 277–298].

R. Griffin explains that "government's policy concerning regulation of business activity plays a crucial role in the way in which organizations are being managed" and that the "theory of management pertaining to companies functioning within heavily regulated branches, such as services of the institutions of public utility, differs a lot from the theory concerning [...] companies active in less regulated branches [Griffin 1999: 68–69]."

These three forces – social, economic and political – resulted in certain manifestations of management appearing in some areas in ancient times. In order to construct large buildings in ancient Egypt, at least three management functions were required: planning, organizing and controlling.

It was five thousand years ago when the Sumerians enacted their legal regulations concerning the way in which a country should be governed. They built ziggurats and created pictographic writing that eventually evolved into the cuneiform; They established and developed astronomy, mathematics, medicine and literature.

The Babylonians had a superbly organized country, whom in times of Hammurabi, legislated a written code including 282 norms that were enclosed in the following chapters: judicature, violations against property, land and development, merchants and mercantile, women, marriage, family property and inheritance, assault and battery, remuneration for professional services and compensations, agriculture, lease stakes and the sale of slaves.

It seems that Alexander the Great owed his brilliant military successes to his wield of army staff structure organization and conducting warfare. The Roman Empire serves as an example of superbly developed structures that were so strong that even an insane person, standing at the front of the aforementioned structures (Caligula is a great example in this case) would have been incapable of destroying them. The Roman Empire owed its strength to notably developed structures which facilitated the circulation of information. The mail service that served the Roman Empire stands for an instantiation of one of the most efficient organizations of the ancient world [Bajka 2007: 11].

Traces of old organizational structures of ancient Rome can be admired not only while admiring buildings as reminders of remote past centuries, but also when looking at designs, as many European cities were built on the basis of old Roman camps (*castrum romanum*). Trier and Strasburg represent operative and management efficiency indicative of ancient Roman capability.

The Chinese Empire used to be managed in a similarly great manner, the proof of which may be found in the teachings of Confucius. He was not only a Chinese clerk but a philosopher and a teacher. Around 500 BC, his students transcribed his knowledge, including information regarding management. At the basis of this knowledge one may find the following assumptions: 1. unequal social relationships are a normal thing; 2. the family stands for a model of every organization; 3. people should treat their neighbors just as they would like to be treated themselves; 4. it is essential for people to be trained, work hard and not to spend more than necessary.

The first European references pertaining to management appeared in ancient Greece. It was Socrates who used to write about practice management methods. Plato indicated virtues of specialization that immediately lead to a conclusion regarding who should perform duties in a given country. He writes *expressis verbis*: "Then what is the next question? Must we not ask who are to be rulers and who subjects? – Certainly. – There can be no doubt that the elder must rule the younger. – Clearly. – And that the best of these must rule. – That is also clear [Plato 2002: 156–157]."

By contrast, Aristotle distinguished components of each system which he indicated in Book IV *Politics* as: deliberating, governing and judicial [Aristotle 2002: 197–198]. Aristotle stated it in the following way: "All constitutions have three elements (…) There is (1) one element which deliberates about public affairs; secondly (2) that concerned with the magistrates – the question being, what they should be, over what they should exercise authority, and what should be the mode of electing to them; and thirdly (3) that which has judicial power [Aristotle 2002: 197–198]." Therefore, the priority of authorship attributed to Montesquieu referring to tripartite division in a given country is unjustified.

In Book 7 it is the same Aristotle who points to the main task of the state. The major indicator of state actions should be happiness and welfare of the man [Aristotle 2002: 305]. This theological approach is, for Aristotle, the core and sense of human actions, including government as well, "...for the wise man, like the wise state, will necessarily regulate his life according to the best end. [...] is best for each individual, and for states and for mankind collectively [Aristotle 2002: 306]." It appears that Aristotle's message refers to organizations on every level, not only the highest.

Book 8 of *Politics*, Aristotle denotes the chief tasks of the state as follows: defense, government, judicature, godly duty. Regarding the governing of the state Aristotle wrote: "...in the order prescribed by nature, who has given to young men strength and to older men wisdom. Such a distribution of duties will be expedient and also just, and is founded upon a principle of conformity to merit... [Aristotle 2002: 323]." It seems that in contemporary Poland the majority of people in charge forgot about the wise advice given by Aristotle and Plato. It is sufficient to rummage among job advertisements in any newspaper to become convinced that most define available roles as part of a "young dynamic team," as if all adults have left Poland. Although numerous studies prove that elderly people have less impressive qualifications than the young, they possess something inaccessible for the young as well – experience.

R. Griffin points out several objective reasons that caused a delay in a few centuries before such a thing as scientific reflection concerning management came into existence. For centuries, actions connected to what we now refer to as management used to be mandated by effectiveness constraints. It was possible for the state as an organization to impose taxes in virtually any amount, and on the whole the state did not have to account for cases of possible wasting of money. Secondly, until the end of the 17th century, there were very few organizations. Their immense increase was related to the Industrial Revolution. Thirdly, it was survival rather than development or even expansion that characterized the beginnings of organizations. As an example one may point out the family as an institution, whose primary concern was survival [Griffin 1999: 71].

Technical inventions along with new technologies, which were applied in the 19th century, led to the common-sense way of solving organizational problems of insufficiency. The first attempt to establish a scientific study concerning problems related to managing organizations was the formulation issued in 1832 by Charles Babbage, a professor of mathematics at Cambridge University, entitled "On the Economy of Machinery and Manufactures," in which he emphasizes the contradiction between developing technology and obsolete forms of labor organizations [Bielski 1997: 7]. The group of management pioneers included Robert Owen, who was probably the first recognized first to recognize the meaning of human resources in an organization. Before him, workers were treated similarly to machines or technical equipment. R. Owen is frequently called a utopian socialist; however, his accounts regarding human resources resulted from sheer economic calculations. In his factory, Lew Lenark Mills introduced what were for those times revolutionary solutions. He assumed that better treatment of workers would result in an increase of productivity. Owen was ahead of his epoch with his ideas. His ideas were returned too much later, along with the shaping of behavioral approach to management. Equally interesting experiments were carried out at the time by James Watt and Matthew R. Boulton. The subject of their research was inter alia, location of the factory depending on the demand, and market research itself [Mikołajczyk 1997: 32].

1.2. Management as a scientific discipline

Several of the most general definitions of management that emphasize diverse aspects of this process have already been connoted. Meanwhile, the birth of management as a scientific discipline was of exceptionally utilitarian nature.

Social development at the turn of 19th and 20th centuries required a continuous increase in production. Depletion of extensive methods resulted in the rise of pressure to find any new ways to increase production. Researchers called on the analysis of management processes as a potential premise that may foster economic growth. Sooner or later, each need would lead to those willing to manage it. Frederic W. Taylor was the first person who managed to turn management into a scientific discipline. He is also considered to be the originator of the notion of "scientific management." It was in 1912 when Taylor received an invitation to the U.S. Congress in order to familiarize deputies with the essence of his research, which proves how important management processes became at the time. It does seem that at the birth of the discipline known as management, one did not distinguish between processes directed to business and public activity. The notion of *management principle* was used for the first time by Elihu Root, a mathematician at Hamilton College, and subsequently a Nobel Prize laureate, who as a secretary in the government of Theodore Roosevelt understood the importance of efficient management for proper functioning of the state. In his exact case the *management principles* referred to a catalogue of cases linked to the modernization of the American Army [Nierenberg 2007: 87]. Peter Drucker, to the modernization of the most distinguished management processes researchers of the 20th century claimed that 90% of problems that an organization deals with is of a general nature, whereas the remaining 10% is determined by mission, history, culture and terminology specific for particular organization [Drucker 2000: 8].

Two trends were shaped by classical management, the first scientific approach in the field: 1. scientific management; 2. administrative management. To put it simply, one can ascertain that insofar as the first trend focused on increasing the effectiveness of the organization by streamlining the worker's jobs, the second one indicated the aspects of operations of people in charge of an organization, who can contribute to the improvement of the entire organization. F. Taylor and other representatives of this trend (Henry Gantt, Harrington Emerson, Frank Gilbreth, Lilian Gilbreth and others) postulated for labor fragmentation, the effect of which was an increase in output. In turn, Henri Fayol elaborated the rules of efficient managing, in which he showed cohesion of bringing out commands and unity of leadership. His accomplishments were the result of his own experiences in the French industry. Fayol was the first to point out specific managerial functions related to: planning, organizing, leadership and controlling [Pringle, Starr 2006: 4]. To this day, most researchers of processes concerning organization and management rely on those systems. In the administrative trend it is also essential to mention achievements of Max Weber, whose research concerning bureaucracy established the foundation of the contemporary theory of organization. It is also essential to

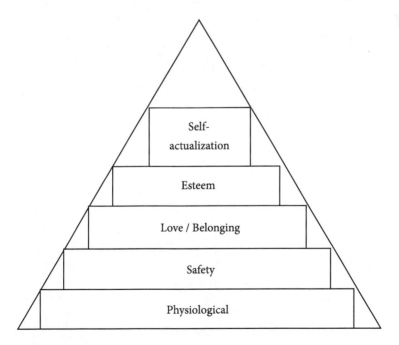

Figure 1. Maslow's hierarchy of needs

Source: Own study based on Maslow 1990: 72–102.

recognize achievements of Lyndalla Urwick, who attempted to merge findings in scientific management with the output of H. Fayol and other representatives of the administrative mainstream [Griffin 1999: 77].

The behavioral approach arose as an opposition to classical management. The reasons for its inception are because of the decrease in work output at the time. Fragmentation of labor proposed by F. Taylor and other representatives of classical management, in fact, increased productivity; however, after some time it stopped increasing and even decreased at times. Factory owners were seeking ways to explain this phenomenon. Hence, research by Elton Mayo, Hugo Münsterberg, and Fritz J. Roethlisberger ensued, out of which it unequivocally emerged that a man, being a part of an organization, is not and must not be treated as a mere cog or addition to a machine. In this way, the *human relations* movement was born, representatives of which, such as Mary P. Follet or Chester I. Barnard explicitly deal with the concept of an "economic man (*homo oeconomicus*)," popularized by theoreticians of the classical approach [Pringle, Starr 2006: 7]. This approach includes works of Douglas McGregor who formulated the X and Y theories, as well as the theory proposed by Abraham H. Maslow in 1943 that said the engine of human action includes needs which are ordered in a given hierarchy. At its bottom of the hierarchy one finds physiological needs, above that, respect and belonging, and at the very top of this pyramid is the need for self-actualization. (Figure 1. Pyramid of needs according to A.H. Maslow).

The complement to the X and Y theories by D. McGregor was theory Z proposed by William G. Ouchie in 1981 [Derrick 2003: 90] which was an attempt to adapt Japanese management methods in America. A description of a General Motors assembly plant in the town of Flint, Michigan served as the canvas of its creation. The theory's essence boils down to the phrase that "engaged workers are the key to an increased productivity [Ouchie 1981: 4]." The book by W.G. Ouchie entitled *Theory Z. How American Business Can Meet the Japanese Challenge* became a bestseller in the American market and as a result, many American enterprises began to emulate Japanese companies, though this management model was imposed on a completely different organizational culture. Thus, some elements were overlooked while others were copied. For instance, workers were allowed to perform different tasks instead of one during a single shift. Trust or concern towards employees became compelling factors of management. As an example, working conditions were improved, workers' sense of self-esteem was enhanced, and social relations in the company were developed and favored [Derrick 2003: 90].

It is worthwhile to note that manifold attitudes towards management do not have to exclude one another nor be mutually contradictory. The systemic approach serves as an attempt to integrate different mainstreams of management, treating an organization as a peculiar system of mutually interrelated elements functioning in unity [Ackoff 1973]. Contrary to closed systems, open systems interact with the environment, and a common feature of each system is the phenomenon of synergy, meaning that within any system two cooperating subsystems may achieve more than a sum of production of each of them working independently [Griffin 1999].

It is the situational approach that plays a crucial role in management sciences, According to which every organization is one of its kind. Hence, representatives of the situational approach movement claimed that universal managerial tools do not exist. Supporters of the situational approach concerning management affirm that the behavior of management should be determined by a particular situation and not by universal dogmas. Merely talent, knowledge and experience of managers should be able to address challenges brought to a given organization by every single situation [Griffin 1999].

Therefore, the question is what challenges will be brought forth by the contemporary world that will determine management in the 21st century? Three substantial determinants are: globalism, unforcedness and networking. Each of these factors impose completely new behavior on organizations, which is not exactly predictable. In this way, management becomes nebulous and uncertain. Gary Hamel even writes about the end of management [Hamel 2008: 9] and implies that the impeachment of old paradigms must naturally lead to a quest to look for new ones: "Management belongs to multi-paradigm disciplines. The disciplines are of particular importance for managers as they include ranges of practices or guidelines which define behaviors and indicate the direction in which one should head toward [Grudzewski et al. 2012: 20]." The same authors refer to these paradigms as systems of management perceived in conceptualization proposed by Robert Kaplan and David Norton who understand this notion as "an integrated set of processes and tools that are used by an enterprise to develop their own strategy, its translation into operational activities and in order to monitor and streamline their efficiency [Kaplan, Norton 1986: 64]."

The aforementioned authors indicate one idiosyncratic paradigm of contemporary times, *sustainability*. This notion is oftentimes associated with ecology; however, in the practice of management it stands for the ability of a company to be reborn again and again in a hyper-dynamic environment. They define *sustainability* as the "ability of an enterprise to continually: learn, adapt and develop, revitalize, reconstruct, reorient in order to maintain a sustainable and distinctive position in the market by offering an outstanding value to purchasers today and in the future (congruous with the paradigm of innovative growth), thanks to an organic variability constituting business models and resulting from creating new possibilities and aims and answering them, while balancing out interests of different groups [Grudzewski et al. 2012: 26–27]."

1.3. Management as a humanistic approach

Some researchers dealing with problems of management favor the opinion that – in the simplest terms – management in economic sciences relates to organizations inclined towards profit, but that the subjects of research in the case of management as a humanistic science are non-commercial organizations. It appears that such a depiction of the problem is not only trivial but also misleading, although some researchers perceive this division as fully justified. R. Griffin distinguishes organizations as either profit-oriented or not profit-oriented. He writes about the former: "a majority of our knowledge about management derives from large, profit-oriented organizations, as their existence for a long time has been dependent upon efficiency and effectiveness." In turn, regarding organizations that are not profit-oriented he states: "The basic role of an organization which is not profit-oriented are oftentimes such fugitive aims as: education, social services, public safety and leisure." According to Griffin such organizations are, e.g., the U.S. Postal Service, International Olympic Committee, scouting, art galleries, museums and systems of broadcasting stations [Griffin 1999: 58–61]. However, the humanistic approach to management seems to be a much more complex problem and is too difficult to be investigated as such a simple and common dichotomy.

Talcott Parsons goes a step further in his considerations. In his opinion, rational and longsighted management is deeply set in the culture of every nation, which creates frames for human needs, aspirations and desires. It is exactly culture that gives consideration to human actions (including management as well) and is favorable to adopting particular norms and values by individuals [Parsons 1969: 112–113].

Management from a humanistic approach places the human being at the center of the process as the subject and essence of the operation. As per this concept, it is not the production norms that lead to the achievement of goals that matter, but the man willing to fulfill them. Given that management is a migration through chaos, this systemic approach brings a sort of order to the "chaos," which does not mean that the human factor in a systemic approach is unimportant. Tadeusz Pszczołowski emphasizes that the "the theory of organization deals with organizations as systems comprising human beings equipped with apparatus, which are linked by certain bonds [Pszczołowski 1978: 150]." In turn, Marcin Bielski states that a "systemic interpretation of an organization (...) treats it as a system that behaves deliberately, i.e. is capable of correcting its aims, and even of their complete change and survive after accomplishing initially established aims [Bielski 1997: 73]." Bielski speculates about relations between culture and organizations, on the basis of research by Bronisław

Malinowski – one of the most distinguished Polish ethnologists and cultural anthropologists. Similar to most researchers dealing with the complexities of management, he claims that people organize themselves in order to achieve their goal. In every community, both primitive and civilized, organizational behaviors create structures with the institution as its basic unit. According to B. Malinowski, each cultural phenomenon is simultaneously an organizational phenomenon; however, it is hard to imagine an organization without diverse cultural expressions. Malinowski displayed that human beings, in contrast to other beings, created a new, secondary environment in order to fulfill their needs, which when "constantly reproduced and maintained is just a mere culture," is a means by which individuals reach their goals a standard of living that is higher than those of other animals. By means of a functional and institutional analysis Malinowski attempted to prove universality of cultural phenomena [Malinowski 1958: 29–52] (Figure 2: Fixed components of an institution according to Bronisław Malinowski).

This functional and institutional analysis made it possible to build a model which, according to Malinowski, explains the essence of organization by people. The primate principle – is a system of values which prejudges whether people are willing to organize or join already existing organizations. Personnel – is comprised of a group of people organized according to rules resulting from the division of work, job description, appointment of functions and power. Norms – technical skills, ethical orders, and customs accepted and applied by members of an organization or enforced. Material devices – material substrate resulting from the activity of an enterprise. Activity – specific conduct of organization members in accordance with established rules (every action leans back on the rules or the ideal). Function – a global outcome of an organization, deriving from an accepted principle and the applied algorithm [Malinowski 1958: 40–42].

Representatives of the humanistic approach in management rightfully notice that one must not apply a simplified, black and white image: economic management – bad, predatory, profit-oriented and humanistic management – positive, respecting people's interests, as the management end beneficiary, and not merely the means of achieving an economic objective (profit). This contorted black and white view has been appearing in reflections of management for at least 50 years. It is sufficient to recall the X and Y theory by Douglas McGregor, and those of Polish researchers Monika Kostera, Lech Witkowski or even Tadeusz Mendel, who used to write about humanizing the management processes [Malinowski 1958: 40–42]. After all, it seems that the development of an ontological understanding should be the aim of each man's activity. In this respect, profit is not necessarily anti-humanistic as profit allows an organization to last. Indeed, it is profit that generates new jobs. Nothing is purely good

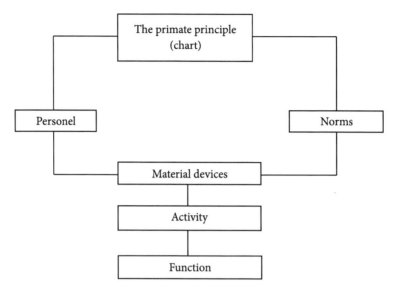

Figure 2. Fixed components of an institution according to B. Malinowski

Source: Malinowski 1958: 40–42.

or bad in itself. Theodor Fontane used to say, "*Alles kommt auf die Beleuch-tung an,*" (everything depends on the lighting). It appears that this thought of a German writer and poet perfectly expresses the gist of investigated problems that refer to management.

In the past, one demonstrated the historical conceptualization of management processes in general. From the standpoint of speculation included in this monograph, the humanistic perspective is of particular interest. The starting point for these considerations is the definition of management proposed by H. Fayol, stating that management stands for the art or practice of the rational use of different methods in order to reach a given goal. It is a criterion of effectiveness that is related to the concept of *homo oeconomicus.* Despite the notion of *oeconomicus,* it has a humanistic derivation, as it is connected with a breakthrough in European culture. It signalized a transition from a medieval theocracy into humanism which puts the human being at the center of all activities. The human, in turn, directed his reason towards nature.

When Adam Smith was writing his *An Inquiry into the Nature and Causes of the Wealth of Nations,* he respected not only human ability to use reason, but also its appreciation of moral values [Smith 2003]. Smith was also the author of *The Theory of Moral Sentiments* in which he introduced the notion of "empathizing."

The birth of capitalism gave rise to three attitudes towards being shaped by those managing the reality. The first of the attitudes was derived from ideals of

Protestantism and served as glorification of the man who does his own planning (*self-made man*). The second is a concept by Joseph Schumpeter meaning that creative entrepreneurs are the major lifeblood of the market. These two concepts were opposed by Thorstein Veblen, especially concerning the idle class. Admittedly, T. Veblen's views have been a source of argument for many varied attitudes and beliefs today (even so opposed as adherents of enlightened dictatorships and gender liberties); however, one may see this as an effort to promulgate civic virtues as a counterbalance to the rapacity of developing capitalism.

With the birth of scientific management at the turn of the 19th and 20th century, it seemed obvious that basing it on the rules of effectiveness was justified, as it is the only way to achieve an aim imposed by an organization. The managerial instruments was drawn by companies from economics and engineering. Those things able to be measured and calculated were of high importance: cost, profit, income, lost working hours, etc. Karol Adamiecki offered to harmonize working hours in such a way to make their loss as minimal as possible. However, contrary to F. W. Taylor's concept, his ideas related to rationalization of teamwork, and they resulted in the announcement of laws by Adamiecki in 1903: harmony of selection; harmony of operation; spiritual harmony. It is especially the third law that has a transparently humanistic context. Adamiecki claimed that it is necessary for an organization to have an emotional bond that connects cooperating people [Kurnal 1978: 408–425].

The classical and humanistic approaches to management are particularly visible in the contemporary media. Journalism exists on the one hand, a creative profession that requires creativity in solving different tasks, and market pressure and the pursuit of higher bars of viewership, audience rating and sales lies on the other. Ryszard Kapuściński served as a great illustration of this dichotomy, as he emphasized that he was a journalist, not a media worker, though he was sensible to changes undergoing in the media at the time [Nierenberg 2008]. It is a global dependency, characteristic not only of Europe or Poland. Similar conclusions have been reached by James W. Redmond who deals with the issues of management on American ground, especially regarding the humanistic mainstream. He also notices a conflict between "idealism" of active journalists and profit-oriented media organizations which employ them [Redmond 2006: 124]. Edward Murrow, one of the most well-known American radio and television journalists, used to finish his broadcast with the famous phrase "*good night, and good luck,*" which became his identification mark. At that time he ascertained that one of the basic problems concerning radio and television resulted from an attempt to combine three things: show business, advertising and information into one [Sperber 1986: 41], when in reality the things do not match at all. Consequently, being a manager in the

21st century is an ability to tie up these seemingly separate things (more widely about it in Chapter 6, Managers and Journalists). J. W. Redmond discusses that contemporary media organizations should possess the ability to combine the demands of upright journalism with commercial aspects of the media organizations' activity. The paramount premise becomes that of fulfilling consumer needs. It requires a detailed testing of auditorium and forming of an offer (formatting) in such a way that it caters to the needs of a specific group of viewers. Redmond vacillates as to how it is possible to maintain an independent opinion in contemporary America, the country where freedom of the press is a foundation, but where profit attained by a media organization is an overriding goal that enables the organization to last. This is particularly true when referring to journalistic opinion formulated against the general opinion [Redmond 2006: 126–128]. Perhaps it requires a renewed definition of media organizations and their purposes, as well as those of their stakeholders.

Media organizations ought to be creative in their nature. Conflict is an inseparable feature of creative organizations and each person has a different solution to this problem. M. P. Follet thought that conflict in an organization is created by differences in potentials, which may be favorable to the company itself. Additionally, there are general problems, or even global issues which are of high importance, especially in the case of media organizations. Therefore, overcoming inner discrepancies of media organizations as well as fostering strong external competition impose new ways of management. One of them may be for instance *management by walking around*. Managers' effort may be directed towards ensuring loyalty in relation to an organization, on advancing values essential for it, on continuous learning, on creating the strength of an organization by dispersion and decentralization. Such a set of activities favors the formation of an organizational culture with high competitiveness as one of its features. When managing a media organization in this manner, it is the human factor that seems to be the key agent. Talent, knowledge and skills, both of managers and employees of media organizations, may serve as factors that facilitate getting advantage over competition in a dramatically changing environment. Contemporary media, especially electronic ones, become supranational, with some gathering even a global dimension. A global Internet network is designed for this purpose, thanks to which even the most local medium receives the features of inclusiveness. On the basis of performed research, Leslie Sklair recognized that the essence of investigating globalization processes does not depend on analyzing civil and economic integration of nations. It depends rather on analyzing the manner in which companies become globalized and on examining the relations between companies becoming globalized and the emerging global elite [Sklair 2002]. For L. Sklair the starting point for these considerations was the three distinguishing concepts of globalization:

1. Nation states as a basic analytical unit,
2. Transnational practices and transnational forces and institutions,
3. Disappearance of nation states.

The most interesting aspect of L. Sklair's concept is the observation of the emerging global elite. It is particularly significant in relation to media organizations, as the product offered by them (without regard to the level of global offer) is of a particular nature. It might be, and frequently is, a tool of social influence or even manipulation. Therefore, one notices a particular responsibility on the part of media organizations, with people in charge in particular. In this context the concept of corporate social responsibility (CSR) in relation to media becomes especially valid. One of the first definitions of this notion, which still remains topical, was offered in the 1970s by Keith Davis. In his opinion, CSR means: "consideration by the company and answer to problems exceeding narrowly understood economic, technical and legal requirements in order to obtain social profits parallel to traditional economic profits [Kostera 2010: 45]." This definition requires some clarifications because according to the neoclassical theory of a company proposed by Milton Friedman, it contains a contradiction. Apologists of neoclassical theories claim that the main aim of each company should be the maximization of profits. Meanwhile, the introduction of the CSR category lowers the profits. And here we touch upon the dispute between adherents of neoliberal theories and their antagonists who affirm that it is improper to focus merely on economic aspects of enterprise activity and offer an idea based on the notion of stakeholders. One may define stakeholders as "each group or individual who can have influence on achieving its goals and who influences achieving its goals by organization [Freeman 1983: 88–106]." Kostera ascertains that the rules of corporate social responsibility majorly consist of the enterprise's undertaking to obey ethical codes, including rules of ethical conduct, and relating to the activities of this company [Kostera 2010: 49]. In this conceptualization the notion of CSR should be applied in case of media organizations in particular. The results of research by Picard and others related to creation of values in organizations, including media organizations, shall be presented in the same meaning in Chapter 8 (*Strategies of Media Organizations*).

In summing up the considerations included in this chapter, one should ascertain that the humanistic perspective with a systemic approach seems to be the most justified look at investigation into problems concerning management in media.

Discussion questions:

1. Discuss origins of management science.
2. Justify the statement of M. McLuhan: "Fish don't know water exists till beached".
3. Indicate differences in classical and humanistic approaches to management.

Chapter 2. Media Systems

Systematic methodology as a way of scientific research was born in the 1930s because of Ludwig von Bertalanffy, who introduced its framework during the course of a psychological seminar at the University of Chicago. However, his methodology was not completely original. Reference to the system concept can be found in the works of Gottfried W. Leibniz, Karl Marx, George W. F. Hegl, Vilfred Paret or Talcott Parsons, and even in the works of ancient philosophers. Aristotle is actually the author of a formulation that says: "In the case of all things which have several parts and in which the totality is not, as it were, a mere heap, but the whole is something beside the parts, there is a cause; for even in bodies contact is the cause of unity in some cases, and in others viscosity or some other such quality [Aristotle 2003: 337]." These words are commonly interpreted as key for systems theory, and denote that *completeness is more than a sum of components.*

2.1. Systemic conceptions

Ludwig von Bertalanffy should be considered the forerunner of the modern systemic method of research. In an article entitled *The Theory of Open Systems in Physics and Biology*, he offered that objects undergoing research should be treated as open systems, i.e. set of elements connected in such a way that they create a new entity standing out in the environment [Bertalanffy 1950: 23–29]. Open systems may be treated as the most general definition of a system. Bertalanffy himself was baffled by the simplicity and universality of the preferred research method. He wrote that if we define the notion of a system properly we will notice that there are models and rules that may be applied to generalized systems independently of their type, their constituents and forces acting on them [Bertalanffy 1984: 63]. Initially unappreciated, the general theory of systems soon gained its adherents. One of its admirers was Kenneth Boulding who wrote to Bertalanffy: "[…] I began with economy and social sciences, not with biology, I have reached more or less the same conclusion as you: that there are frameworks of the thing which I refer to as general empirical theory, or what in your excellent terminology is known as the general systems theory, which finds vast application in various disciplines [Bertalanffy 1984: 43]." In response to these commendations, it was ascertained that the general systems theory should become an important normative tool in science. The existence of a similarly structured law in various domains enables the use of simpler or better known models for analyzing phenomena that is more complicated and more difficult to explain [ibid.].

Boulding, while continuing his work upon a new theory, distinguished eight types of systems beginning with static ones, such as a stone, then to simple mechanisms like a loom, then to more complicated ones, such as actuators, and then to the level at which there is a separation of life from the inanimate matter, and finally to human and community. At this level he distinguished socio-cultural systems. Along with this classification, especially concerning the latter level, comes the affirmation of Leszek Krzyżanowski that the study of an organization and management encompasses "the highest rank of reality development: human society [Krzyżanowski 1992: 166–170]." His observations led him to overly humanistic conclusions. According to Krzyżanowski, the aim of his studies are not, as a matter of fact, social or socio-technical, cultural systems, etc., but "organizations created by people and for people [ibid.]." It seems that people should take advantage of the effects of proper choice and the adequate combination of all the subsystems included in a given system. Contributing to this connection, one achieves a synergistic result, i.e. obtainment of an effect that is larger than the effect that results from summing up elements constituting the system.

Here, one should indicate that the systemic approach, and particularly the synergy effect which is inseparable, is not the only "proper one." The Ringelmann effect denotes a phenomenon that is the opposite of the synergy effect. In the 19th century Ringelmann carried out an experiment which proved that a collective operation may bring smaller effects than those that result from a simple adding up of constituents. Ringelmann's experiment consisted in measuring the strength by which different groups of people pulled a line. Two people put in 93% of a single person's effort. Three of them indicated 85%, and four, only 77% of a single person's commitment. In the case of a group consisting of eight people the involvement declined to 50%. With this experiment Ringelmann proved that being lazy is a natural tendency of human beings. However, the researcher also allowed for such an interpretation of this experiment which indicated that smaller involvement of a larger number of people executing a particular task did not necessarily result in laziness but in bad coordination while carrying out a task. This bad coordination lowered individual motivation and encouraged participants in the experiment to lessen efforts [Ringelmann 1913: 2–39]. This same experiment was repeated by A. G.

Ingham in the 1970s. The Washington University professor modified it slightly by introducing some people already initiated in the aim of the research and by blindfolding the participants. In each phase of the experiment there was only one person who was not initiated, who lost motivation to a large effort along with an increase in number of the experiment's participants [Ingham 1974: 371–384]. This aspect should, undoubtedly, be taken into consideration by the management; however, one should not pay too much attention, as contemporary managerial tools in general allow the evaluation of employee involvement in the realization of common projects.

It is crucial to say that not all researchers recognize systemic methodology as a useful research instrument. An excessive formalization of descriptions and quantitative analyses (modeling and simulation) favors leaving out qualitative phenomena accompanying the process being researched. However, one must not neglect objections that seem applicable only in relation to systemic analysis in a static approach and refer to closed systems. Meanwhile, open systems are the essence of systemic analysis and intrinsically perform a continual exchange with the environment. Finally, open systems have an ability to eliminate the effects of disruptions by the self-regulatory processes [Ackoff 1973; Gościński 1977; Bielski 1997].

2.2. Media systems

There are few researchers in Poland who deal with media in a systemic approach and there is almost no one who deals with systemic management. Bartłomiej Golka was first in the scientific fields in Poland to address the systemic research of media processes. He demanded using the notion of the "mass-information system" which, in his opinion, can be investigated from two perspectives: political science and journalism. The first perspective means connecting the mass media in a given country with its political system. The second shows the location of media organizations in the social system. Golka, while referring to dependencies of "mass information systems" on the manner of governing in a given country, distinguished two basic media types: democratic and authoritarian [Golka 1996: 7–9].

It is also essential to notice that many researchers claim that a media system is impossible to define due to lack of homogeneity. For instance, Denis McQuail writes that "in most countries, media is not constituted in a single system of one defined aim or philosophy, but is comprised of many separate but overlapping, frequently contradictory elements, differing in the scope of normative anticipation and binding legal regulations [McQuail 2007: 133]." Nevertheless, the systemic way of thinking is exactly the quest to find either differences or common features which allow to answer three fundamental questions formulated by Gerald M. Weinberg [Weinberg 1979: 230]:

1. Why do I see what I see?
2. Why do things remain the same?
3. Why do things change?

To address the needs of these queries, in spite of various objections, one could use the definition of a media system offered by Witold Kieżun: "A system is a separate part of its surrounding reality that has a certain inner structure, and therefore consists of parts arranged according to rules that define mutual relations [Kieżun 1997: 13]." In this context, considerations of Maciej Mrozowski deserve attention as he focuses his scientific interests around the system of mass communication. In support of Jürgen Habermas, the aforementioned author adopts Habermas' conceptual system which relates to the country and society. In a system of national organization there are two functioning subsystems: political and economic. This division is derived from the notion scheme by Habermas and allows the possibility of distinguishing three realms within the structure of a contemporary country: private, public and institutional; Information circulates effectively between them [Mrozowski 2001: 119].

Contemporary media systems go beyond the boundaries of a given country, which is undoubtedly impacted by global phenomena, as well as new methods of communication, for which national borders are generally a weak barrier in disseminating information. Admittedly, some totalitarian countries attempt to impose censorship on the Internet, but in the present world, censorship is quite an elusive muzzle. Mere knowledge of foreign languages is sufficient to find information that totalitarian authorities try to conceal from citizens. Consider this famous passage from a poem by Brecht, *The Solution*: "would it not be simpler, if the government simply dissolved the people, and elected another? [Brecht 1954: 66]."

Substantive research on media systems in the world were carried out by Daniel C. Hallin and Paolo Mancini, printed in a monograph called "Comparing Media Systems: Three Models of Media and Politics." Their work has unquestionably contributed to the understanding of the complexity of media systems not only in the world, but also in Poland, although the authors did not include the Polish media system in their research [Hallin, Mancini 2007].

The beginnings of systemic considerations relating to the media can be found in the monograph *Four Theories of the Press* by Fred S. Siebert, Theodore Peterson and Wilbur Schramm. The aforementioned authors indirectly refer to one of the basic systemic research tools formulated by G. Weinberg [Wienberg 1988]. The systemic exploratory apparatus served as a means for the authors to verify their thesis, which says "the press always takes on the form and coloration of the social and political structures within which it operates [Siebert, Peterson, Schramm 1957: 1–2]." Hallin and Mancini followed the lead of Siebert, Peterson, Schramm and attempted to demonstrate that individual models of media are deeply ingrained in economic and political structures of their respective countries. In contrast to the authors of *Four Theories of the Press*, Hallin and Mancini left one matter open. Namely, they recognized that adopting the Marxist scientific point of view concerning the basis and superstructure, according to which media constitute a variable dependent on the attitude towards the system of civil monitoring in a systemic conceptualization, would be invalid. Even if for the fact that media systems are not only a reflection of the social structure but the media also affects social structures, for which there is a lot of convincing evidence [Hallin, Mancini 2007: 9].

The comparative analysis served for Hallin and Mancini as a basic tool, which in their opinion would be most useful while studying media systems. Therefore, they attracted attention to the uselessness of ethnocentrism in systemic media graphic research, as generalizing research referring exclusively to one country seems to be methodological abuse. Moreover, the ethnocentric perspective does not address, according to Hallin and Mancini, a basic question from the standpoint of systemic research: why are the media the way they are? Both authors rightfully emphasize the importance of comparative analysis for social research, Emil Durkheim who claimed that we can prove that a given phenomenon is the cause of another phenomenon only through the comparison of events in which they are simultaneously present and absent [Durkheim 2000]. As exemplification of usefulness of comparative analysis for the problems being discussed, Hallin and Mancini referred to the example of Jeffrey Alexander, a man who attempted to explain strong professional autonomy of journalists in the USA. The comparative research carried out by this man who referred to the history of press in Great Britain, France and in the US, clearly stated that the development of independent, professional American journalism arose from the lack of workers' press in the local market [Hallin, Mancini 2007: 4–5, 21, 67].

For the sake of comparative analysis aiming at identifying individual media systems in most countries of Western Europe, the United States and Canada, Hallin and Mancini adopted the following parameters [ibid., 21]:

1. Development of media markets with particular impact on mass press development;

2. Political parallelism, reflecting the level of connections between media and political parties;
3. Development of journalistic professionalism;
4. Rank and nature of state intervention into media system.

The application of the accepted indicators in the case of comparative analysis are presented in Chart 1: Diversification of media systems according to four parameters. On the basis of criteria formulated in this way, Hallin and Mancini distinguished three models of media systems in the countries where they carried out their research [ibid., 67]:

1. Mediterranean or of polarized pluralism;
2. Northern European and Central European or democratic corporatism;
3. North Atlantic or liberal.

I must remind you that Hallin and Mancini observed a majority of West European countries, the United States and Canada. Consequently, it would be proper to add at least one more model, characteristic for totalitarian countries. In this totalitarian model, the level of parallelism concerning political and media systems is very high, if not identical. Additionally, the case is similar regarding the level of state intervention. Undoubtedly, it would be advisable to introduce distinctions between utterly subordinate media in North Korea, censorship in Cuba and Honduras, as well as the dictatorial impetus of Hugo Chavez with his attempts to subjugate the Venezuelan media. These are only distinct hues of the same system that could be called totalitarian or authoritarian. This identified gap dealing with media systems is complemented by works of other authors [Nierenberg 2011; Jędrzejewski 2003, 2010]. As a starting point in differentiating media systems, in this specific case radio systems, Stanisław Jędrzejewski took on the degree and the range of media sector regulated by the state and the manner of it's financing at the moment of its founding. On this basis Jędrzejewski distinguished four radio systems [Jędrzejewski 2010: 52]:

1. Monopolistic radio system wholly controlled by the state;
2. Monopolistic radio system, within which there is a corporation established and managed by the state;
3. Affiliate system, a dual system in which the public radio corporation co-exists with the private;
4. System with stations under private management.

Table 1. Diversification of media systems according to four criteria

	Model of polarized pluralism	Model of demo-cratic corporatism	Liberal model
Development of mass press	Low	High	High
Level of political parallelism	High	High	Low
Level of professionalization	Low	High	High
Level of state intervention	High	High	Low

Source: D.C. Hallin, P. Mancini, *Systemy medialne. Trzy modele mediów i polityki w ujęciu porównaw-czym.* Wyd. Uniwersytetu Jagiellońskiego, Kraków 2007, p. 305.

As indicated before, Hallin and Mancini pointed out four determinants on which they introduced their systemic typology. [Hallin, Mancini 2007: 305]. On the other hand, Jędrzejewski, following Crook, denoted seven factors that were important while developing radio systems in individual countries [Jędrzejewski 2010: 52]:

1. Social and political system,
2. Tradition and government,
3. Religion,
4. Culture,
5. Ethnography,
6. Scale of the economy,
7. Individual vision of John Reith.[1]

The selection of criteria, serving as the basis of the created systemic typology is predestines the selection of determinants for constructing models that reflect given media systems.

2.2.1. Selected media systems

As previously indicated, Hallin and Mancini examined a majority of the West European countries, the United States and Canada. However, neither countries from Central and Eastern Europe, nor the Far East were included in that research. Therefore, this monograph recognizes that it is essential to fill this gap and choose three countries from the area unexamined by Hallin and Mancini: Japan, Russia and Poland. The aim of this measure was to elaborate on the

---

[1] John Reith – a charismatic designer and the first CEO of the BBC.

media systems in those countries and accentuate any similarities to the three media systems studied by the aforementioned researchers.

Japan. The Japanese media system was formed under the influence of events that took place in the middle of the 19th century. Previously, Japanese borders used to be closed to foreigners, which fostered the creation of a homogenous society where only one language was spoken. Two events preceded Japan's opening to the outer world: demonstration of the power of American naval vessels and Mutsuhito's ascension to the throne, who was posthumously named Meiji, a title which also refers to the period of his hegemony. These events contributed to the dynamic development of the Japanese press. To this day, Japan has one of the largest newspaper circulations in the world. As of 2008, these were the daily papers referred to as the "Big Three":

• "Yomiuri Shimbun" – ca. 10 million copies,
• "Asahi Shimbun" – ca. 8 million copies,
• "Mainichi Shimbun" – ca. 4 million copies.

Comic books, also known as manga, testify to the peculiarity of the Japanese publishing market. Some people consider them a separate mass medium. Manga dates back to the 18th century, yet the peak of its popularity was achieved in the 1990s. In 1995, the printing of the teenage weekly *Shukan Shonen Jump* reached 6.5 million copies [Merklejn 2008: 274]. Manga is not only a manifestation of popular culture, it is also an inspiration and a device for many notable Japanese artists. Presently there has been a decrease in interest in manga, which is attributed mainly to the development of the Internet and computer games which compete with to manga in their aesthetics.

The press imposed a huge influence on the formation and present shape of the Japanese electronic media. Even the American domination after World War II and American antitrust activities were unable to change it. Japanese radio in the 1950s and 1960s lost its listeners to television. However, radio has still been performing an important function in Japan. For instance, during natural disasters when power is cut off immediately, radios still function. The first commercial TV station NTV (*Nihon Terebi*) came from the press entity that issues "Yomiuri Shimbun". This station was founded in 1953, based on legal framework introduced by occupants. In the same year, Japanese public television – NHK (*Nippon Hoso Kyokai*) – came into existence. This institution is an institution for the management of public issues, similar to the BBC, which survives solely on licensing fees. The supervisory board of NHK is appointed by the prime minister in agreement with the parliament. However, the beginnings of NHK date back to 1926 and the first radio signal was transmitted one year earlier. During the 1930s and 1940s, Japanese radio was subject to the authority of the state and the military [ibid., 275].

Public media play a crucial role in the Japanese media system, but a series of scandals in 2004 involving embezzlement of money devoted to the production of missionary programs led to suspicions of deputies' manipulations of programming content on Japanese public television. This debilitated their reputation to such an extent that a considerable number of Japanese consumers cancelled their subscriptions. Moreover, it gave rise to a discussion concerning the possible privatization of NHK. Albeit, the position of Japanese public TV in the local market is still very strong.

Conglomerates, also known as *keiretsu* are a characteristic feature of the Japanese media system. They were shaped under the influence of structures functioning in other divisions of the Japanese economy. The idea of *keiretsu* is that the mother company, serving as a basis of this economic conglomerate, is surrounded by numerous minor enterprises that are connected with each other and are mutually dependent. It recalls vividly an organization defined as a system.

An individual approach has to be implemented by the Japanese journalistic environment. A peculiar topic regarding the Japanese system is that most information is released by the so-called journalists' clubs (*kisha kurabu*). Their origin dates back to the 19th century when representatives of authority treated media representatives with disrespect. Therefore, this was a form of vocational self-organization. Nowadays, Nagata, Kasumi and Hirakawa form the three most prominent clubs. They are dominated by the 15 largest entities of the Japanese media: 5 prominent nationwide newspapers, 3 regional papers, 6 TV stations (NHK and 5 commercial stations) and 2 press agencies. The clubs of journalists are of an exclusive nature. They are inaccessible to other journalists and club fees are collected from their members. This system cultivates favorable relations with politicians. The activity of Japanese journalistic clubs has been repeatedly contested by different foreign media groups, including European Union representatives [ibid., 285–286].

Freedom of media in the Japanese system is granted by law. Censorship does not exist. However, there are certain factors that create boundaries regarding freedom of speech. They are: the protection of good reputation and privacy, censorship and Comstockery, and the protection of personal data. Comstockery results from Article 175 of the Japanese Penal Code says that it is considered indecent to show genitals and pubic hair. Yet, one should notice that social consent for pornography in Japan is relatively high [ibid., 287–289].

Constitutional monarchy is the political system of Japan. However, the chief of state (emperor) does not exercise real power; he performs only symbolic and representative functions. A trisection of power, referred to by Aristotle, is binding in Japan. The parliament is comprised of two chambers: the

Table 2. Media system in Japan according to criteria by Hallin and Mancini

	Appearance of a distinguishing feature of given model	
	On a high or moderate level *	On a low or moderate level*
Mass-press development	+++	
Level of political parallelism	++	–
Level of professionalization	++	–
Level of state intervention	+	– –

Source: own study (* – number of symbols stands for the intensity with which a particular feature occurs).

upper house (the House of Counsellors) and the lower house (the House of Representatives). The Supreme Court concurrently performs the function of a constitutional court. A constitution was enacted underneath the American occupational authority in 1946 and is still binding. Solutions contained in it are modeled after the American constitution.

The Japanese economic system stands as an idiosyncrasy for the Europeans and the Americans. Japan has one of strongest economies in the world, despite being an outcome of tight cooperation between government and business, and is in some respects a planned economy.

All these factors influence the Japanese media system. The analysis of Table 2: Media system in Japan according to Hallin and Mancini's criteria, indicates that the Japanese media system is located closest to the model of democratic corporatism, yet it reveals features of liberal models and even polarized pluralism.

Russian Federation. Russia is a federation and its political system is referred to as presidential. Nonetheless, from December 1922 to December 1991, it was the most important constituent of the Union of Soviet Socialist Republics (USSR). Communism, which had been functioning in Russia for over 70 years, must have left an imprint on the country's media system as well. The press, radio and television all developed during the times of totalitarian rule in Russia. Therefore, the informative functions of media were obtrusive propaganda. In 1992, after the disintegration of the USSR, the Russian media market began to rise, some researchers predicated that many press titles were still strongly dependent on the authorities [Szurmiński 2008: 219], however, Russian researchers have challenged this view. Alexei Bykov, invoking the words of Yuri Mamczur of Discovery Institute in Seattle, affirmed that "not everything looks bad in modern Russia and American press is wrong showing Russian reality only in dark colors [Bykov 2007: 65]."

Putting aside the argument of whose opinion defines the essence of media systems in Russia, it is an indisputable matter that in 1992, after the dissolution of the USSR, a fundamental stage in forming a contemporary media system in Russia began. This was a period of transformation for the Russian media. The beginning of this process goes back to the time when Mikhail Gorbachev came to power. However, *perestroika* referred more to the press than electronic media [Adamowski 2002: 35]. The reform of Russian radio and television commenced with the elimination of the State Broadcasting Committee of the Soviet Union. Afterwards, a threefold market was shaped in Russia with three types of enterprises: state controlled, state and private, and private [Nierenberg 2007: 35].

The first Russian radio station began broadcasting regularly in 1922, leading to the first Soviet broadcasting program. The importance of radio, and later television, can be seen in the fact that the Inter-Soviet Committee for Broadcasting was subject to direct control of the Council of People's Commissars of the USSR. This control was maintained until December 27, 1991, i.e. the dissolution of the USSR. Radio had a privileged position in the Russian Federation and it was granted concessions for broadcasting frequencies by virtue of law, similar to national television). However, as a result, radio became involved in a network of political dependencies. Oddly enough, a characteristic feature of Russian commercial radio is its lenient apolitically. Between 1991 and 1995 national radio and television functioned within the Russian State Broadcasting Company *Ostankino* [Szurmiński 2008: 232–233].

The first experimental transmission of television signals in the USSR took place in 1932. TV programming started regular broadcasting on March 10, 1939. Throughout the entire period of communist dictatorship, TV in particular was monitored by totalitarian authority. It was Gorbachev's *perestroika* along with his *głasnost* (clarity) that allowed broadcasts describing Soviet reality deprived of propaganda congratulatory scrolls (an informative and journalistic program TNS) to appear alongside propaganda informative programs (*Wremja*). Still, the symptoms of temporary liberalization at the end of the 1980s began to disappear. The years between 1991 and 1995 were a period when "Ostankino" was being transformed into ORT, also a state broadcaster. The idea of Novum was that not all the state's treasure belonged to the state (although the majority of it did). Those were the times of criminogenic, or simply criminal privatization. A good deal of "Ostankino" employees enfranchised on the property of state television. The "knock-on effect" of this process peaked with the formation of TV producers' market [Adamowski 2002: 51].

The first non-state TV station in Russia emerged in 1992. It was a merger of Moscow Independent Broadcasting Corporation with Turner Broadcasting System. However, its owner, Ted Turner, was forced to withdraw from the

Table 3. Media system in Russia according to criteria by Hallin and Mancini

	Appearance of a distinguishing feature of given model	
	On a high or moderate level*	On a low or moderate level*
Mass-press development	+	– –
Level of political parallelism	+++	
Level of professionalization	+	– –
Level of state intervention	+++	

Source: own study (* – number of symbols stands for the intensity with which a particular feature occurs).

Russian media market. NTW, the second commercial station, emerged in 1993; Władimir Gusinski, a media magnate, was its owner. He was also forced to resell his TV shares and escape to Spain. However, it would be incorrect to consider him an innocent victim of persecution, as Gusinski actively participated in the formation of systems of oligarchic influences. A new station, ORT, was created in 1994 as a result of the fusion of state and private capitals. The State Treasury holds 51% of shares and the remaining 49% belong to a consortium of large banks, Łogo-WAZ and Gazprom [ibid.].

An extremely high influence of politicians and media interest groups, especially electronic, is visible in Russia. This influence stands not only for a direct interference with journalistic materials, but also with applying criminal methods to journalists and media owners, including intimidation, unlawful arrests, obscure sentences and even murders. The most notorious cases are the murder of Vladislav Listiew, a well-known journalist and the first director of ORT and the murder of Anna Politkowska, the "Novaya Gazeta" reporter, who was an author of critical articles about Russian crimes in Chechnya. An excessive exercise of independence within the Russian media market may also end up with a longstanding prison sentence or the loss of property. The instance of Vladimir Gusinski or other Russian oligarchs is highly distinctive in this case.

Therefore, the Russian media system is characterized by a high level of political parallelism along with a high level of state interference in the functioning of the media. This interference pertains to all kinds of media, both public and commercial. The indicated factors place the Russian media system according to criteria proposed by Hallin and Mancini, in the category of polarized pluralism. In the Russian Federation media system, one may also distinguish elements typical for authoritarian countries (Table 3: Media system in Russia according to criteria by Hallin and Mancini).

Poland. As previously mentioned, several Polish researchers described diverse media systems, both European and more remote continents. Meanwhile, in the Polish market there has never been a coherent thesis referring to the Polish media system. It appears that this lack ought to be supplemented as soon as possible. The discussion below constitutes only an attempt to illustrate problems that motivate wider elaboration.

The Polish media system in its present shape is eclectic. The source of this electivity should be identified in the lack of sovereignty in the 19th century, i.e. times when foundations of most media systems we are dealing with nowadays were being formed. Then the Polish press used to adopt models imperialist countries were operating. It was only electronic media that developed differently. The radio, as a broadcasting organization, was formed in free Poland in 1925, and in the initial period, was of private capital company nature. Subsequently, most of the shares were taken over by the state. After World War II, both the press and the radio, and later television, belonged to the state (they were actually in the hands of the communists in power at the time). However, rare press titles that did not belong to the state were completely subdued by the system of censorship and the rationing of paper on which newspapers could be printed. The Broadcasting Act of 1992 introduced a dual system into the Polish electronic media market, i.e. public and commercial media, and afterwards, social media.

Poland is currently a democratic country. The framework of the contemporary political system was formed in 1989 at the Round Table. Nevertheless, the entire 19th century was marked by a lack of sovereignty. The interwar period (1918–1939) had features of a democratic state only until 1926 (the May Coup). The subsequent period was of an authoritarian nature. After World War II, the communist system imposed in Poland was of a totalitarian nature with a democratic facade. Thanks to processes initiated in 1989, democracy was brought back to Poland. It is evident that these political factors had repercussions on the media system.

Table 4. Media system in Poland according to criteria by Hallin and Mancini

	Appearance of a distinguishing feature of given model	
	On a high or moderate level*	On a low or moderate level*
Mass-press development	+	– –
Level of political parallelism	++	–
Level of professionalization	+	– –
Level of state intervention	++	–

Source: own study (* – number of symbols stands for the intensity with which a particular feature occurs).

The lack of own statehood or own sovereignty meant that the media generally tended to perform purely propagandist, tertiary functions towards the government. It was difficult to imagine the development of a fully professional journalism industry in such conditions. The press from the anti-communist opposition performed propaganda functions *à rebours* as well. In these conditions resembling a conspiracy, or even being a conspiracy, it is hard to maintain the requirements of professional journalism. It was just after 1989, after almost two centuries of more or less bothersome enslavement, that it became possible to begin the formation of a media system characteristic of democratic countries. The Constitution of April 2, 1997 states that Poland is a democratic legal state that guarantees freedom of speech. In Poland censorship does not exist, and the Broadcasting Act of December 29, 1992 introduced a dual system of electronic media in Poland and replaced national media with public media. Formal records that guarantee media independence and abolish censorship are frequently only a facade behind which politicians are aiming to subdue media, the public media in particular.

The contemporary Polish media market is distinguished by a high level of political parallelism, referring not only to public media. The role of the state in the media system also seems to be significant. As a result, our media system should be considered a model of polarized pluralism, characteristic of European Mediterranean countries (Table 4: Media system in Poland according to criteria by Hallin and Mancini).

2.2.2. Selected models of media systems

As previously mentioned, models make up one of the most essential research tools in the theory of systems. Literature of the subject deals most frequently with models of public media. It is primarily related to a lack of consensus regarding the tasks that the public media is supposed to fulfil. In his monograph entitled notably *Public Media? Beginning of the End or New Opening*, Karol Jakubowicz characterized the most frequently-occurring models of public media nowadays (Table 5).

The current state of the matter within the area of electronic media is conducive neither to public nor commercial broadcasters. The latter stipulate totally distinct models of public media (Table 6: Models of public media stipulated by commercial sector).

Adherents are divided into those being in favor either of pure mission, or of the complete offer (Table 7: Models proposed by adherents of public media). The first model, offered by supporters of public media, despite distinct intentions, resembles an "enclosed" model, demanded by the commercial sector. Jakubowicz, postulating the mission of public broadcaster and objectives, states that the mission and objectives may only be achieved in the "full offer" model [Jakubowicz 2007: 156].

Table 5. Models of public media present nowadays

Classical model	Broadcasters attempt to combine mission with a challenge to participate in an auditorium (and possibly in the advertising market).
Quasi-commercial model	Broadcasters dependent on funding from advertising on a level determining their program policy are forced to compete with commercial broadcasters upon the share in advertising market by means of a very similar program (phenomenon known as program convergence between public and commercial broadcasters).
Model of pluralist public service	Co-occurrence of two or more equivalent public broadcasters in the same markets.
Broadcasters of specialist channels	Broadcasters of "bunches" of specialist programs or addressed to various viewers (e.g. digital channels BBC or France 2 and France 3).

Source: Jakubowicz 2007: 155.

Table 6. Models of public media postulated by commercial sector

Model of retained evolution	Public broadcasters should not make use of new technologies, including the Internet, or change the traditional universal formula of the program.
Enclosed model	Public broadcasters should not be niche ones, complementing the commercial offer by focusing on genres that private broadcasters are not allowed to televise commercially.
Model of dispersed public service	The public duty mission should be distinguished from institutions created for its production. It can be assured by market methods, by commissioning production and emission of appropriate contents to all market-based subjects.

Source: Jakubowicz 2007: 155.

Table 7. Models proposed by adherents of public media

Model of pure mission	Program focused on mission and non-tainted by commercialization – by means of traditional television and new technologies. The aim is to maintain particular *distinctiveness* of public media and preventing commercialization. Though proposed from a different intention, in fact is close to the enclosed model.
Model of full offer	A full offer of universal and specialized programs and services making use of new technologies. Policy tasks adjusted to the new social and cultural situation.

Source: Jakubowicz 2007: 155.

The concept of Triangle of Media Powers (TMP) [Nierenberg 2007: 152–218] was at some point an offer of a non-political evaluation of public broadcasters' accomplishments. The presented basics of constructing the TMP model in the monograph entitled *Public Media Enterprise. Determinants, Systems,*

Models have a solid foundation, both theoretical and practical. They enable the use of the cause and effect forecasting method. In essence, the basis of the TMP model consists in determining a model that would explain the mechanism of changes in endogenous variables. Such a cause and effect model is applied to research both past events and for forecasting [Welfe 2004: 12]. Model variables are assorted on the basis of a test characteristic for a given fragment of reality. The TMP model assumes that the media system of a particular country affects other systems such as authority, public opinion and market. According to the model, the state (legislative and executive competencies) represents the "authority," media audiences' represent the "public opinion," and the advertisers are representatives of the "market." The aim of the econometric model was to verify the research hypothesis stating: media fully accomplish their public function provided that the three basic powers which influence it, represented by the state authority, advertisers and media customers, remain in balance. The model's authenticity was verified by investigating regional radio stations in Poland.

It was assumed that the "powers" of authority represent, in the TMP model, decisions of the constitutional body – National Broadcasting Council. The influence of this body on the public radio has multiple impacts:

1. Resulting ordinances concerning radio functioning (these ordinances pertain equally to all radio broadcasting stations and therefore might be omitted),
2. Subscription installment (SI) granted by the National Broadcasting Council to public radio broadcasting stations according to a specific algorithm,
3. "Forces" of media customers would be expressed by the "listening rate" (LR), i.e. the number of listeners of a given station at a given time.

Market "forces" would depict advertising revenues of the individual public radio stations (Adv.).

Therefore:

$$TMP = a_0 + a_1 SI + a_2 LR + a_3 Adv. + \xi$$

where:
SI – subscription instalment
LR – listening rate
Adv. – advertising
a_0; a_1; a_2; a_3 – structural parameters
ξ – random element

A synthetic variable has been constructed in order to receive comparable data. The basis of this variable was a set of diagnostic variables. As a result, a matrix of standardized features was formed [Nierenberg 2007: 181–184]. Such matrices were constructed for sixteen regional radio broadcasting stations of the Polish Radio (Polskie Radio). Next, calculations were carried out which made it possible to receive model structural parameters and the determination coefficient for individual voivodeships with broadcasting public radio stations (Table 8).

In order to depict calculation results for individual regional public radio broadcasting stations, adequate drawings have been made to find out whether impactful "forces" remain in balance in a given situation. Three categories of broadcasting stations are:

1. "insensitive" to advertising (Chart 1),
2. "insensitive" to subscription (Chart 2),
3. "sensitive" to TMP (Chart 3).

On the basis of research, the first model (regional radio stations insensitive to advertising) includes 6 regional stations of the Polish Radio; in Zielona Góra, Łódź, Rzeszów, Gdańsk, Kielce and Szczecin. These broadcasting stations operated similarly to public institutions, such as libraries, schools or museums.

Table 8. Model structural parameters and determination coefficient for individual provinces

Provinces	Model structural parameters				Determination coefficient
	a_3	a_2	a_1	a_0	
Lower Silesia	0.045	0.098	0.059	0.227	0.885
Kuyavia-Pomerania	0.082	0.089	0.062	0.204	0.873
Lublin	0.022	0.127	0.101	0.243	0.824
Lubusz	0.101	–	0.054	0.227	0.772
Łódzkie	0.082	–	0.060	0.231	0.932
Lesser Poland	0.112	0.129	0.090	0.331	0.881
Masovia	0.066	0.095	0.080	0.258	0.893
Opole	0.065	0.064	–	0.212	0.970
Subcarpathia	0.098	–	0.120	0.198	0.778
Podlaskie	0.019	0.114	0.108	0.299	0.949
Pomeranian	0.083	–	0.066	0.340	0.946
Silesia	0.044	0.103	0.061	0.231	0.926
Świętokrzyskie	0.030	–	0.072	0.210	0.911
Warmia-Masuria	0.064	0.112	0.103	0.307	0.912
Greater Poland	0.064	0.105	0.079	0.315	0.948
West Pomerania	0.080	–	0.089	0.287	0.951

Source: Nierenberg 2007: 188.

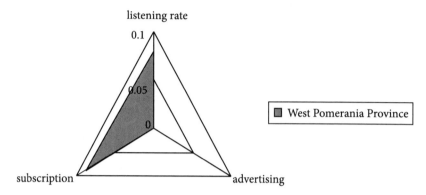

Chart 1. TMP for Radio Szczecin S.A.

Source: Nierenberg 2007: 198.

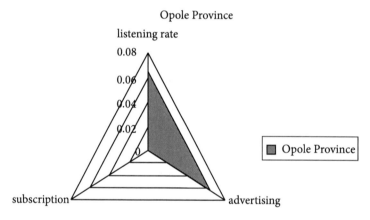

Chart 2. TMP for Radio Opole S.A.

Source: Nierenberg 2007: 203.

The model of broadcasting stations that are insensitive to subscription includes only one station: Radio Opole. In the case of Radio Opole S.A., there was a dependency characteristic for a commercial radio (almost a linear dependency between an advertisement and listening rate; Chart 2).

The group that fulfils the requirements of the TMP model includes 9 regional radio stations of the Polish Radio stations in Białystok, Bydgoszcz, Katowice, Krakow, Lublin, Olsztyn, Poznań, Warsaw and Wrocław.

The calculated determination coefficient for the econometric TMP model, being the measure of adjusting the model to empirical data, was in many cases close to one (Table 8), which means a high model adjustment to real data.

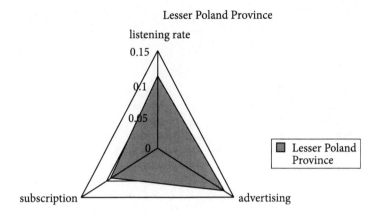

Chart 3. TMP for Radio Kraków S.A.

Source: Nierenberg 2007: 201.

The presented geometrical model could serve as a useful tool for decision-makers evaluating work of regional broadcasting stations of the Polish Radio. It would allow for an evaluation of their work in a possibly objective way, without any additional burdens, especially political ones. However, the model did not win the attention of either the National Broadcasting Council or the members of Parliament.

Discussion questions:

1. Discuss the essence of the systemic study.
2. Hallin and Mancini distinguished three media systems. Indicate differences among them.
3. What are the characteristics of the concept of Triangle of Media Powers (TMP) of Nierenberg?
4. What models of public media are offered by their adherents and antagonists?

Chapter 3. The Essence of Media Management – Dual Nature of the Media

Media organizations constitute the basis of a media market. The nature of such organizations differ from other enterprises, taking into account their dual nature [Picard 1989]. The analysis included in this chapter shall connote previous concepts as well, referring to pre-systemic interpretations. However, the systemic analysis of media organizations in a management context will to serve as the basic concept.

3.1. Media management in historical and methodological contexts

Research concerning media management primarily has its roots in the United States. The research was related to the rise of huge media concerns, firstly the printing press, and then radio and television concerns. For Alan B. Albarran the need for researching the areas connected with media management lies in the uniqueness of the media industry. For every society, the media is the main supplier of information and entertainment [Albarran 2006: 3]. John M. Lavine and Daniel B. Wackman [1988: 7] identified five characteristic features that distinguish the media from all other industries:

1. The media deliver "perishable" products,
2. The media employ highly creative workers,
3. The media have a distinct organizational structure,
4. The media play a socially-substantial role (they have an effect on audience consciousness, may serve as a tool of influence, etc.),
5. The differences among traditional media become bleared.

Even considering the unique nature of the media, research pertaining to media management has been developing in a historical context just like other disciplines. Currently, the research is of a global and interdisciplinary nature to a large extent, just as are contemporary media. However, Albarran [2006: 3] propounds that media management should be perceived through previous research accomplishments. This kind of review of basic currents in management was performed previously, in Chapter 1. Nevertheless, one ought to recall at this point that making use of the output of American researchers requires specific knowledge relative to the US market and its historical conditioning, which influenced the shaping of notions referring to management.

Widely, management is associated with commercialism and with profit-oriented organizations. Yet, it is worth remembering that while delivering a speech to the U.S. Congress in 1912, Frederic W. Taylor talked about management wielded by the example of Elton Mayo's clinic, an organization which was not profit-oriented. Also, the notion of management principles was used for the first time in reference to a completely non-commercial organization (American Army) by Elihu Root, Secretary of War in Theodore Roosevelt's government. The term management used to have a negative association for Americans, especially in the times of the Great Depression. In order to avoid bad connotations, the notion of public administration was introduced – a term which in fact denotes management in the public sector [Drucker 2000: 6].

It seems that a contemporary manager should concentrate on efficiency and achieving goals, and in order to reach these goals, they need knowledge and skills from diverse domains, without giving any special thought to what makes business management different from non-business management. Drucker candidly claims that 90% of the problems organizations deal with is of a general nature, and the remaining 10% is determined by mission, history, culture and terminology specific to a given organization [Drucker 2002: 29].

Research carried out by Albarran stands in opposition to such a perception of management, and the media in particular. In his opinion, the unique nature of the media makes it impossible to accept any universal theory of media management. Managing a TV station, a newspaper, or a cable network, requires separate abilities and distinct managerial tools. A media enterprise works in a turbulent environment, and additionally asks for new technical and technological solutions, a ceaseless market analysis etc. [Albarran 2006: 11]. Anyone who has had the opportunity to observe the work of either a radio station, TV station, or a team of editors must agree with Albarran. This environment is, to a large extent, connected with the convergence process, being the *in statu nascendi* process.

Gracie Lawson-Borders was one of the first who dealt with the research on convergence processes on a large scale. Three huge media corporations: Tribune, Belo and Media General became the subject of her research. She did a very good job elaborating the research methodology that enables evaluation of processes and convergence levels. G. Lawson-Borders [2003: 91–99] outlined several research areas, the penetration of which made it possible to conclude about the convergence level. The research areas were: communication, culture, competition, cooperation, obligations, compensation and media receivers.

Based on an overview of the literature, conducted research, and his own knowledge of the scope of media management, Albarran indicated four presumptions that may be helpful while appointing research direction for media management [Albarran 2006: 16]:

1. The literature pertaining to media management, both theoretical and practical, is relatively limited to literature covering the entire discipline of management. Many elaborations, especially earlier ones (before 1990), are of a descriptive nature, but make it possible be become acquainted with media management and comprise a solid basis for future research in this field;
2. There is no consent among scientists dealing with the problematic aspect regarding which research approach is optimal. Most researchers aimed to study the managerial processes of the highest levels of management in the media (press publishing, radio stations or TV stations, etc.), omitting the lower levels;
3. The research methods applied while studying media management in its early stage used to be limited surveys, interviews, or analyzing of secondary research sources. Beginning with the latter half of the 1990s, exploratory methods became more sophisticated;
4. Media management as a subject of research has matured to seeking new research methods and developing new theoretical approaches.

In Albarran's opinion, the discipline of media management should concentrate on the following eight research areas [Albarran 2006: 16–17]:

1. Media management ought to be analyzed on different levels complying with the different implications resulting from macro and global phenomena, as well as multicultural. This analysis is associated with the fact that media organizations in their operations often surpass the borders of their own country. Media management should follow all occurring trends, both micro and macro;
2. The research carried out in the scope of media management should have a theoretical framework and ought to underscore methodological rigor in order to enable us to broaden our knowledge within this scope. Researchers should undertake the risk of testing new theoretical assumptions, which could possibly shift existing paradigms;

3. It is essential to carry out intensive research related to alterations in the type of management created by a media convergence in all possible dimensions of the phenomenon;
4. One ought to carry out research founded on the effects of applying various strategies in media management, in order to increase market share. This can be accomplished by developing new business models and media products, implementing new technologies, and reacting to the moves of competition and other external forces;
5. The research carried out should clarify which forces have an effect and which dependencies take place in management, economics, media regulation and society;
6. Future research should exceed single case studies in favor of vertical studies which are a source of greater amount of data for comparative analyses;
7. It is essential for future research to be of interdisciplinary character and to consider cooperation between academia and media organizations;
8. Academia should show concern for widely spreading scientific output not only at traditional conferences or in academic monographs, but also by bringing information into general use via the Internet, for example.

An equally interesting research perspective was offered by Manuel Puppis [2010: 134–149]. In his opinion, public usefulness of the systemic approach for research concerning t management should be extended with diverse new theoretic conceptualizations of this topic, chiefly communicative, based on sociology. M. Puppis calls it media governance which can be defined as a set of broad-based policies and forms of media management. Nevertheless, it seems that the concept proposed by Puppis outreaches the frames of this monograph.

3.2. Theoretical concepts of media management

Clayton Christensen and Michael Raynor rightly notice that theories are formed as a result of conducted research and observations, and are acknowledged by further experiments. Theory extends resources of our knowledge about the surrounding world, schematizes and structures it, which makes it possible not only to explain past events but also to predict future ones [Christensen, Raynor 2003: 67–74]. However, Denis McQuail and Sven Windahl point out the role of models in verifying communication theories. On the other hand, models which reaffirmed the authors of heir given communication theories, in the correctness of their results, encouraged others to look for new solutions [McQuail, Windahl 1993: 17–26].

Undoubtedly, both the economics of media and media management (combining these two notions is characteristic among current research trends; the most important world conference that groups paramount explorers of this research is called the *World Media Economics and Media Management*, the research team of the Polish Communication Association is known as: *Media Economics and Media Management*) have been seeking their place in the major research trends. It is rather certain that sooner or later *media economics* is going to diverge from *media management*.

Two researchers, Bożena Mierzejewska and Ann Hollifield, who deal with media management, took steps to organize the knowledge within this area and performed an overview of the most compelling theoretical concepts that used to be harnessed by scientists dealing with media management. The basis for their analysis was 309 papers published in the "Journal of Media Economics" and "The International Journal on Media Management," between the years 1988 and 2003. Neither the choice of periodicals for the analysis nor the time were accidental. The "Journal of Media Economics" was the first scientific periodical in the world entirely devoted to the problems of media economics and media management [Mierzejewska, Hollifeild 2006: 40].

According to the mentioned researchers, the most widely applied concept was the examination of strategic management. A case study of a particular media institution was used in order to describe the phenomena undergoing research. As a result, it was possible to explicate why some media organizations get along better in the market than others. One described some applied strategies for concentration in media and adaptations to changing conditions. Allan Albarran, Robert Picard, Sylvie Chan-Olmsted and Richard Gershon found themselves among the authors who published the effects of their research in this field. In their publications, Mierzejewska and Hollifield distinguished three approaches. The first refers to the influence of a structure on an organization's performance (*structure-conduct-performance* SCP); The second pertains to the view that every company has a set of unique resources that should be its base when constructing a strategy (*resource-based-view* RBV); The third consists of implementing the well-known biological *niche theory*, according to which every creature tends to look for a niche in a new environment. In a similar way, media organizations ought to harness gaps and market niches with their adopted strategy [ibid., 41–42].

The structural approach is another strategy concerning media organizations. Mierzejewska and Hollifield remark that within the area they studied it was very rare for scientists to notice the influence of an organization's structure on its activity. However, the influence of a proprietary structure on adopted strategies tended to undergo research frequently. The majority of researchers focused rather on investigating the structure of press property than on the electronic media, resulting in a substantial gap [ibid., 43–44].

An exploratory area related to managing international and global media organizations began to grow rapidly within the last two decades. The research carried out within the scope of the organizations and managerial activities was verified by economic rationality, structure, and organizational culture. The research of such figures as Stephen Lacy, Alan Blanchard, Sylvie Chan-Olmsted, and Richard Gershon dealt with the aforementioned issues [ibid., 44–45].

An approach connected with organizational culture used to be applied, relatively rarely as a description tool of an organization itself and its management. It dealt mainly with comparative analysis of vocational roles and organizational culture, and chiefly the influence of organizational culture on the ability of media organizations to adjust to the changing environment or the impact of organizational culture on disclosing spurious news or plagiarism (this particular case referred to Jayson Blair who wrote articles for *The New York Times* based on fabricated facts or plagiarism). Lucy Küng, George Sylvie, Lee B. Becker, Gerald M. Kosicki were mainly who dealt with problems [ibid., 46–47].

New technologies, innovations and creativity were the focus of over 60% of the articles inserted in scientific journals dealing with media economics and media management. The influence of new technologies on all media manifestations is overwhelming. Nevertheless, the initial stage of research in this scope was characterized by a definitional mess. Research by Karlene Roberts and Martha Grabowski in the 1990s demonstrated that scholars applied seven different definitions of technology [Roberts, Grabowski 1996: 409–423]. Similar definitional problems dealt with the notion of innovation or the new media. The lack of such a taxonomy aggravated the assimilation of research carried out by diverse researchers and in various places. An attempt to abandon this deadlock was an indication of which research areas refer to the description of new technologies. Such areas include the following technology frames: economic, strategic management, new product development, diffusion, gratification and benefits, creativity. Creativity in particular was an acutely analyzed agent. It was just due to the fact that it is (a determinant extremely difficult to predict) the main "ingredient" of a media product, whereas investments into media organizations require immense expenditures [Mierzejewska, Hollifield 2006: 48–52].

In their publication, Mierzejewska and Hollifield point out that leadership, as a subject of research within the scope of media management, is one of the most neglected topics. It is even more bizarre that the research of leadership contains a good deal of weighty research topics, such as the motivations of media managers, management styles, methods of decision-making, changes in management, organizational behaviors, etc. Media organizations operate under persistent change and a high level of uncertainty, which in turn leads to high employee turnover. For people in media management, this is undoubtedly a challenge. It is also a challenge for researchers who handle the media [ibid., 52–54].

Investigating leadership in media organizations is strictly connected with human resources. A media product is dependent on knowledge, talent, and the creativity of its creators. In the year 2000, the salaries of workers employed in American TV stations constituted the largest single position, which amounted to 42.4% of the entire budget. Long-standing research projects carried out in the US resulted in a large number of publications in this field. Thanks to these publications, not only is the demographic structure well recognized, but the structure of income, political views, satisfaction of performed work, manner of performance, acquisition of information sources, etc. Thus, one is able to discover dependencies between the profile of students who graduate from journalism and their employment level. These dependencies are also related to job market research within media areas. This area also contains research on gender type which as an example pertains to the status of women or national and ethnic minorities in media organizations. Nevertheless, this kind of research tended to be carried out by the representatives of other disciplines rather than media management [ibid., 55–56].

While Mierzejewska and Hollifield did not favor any particular research method while performing their review of research fields and approaches, they only indicated what to study, not how to convey research. In the introduction to their considerations they brought up the vast usefulness of varied models which inherently constitute a basic exploratory tool of systemic theory.

3.3. Media management in the systemic approach

In order to explain various phenomena referring to media management, adopting a systemic methodology is justified. According to systemic theory, the investigated phenomena should be perceived as a whole, either directly or indirectly related. It is substantial to bear in mind, while describing these phenomena, the aforementioned three key questions from Weinberg: Why do I see what I see? Why are things the way they are? Why do things change?

In this conceptualization, an organization is a structured system, i.e. organized in a certain way that assigns a socio-technical framework [Kast, Rosenzweig 1972]. The theory of systems assumes that an organization, including the media, constitutes an organism that functions in a specific environment from which it gets reserves, and where the effects of its activities drift (entrance, exit). It is possible to distinguish five subsystems within this system [Bielski 1997; Nierenberg 2007]:

1. subsystem of aims and values,
2. psychosocial subsystem,
3. technical subsystem,
4. structure subsystem,
5. subsystem of media management.

Distinguishing individual subsystems, typical for a systemic approach of an organization, allows for a better understanding of its essence. In this conceptualization it is the systemic definition of an organization by Russell L. Ackoff that seems to be the most useful:

> An organization is a system that behaves deliberately, containing at least two components which behave deliberately, which have a common intention, on the grounds of which a functional division of work takes place; its functionally separate components may react to one another's behavior by means of observation or connection and at least one sub-combination performs a monitoring-managerial function [Ackoff 1973].

It also facilitates the use of one of the most characteristic tools applied in systemic research – models. Let us recollect that a model is a simplified mapping of reality. When examining processes related to the management of organizations, it is customary to make use of these types of models:

1. schematic: reflecting structures and links in an organization, and,
2. mathematical: typically econometric models which make it possible to reveal dependencies among respective forces functioning in an organization.

On the basis of Kast and Rosenzweig's concept, as well as the one developed by Bielski and the present author, the systemic model of media organization has been presented (Figure 3).

A systemic study of an organization resembles a Russian matryoshka, or a story within a story (The French refer to it as a drawer novel). These references stand for determining given subsystems within a particular system. In turn, within these subsystems one may distinguish other subsystems. As an example, the notion of "subsystem of aims and values" in an organization, exemplifies the mission that an organization realizes in a specific situation, and its strategy. It is a function that on one hand appoints fulfilling definite social needs, and on the other means feeding the organization from the environment which, in turn, makes its survival and development possible.

The systemic analysis of an organization shows that under no circumstances should it be limited to merely describing and investigating its sole structure. An analysis should bring out the "quiddity" – as Weinberg wrote about in his

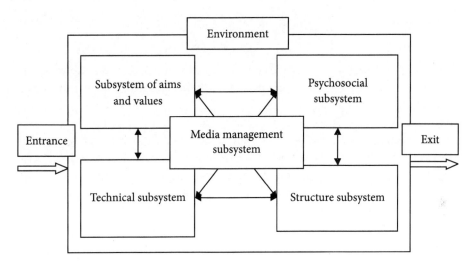

Figure 3. Systemic model of media organizations

Source: own study based on Bielski 1997: 81; Nierenberg 2007: 163.

systemic examination. The previously mentioned Hallin and Mancini did such an analysis. They did not limit themselves merely to describing investigated structures, but looked for dependencies occurring among the phenomena.

Research on the economic aspects of media organizations' activities arose earlier than documented processes related to their management. The case was similar to the classical science of management which was codified exclusively at the turn of the 19th and 20th centuries, yet managerial processes are as old as civilization itself. Almost from the dawn of history, human beings engaged in management, however unaware of it. Media management, a new and not fully crystallized research discipline appeared along with media economics. Some researchers dealing with these issues claim that joining research in the area of media economics with media management would be favorable [Albarran, Chan-Olmsted, Wirth 2006: 2–7]. However, it appears that scientific management detached itself from classic economy, in the same way media management shall dissociate itself from media economics. This is principally because media management, due to its social mission, should be close to the humanistic aspects of this process. It seems that research in the world is headed in this direction.

It seems that the systemic approach, in terms of studying media management, would be useful for scientific identification of this area, as it is just the beginning of a formation of research tools. Studies in this field are still scanty, yet becoming more frequent year by year.

3.4. Range and subject of media management

The study of media comprises a compelling part of the diverse domains described by sociology, political science, economics and many others; however, it is still not officially approved as a scientific discipline in Poland. One of the most essential research questions related to this domain is media management. The mentioned management should be understood both in a wider context, referring to the media perceived as a realm concerning social, political and economic phenomena, and in a narrower conceptualization, understood as media enterprise management that functions in a particular environment. Investigating these questions is difficult, as up to now the research has not been recognized well and requires creating a certain notion apparatus, adequate research tools, determination of parallel and separate questions as compared to classical management.

A media enterprise deals with the manufacturing of a specific good or providing services that are of a dual nature [Picard 1989]. Therefore, media management, in a blinkered view would be a process in which that dual good would be subject to specific actions. Consequently, in the context of previous speculations, the following definition would be the right one: media management (in a systemic approach) stands for a set of mutually connected processes and actions which include planning, organizing, leading, motivating and controlling, that apply to all manifestations and levels of the media system. It appears that the proposed definition is capacious enough to embrace all areas related to the defined questions, and also sufficient to determine what constitutes media management and what does not.

It has been mentioned that investigating the economic aspects of media activity and media organizations appeared earlier than study of processes connected with media management. A new, not entirely crystallized research subdiscipline emerged following media economics. Some researchers dealing with these problems express the opinion that combining research in scope of media economics and media management would be favorable [Albarran, Chan-Olmsted, Wirth 2006: 2–7], as according to many a rigorous separation of economics from management is impossible. Nonetheless, let us emphasize once again that in the same way the scientific management detached itself from classical economy, the media management itself shall dissociate itself from media economics. It is indispensable to create an individual academic instrumentation and researchers who will deal with this research area. Apparently, the border between media management and media economics shall be misty yet present.

The setup of public media in Poland, along with its problems, favors media management and economics. It seems that Polish researchers who deal with media economics in a natural way are headed towards commercial media, finding a multitude of research difficulties there, whereas those who are mainly concerned with problems in the field of management will be looking for research areas in the sphere of the public media. Perhaps in the long run, it is likely to change, but the forthcoming years seem to be outlining this differentiation in research areas. It also appears that within public media management, one of the chief tasks will be the implementation of its major targets, i.e. the thing referred to as the mission of the public media.

Public and commercial organizations offer their current and potential consumers either private or public goods. The easiest method to identify them is to assume that a private good is the one that can be consumed by one person and then cannot be used by someone else (e.g. a cookie, a shirt or a bike). In contrast, it is possible for a public good to be consumed simultaneously by many people without causing damage to any of them (the air we are breathing, national healthcare or state defense). It can be ascertained that the subject of management is some type of specific good. In case of the media it would be a media good.

3.4.1. The media good as a subject of management

A contemporary person is deprived of humility. According to them, he or she creates the utmost and greatest works, and he or she is the maker of the information revolution. Nevertheless, the current revolution is the fourth one in history. The first of them was related to the invention of writing in Mesopotamia about 5,000–6,000 years ago. The second one began around 3,500 years ago in China along with the invention of the book. The third one was initiated in 1456 by Gutenberg with his invention of the movable type printing [Drucker 2000: 104–113].

Drucker, who argued that the 21st century is the age of information, emphasizes noteworthy properties of information as a source that absconds basic economic rules:

> If I sell a thing, e.g. a book, it means that I no longer have it. If I release information to somebody, I still have it. Actually, information becomes more valuable as it becomes known to a greater number of people. As the number of information recipients increases, its value grows" [Drucker 2000: 27].

At this point it would be advisable to notice that all media without regard to their nature and type of carrier, have two functions [Picard 1989: 17]:

1. social,
2. commercial.

Moreover, Picard proposed to treat media, on the grounds of their duality, as a specific market goodness (Figure 4: Media as a good or a market service). This division proposed by R. Picard has profound consequences. This means that the media are not "common" enterprises whose aim is to bring profit to their owners. McQuail [2007: 242] announces: "Media [are] not just any other business" due to the aspect of social interest. It also seems that the duality of the media as indicated by Picard, referring mostly to the content product and the economic aspect for advertisers, also enables us to say that they are not a business like others.

Picard's economic view regarding the media raises a stark objection amongst those who are unaccustomed with its essence. How is it possible – they would say – for instance for the BBC to perform not only a social but also a commercial role, if they do not broadcast commercials at all? To answer such charges referring to the CPT (*cost per thousand*) indicator is sufficient – at the expense of reaching thousands of viewers of a given commercial. Let us imagine a program broadcast by the BBC, watched by three million viewers. Is it possible for the said three million to watch a program on a commercial TV station? No, they cannot. Therefore, if there was neither such a program, nor the BBC, then surely some of the viewers – perhaps a considerable number – would be watching a program on commercial television. Thereby, its audience would increase and its CPT index would diminish. This is what advertisers are especially interested in. Hence, the BBC, despite not airing commercials, also serves a commercial role on the media market.

Let us return to the main thread that reflects the ideas of Drucker, who drew attention to peculiar properties of information as a source drawn from basic economic rules. It seems that it is impossible to explain this paradox without referring to the research carried out by Picard. Drucker claimed that information becomes even more valuable with increased universality [Drucker 2000: 27]. Conversely, classical economics assumes that the more scarce a particular

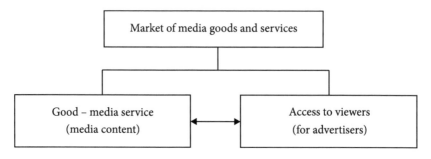

Figure 4. Media as a good or a market service

Source: Picard 1989: 18.

good the more valuable it is and vice versa. The commonness of a particular good lowers its price. Meanwhile, Drucker topples our previous understanding of the most cardinal principles of economics. This ostensible contradiction may be explained by referring to the duality of the media market formulated by Picard (Figure 4) and to the formula of "information and media buttons" created by the author of this monograph.

For the purpose of illustrating this argument the author buttons on a shirt and their informational equivalents. It is also necessary to differentiate between a classical enterprise and a media enterprise. Let us assume that the classical enterprise is a factory that produces real buttons, whereas the media enterprise is an organization (e.g. some editorial office) which delivers "media buttons" (information). If the author of this monograph stood on a slope, wearing a ski suit, there would probably not be anyone wanting to place advertisements on his outfit. On the other hand, if he was the world champion in ski jumping, then each square centimeter of his suit would be worth quite a lot of money. In this case, the author of this thesis depicts an enterprise which produces ordinary buttons, whereas the world champion in ski jumping, depicts a media enterprise, which not only delivers a certain media product ("media buttons") but also has an ability to collect a rare a good, namely capturing the viewers' attention. Hence, the rules of classical economics apply to the first enterprise, whereas they do not apply to the second one. In this instance this means that the information is more valuable the more common it becomes. At this point, one should use analogic reasoning. If two newspapers were published on a market, let us call them: A and B, containing exactly the same 100 "media buttons" and newspaper A sold a circulation of 1,000 copies, and newspaper B a circulation of 1,000,000 copies, then the question of which buttons are more precious would be rhetorical. Of course, the newspaper which managed to sell more copies. Larger circulation means that a newspaper offers rarer good to its advertisers, meaning the attention of its readers. Therefore, this signifies that Drucker's statement that information is more valuable the more common it is was proven right.

The way of thinking described here proves that the interdisciplinary nature of media management requires new research tools and a new description, which could be created by researchers possessing interdisciplinary skills. Traditional instruments relating to information as a media good seem to have limited usage.

In the case of commercial media enterprises, the basic issue is that of an organizational management focusing on preserving and respecting the business of both the owners and viewers. This focus is often very difficult to implement in practice, as there are situations when social interest and the interest of the owners are conflicting. This particularly concerns small media enterprises whose economic existence depends for instance on one advertiser that operates in a given region. It may be both a local government unit as well as the only enterprise operating in a given region.

In the case of the public media (generally the electronic media) the basic managerial matter is making these media independent of political influences. In general, the political interest is divergent from the social interest. From the point of view of matters considered here, an essential issue arises: whether it is necessary to implement special managerial forms and tools in the case of this organizational dualism and subject management of public media enterprise. Its settlement requires the primarily designation of tasks to be observed and an understanding of public management.

A highly symptomatic example is that of the commission appointed by the British government to elaborate on the concept of BBC digitization, including redefining the substance of British public broadcasting. In their final report entitled *The Future Funding of the BBC: Report of the Independent Review Panel*, they wrote: "We have not managed anything so ambitious in the six months we have had at our disposal. When we each tried to define public service broadcasting, some very familiar words started to appear – information, education, extension of horizons, impartiality, independence, universal access, inclusivity, service of minorities, lack of commercial motivation, etc. We decided that we may not be able to offer a tight new definition of public service broadcasting, but we nevertheless each felt that we knew it when we saw it."

The report, *Review of Public Broadcasting around the World of 2004* indicated three major orientations concerning the level of state interference in the media:

1. Minimalistic – appearing in countries where the commercial media content is not regulated and the public funding of the public media does not exceed USD 30 per capita (Italy, New Zealand, Portugal, Spain, the US);
2. The media as a "cultural exception" – commercial broadcasters are obliged to produce programs that enhance national identity and the public funding does not exceed USD 30 per capita;
3. A large degree of interference – intervention in the program is justified by public business and public funding does not exceed USD 50 per capita (Germany, Holland, Sweden, Great Britain).

It seems that in the case of public media management, one of the most vital elements is a lack of commercial motivation. It is feasible only when public media is not forced to look for means in the commercial market. In such countries as: Great Britain, Denmark, Norway, Sweden or Japan, the contribution of public money to the revenue of public media institutions amounts to nearly 100% [Jędrzejewski 2003: 39]. In Poland, public media enterprises are forced to look for sources of funding in the commercial market. The share of public means, while implementing tasks of public authority, amounts a yearly average ranging from about 27–28% (public television) to about 72–73% (public radio) [www.krrit.gov.pl].

Taking the existing laws into consideration, managing Polish public media must be comprised of a combination of two interests: commercial and public. Polish public media were shaped into profit-oriented companies. In any case, such companies are required by the Secretary of the Treasury who performs proprietary functions in relation to media companies. Yet, on the other hand, Polish public media are subject to the Broadcasting Act that included a description of the public interest (mission – Polish Broadcasting Act of 1992). For many years the Polish government has been attempting to solve this, but it has generally ended up with announcements and taking influences over the public media. K. Jakubowicz [2007: 252] wrote explicitly about the validity crisis of the public media's existence. According to research, the viewers on the one hand declare the necessity of their existence and on the other hand are disenchanted by the media's practices.

Contemporary media are characterized by an ever larger degree of convergence, and also by technical opportunities of independent program adjustments by the audience. Technical progress provides options which media customers were never given before. It stands for a brand new attitude to media management. The shape of media and their content is no longer subject to only media pilots. Contemporary media is subject to audience management of the stream of media information as well.

Media management is a relatively new research sub-discipline of modest scientific output. It demands the formation of a new exploratory apparatus, a creative adaptation of a existing notions towards research requirements and also an indication of a research area in the new discipline that media management is likely to become. It appears that the immediate years will see an intensifying interest in media management both in the scientific environment and among current and potential researchers and students, but in the political and business communities. It has and is going to have its roots in an ever increasing significance of media industries.

Problems concerning media management seem to be an attractive exploratory field, in relation to both commercial and public media. It seems that in the future, public media are likely to drift away from politics. Its place shall be taken over by culture understood as a sense and essence of basic public media tasks. Even nowadays, lots of cultural or even artistic ventures have an artistic dimension. Virtual museums or libraries serve as an example. This mutual diffusion of culture and media shall lead to the appearance of more research areas.

The media are becoming a sort of network and this means that media pilots are likely to lose their monopoly on management. Manuel Castells [2003: 11–12] pointed out the advantages of social networking organizations, "For most of human history, unlike biological evolution, networks were outperformed as tools of instrumentality by organizations able to muster resources around centrally defined goals…"

Discussion questions:

1. Discuss media management in a historical perspective.
2. What does the dual nature of management in media organizations consist of?
3. Why do the rules of classic economy have no application in relation to information?

Part 2

Chapter 4. Systems and Information Markets

4.1. Systemic and economic aspects of information

For a long time, information as a subject of scientific description remained the domain of IT specialists. Only on rare occasions, was it of interest to economists, sociologists, cultural experts or political scientists. Nowadays, information in its various expressions has become the object of scientific interest in different disciplines. This phenomenon is encouraging as the present state of social development seems to be temporary. The Industrial Age gave rise to a mass society which has been heading in the direction in which a new resource of information became easily accessible. It appears that an analysis of this phenomenon is impossible without referring to the past.

From an economic standpoint, a civilization begins when human beings have an excess of things they consume. This surplus becomes the subject of a swap. As a result, we are able to indicate that human development has embraced three stages: 1. collecting (consuming things assured by nature); 2. production for one's own needs; 3. swap (successive stages of a swap, ranging from an immediate form of bartering to an indirect form of exchanging money). Meanwhile, by means of the Internet and other electronic methods of communication, contemporary individuals are capable of constructing their own media, most satisfying for themselves. Here, apart from the common process of exchange, one faces a return to the "production for one's own needs." What shall be the consequences of such a phenomenon? It is difficult to predicate now, but undoubtedly it has and is bound to have a huge impact on social relations, on the way politics is practiced, and, most of all, on the media market and the goods offered [Nierenberg 2009: 79–88].

Researchers of issues described here agree that management is a process which involves planning, organizing, leading, managing, and controlling. As previously indicated, for the sake of this thesis, the systemic methodology is the most useful of the various current forms of management. Its basis is to be found in Aristotle's axiom that concerns completeness as something more than the sum of its components. Such a conceptualization of phenomena has prolific results for the description of organizational and managerial processes. This organizational systemic completeness takes from four basic environmental resources: factual, human, financial and informational. In the case of traditional enterprises, information is necessary for a proper disposal of three sources: factual, human and financial. Then, in the case of a media institution, information appears with a double meaning: a source of *sensu stricto* and *sensu largo*, i.e. particular knowledge (thus also a characteristic resource), essential to properly dispose of the first resource mentioned. Supported by most original notions, information is hard to define. Władysław Kopaliński [1983: 188] pins information down by means of such notions as a message, news, novelty, thing communicated, notification, dispatch, caution, information and data. The same author considers "information theory" as a "branch of mathematics which deals with studying how much information is included in a given set (e.g. in a sentence, book, TV image, code record)." Following this lead we reach the notion of a "bit," i.e. the smallest unit of digital information record – the choice of one of possibilities: "yes" or "no," "0" or "1."

Alternatively, according to Tetelowska [1972: 46], information is a press genre that

> describes and realizes a fact or the *status quo*, refers to it by means of which it enables the reader who recaptures the outcome of the reporter's cognitive activity to perceive this fact. Information is accomplished by words functioning as notification, thereby building clear-cut semantic intentions.

Oleński [2003: 39] points out the processes connected with information. In his opinion, the information process encompasses semiotic, economic and technological aspects which cover at least one of the following functions:

- generating information,
- collecting information,
- storage of information,
- conveying information,
- processing information,
- facilitating information,
- interpreting information,
- depleting information.

At the same time, Oleński [2003: 193] notes that one should distinguish information perceived in gnoseological categories from information interpreted in an economic context, i.e. "information perceived within a given socioeconomic system as a resource, production factor, product, good, consumer goods (…)."

Summing up, these definitional attempts could be declared by means of tautology that information is the result of an informing process.

In the contemporary world information has become a highly desired resource. Drucker claimed that the 21st century was going to be the age in which information became common stock. It was chiefly media that contributed to the growth in importance of this resource, both the traditional media such as the press, radio and television, but first and foremost, the Internet. Recently, someone maliciously recapitulated the contemporary men's fascination with computers using the following words: "a computer stands for a device which helps us carry out certain work we would never have if there were no computers at all." However, this jocular statement contains some grain of rationality as once I observed students who were in the same building send e-mails to each other instead of having a simple conversation. This addiction to computers is still growing, thanks to technological innovation and new devices that facilitate communication (that is the media in a technical sense) and information about the surrounding world.

Modern Americans devote an average of 70 minutes a day to the media. Chart 4 illustrates a clear declining role of traditional media, whether it be

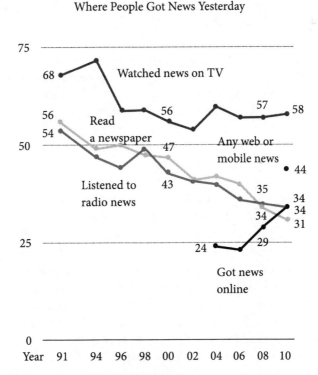

Where People Got News Yesterday

Chart 4. Where Americans get their information

Source: http://pl.ejo-online.eu/?p=1138; date of access 20.01.2011.

the press, radio or television, and an increasing role of new media. The growing importance of the Internet and mobile devices that enable the use of network information is visible. This growth has led to a rise to the development of a huge market of information services.

4.2. Information as stock

Assuming the macroeconomics division embedded into main markets, the informational market ought to be classified as a market of goods and services. Considering the informational market's specification, it has been the subject of inspection in many disciplines: economics, political science, semiotics, sociology, management sciences, computer science, etc. However, from both the methodological and practical point of view, the definition of information market is the most expressive on the grounds of economics. In this approach the information market incorporates the processes of production, exchange, and information [Oleński 2003: 199–203].

Information as a good or a service offered in the market is, contrary to common opinions, the subject of considerable interventionism, including that by the state; Information is subject to substantial institutional regulations. The vast majority of products and information services are licensed, and fees are charged for specific services in the information market. According to Oleński, the law of the market is applicable to information. In his opinion, one deals with classical categories in the information market: supply, demand, and price.

It is at odds with a postulate declared by Drucker [2000: 104–105] that information as stock is not subject to basic economic rights. This contradiction asks for a clarification. The argument referring to the postulate declared by Drucker belongs to one of the most essential themes of this monograph. Adopting the manner of reasoning and arguments proposed by the author of this publication is decisive regarding things considered here.

It seems to be a legitimate affirmation that the history of civilization has determined the resources that have shaped individual stages of human development. The present time, as Drucker claimed [ibid.], appoints stock known as information. Information is exactly the most desired resource in the contemporary world. If something is a target of desire, it usually releases intense emotions.

In the past, wars were waged over basic stocks that were desired. Originally, workforce was this stock. In ancient times machines were relatively rare, hence "hands for work" constituted the most wanted resource. Working the land or building pyramids was impossible without countless workers. The problem of meeting demand for a socially-desired good, being "hands for work" in this instance, could have been solved in three ways: striving for the largest birth rate possible, resulting in an increase of the workforce; purchasing slaves or falling into slavery due to debt; going to war as a result of which captives become slaves. Each of these solutions had its advantages and disadvantages. However, from the ancient peoples' point of view, the third way of capturing a cheap workforce was the most effective. Even in the 20th century many tyrants used this method with conquered people, and even with people of their own nation.

In the Middle Ages and later, land became the most desirable stock, which, as Smith wrote [2003: 213–235], gave golden ducats as a result of the exchange. The ruler who possessed more land was more powerful than the one who had only a little land. Therefore, wars were waged over land. Poland was a notable victim of this greed as practiced by its neighbors in the epoch of partitions.

Afterwards, thanks to James Watt (he only improved Thomas Newcomen's atmospheric steam engine, but he is considered to be the inventor) and Edmund Cartwright (he patented a mechanic loom), whose inventions catalyzed the Industrial Revolution, raw materials indispensable in the production process became the universally desired stocks. Wars were waged not only over resources but also markets.

These days, wars are fought over energy media. Even for those of us who are optimists, it was hard to believe that the war in Iraq took place for the sake of democratic ideals. The reason for this war was oil, or rather the fact that oil supplies are shrinking all over the world. Consequently, it is about who has and is going to have (until when is not known) the widest access to this medium of energy.

The contemporary world has another problem to solve. Provided that Drucker is right in theorizing that information shall remain the basic resource in the 21st century, then we will undoubtedly witness wars over information resources in the future. Actually, we already are. When the president of Georgia decided to take advantage of the opening of Olympic Games in order to get even in the war with Russia, Russian hackers (it is highly probable that they were government-related), attacked Georgian governmental servers [www.moje-militaria.pl/Cyberwar.html].

The US, the only global superpower left after the events of 1989, may be losing its cyberwar against the Chinese and the Russians. China is becoming a power threat in this domain; its cyber soldiers have not only succeeded in bypassing the safeguard of the governmental servers, but also the financial servers of the US, France, Germany, Great Britain and the Republic of Korea (South Korea). Additionally, the Russians have demonstrated their power not only in Georgia, but also in Estonia, the government of which was attacked in cyberspace the moment they were about to remove the monument to Red Army soldiers from the center of Tallin [ibid.].

In the fall of 2010, the media reported the following attack in cyberspace: By means of a virus called Stuxnet, they attacked software of an Iranian nuclear power station in Bushehr. American experts estimate that it may delay the construction of Iranian nuclear bomb. According to specialists at Kaspersky Lab in Russia, "Stuxnet is the first real cyber weapon [...], it is so complex and intelligent that it must have been written only by computer experts working for someone without financial constraints. That is for the state [Węglarczyk 2010: 1]." Yet, no country confessed to this attack. Academics and journalists considered various options. One German expert found inside the virus the word "Myrtus" which in the Middle East stands for a common bush and indicated that it may have some connotations with a legend known from the Old Testament. The thing is that in Hebrew the word "myrtle" sounds almost identical to "Hadassah" – the original name of the biblical Esther, a Jewish wife of the Persian king Xerxes I. Having found out about a courtly intrigue, the aim of which was to be the extermination of Jews living in Persia, the Jews executed a preventive attack during which they murdered 75,000 of their enemy.

The mentioned examples prove that information as stock has already become an object and a tool of war. Similarly to previous resources, information has become a desired object. Contemporary cyberwar takes different forms than earlier wars, but is equally ruthless and fierce as all its predecessors.

Neil Postman [1985] and Wiesław Godzic [1986] point out cultural aspects of information. They employ an analysis of probably the two greatest depictions of dystopia in the 20th century: George Orwell's *1984* and *Brave New World* by Aldous Huxley. "Orwell used to be afraid of those who deprive us of information, whereas Huxley feared the ones who give us so much that we shall become passive and selfish [Godzic 1996: 8]." Godzic recalls a thesis by Postman, that according to Orwell, the things we hate shall lead us to destruction. On the other hand, Huxley dreaded that we will be destroyed by the things we love [ibid.].

4.2.1. Informational system

An informational system can be examined using a quantitative or qualitative approach. A qualitative approach stands for defining an informational system by means of its quantification or measurable features. It is an apprehension characteristic for economic information, including management sciences.

The qualitative approach to defining an informational system emphasizes specific features of informational systems such as [Oleński 2003: 139–141]:

- content,
- adequacy,
- reliability,
- validity,
- usefulness,
- transparency,
- level of users' satisfaction of needs,
- relevance,
- pertinence,
- availability.

One could indicate more qualitative features. Each of the researchers dealing with the qualitative aspects of information emphasizes different things, pointing out unlikely features and attributing more significant meaning to other features. Hence, the quantitative approach of information as a resource seems to be more applicative from a perspective of investigated questions. In this formulation Oleński [2003: 141] defines an information system as a set of interrelated information processes. The notion of processes constituting a particular information system is connected with specified functions and aims. At this point Oleński points out that most information processes do not have defined aims, but only functions. For instance, information processes which appear in payment systems do not have any individual aims, though they perform significant economic functions. Occasionally it is possible to distinguish aims in information processes and at such times they are convergent with functions. As an example, the activity of a party (a person or an organization) may be profit-generating simply by possessing a particular image. For instance, a politician, a political party or a non-profit organization may build success upon profits as a direct result of preserving a given image. New media systems make it possible to multiply such an image at a rapid pace in the information market.

4.2.2. Information management

The notion of "information management" may result in defiance among some readers. Any sort of adjective juxtaposed with the word information perhaps apart from "honest," "objective," and "solid" – evokes objection. The term "management" as combined with "information," in everyday understanding, is interpreted too closely to the word "manipulating." If then somebody talks about information management they should explain to the reader what he or she should understand by the notion of "management" and "information" (both concepts have been previously defined in this monograph). It is even more important as many prominent media researchers who deal with media management mean rather "managing" or "exerting influence," frequently expressed by the writers *expressis verbis*, which again positions us dangerously close to the word "manipulation." In his lapidary *Mass Communication Theory*, Denis McQuail [2007: 241–242] explicitly states:

> The manner in which the media are controlled in democratic societies reflects both their indispensability (taken as a whole) for business, politics and everyday social and cultural life, and also their relative immunity to government regulation. Some controls, limitations and prescriptions are necessary, but principles of freedom (of speech and markets) require a cautious, even minimal, approach to regulatory control. It makes sense to use the term governance, in this context to describe the overall set of laws, regulations, rules and conventions which serve the purposes of control in general interest, including that of media industries.

Economic instruments became tools of control for governments of many countries, which also concerns democratic nations. Don Pember [1974: 268] contends that in a view of the liberal doctrine, derived from democratic systems, any direct control of the media by the governing administration is unacceptable. But even when media remain politically independent from the government, they are not completely excluded from state regulation.

A distinct perspective on "management" was presented by Marek Chyliński and Stephan Rus-Mohl [2007: 198] when they said: "...it is time to discuss structure and process of work, in particular organization, division of work and management, but also relations with the recipients, i.e. so-called editorial marketing." This perspective results from the foregoing quotation that management is a part of marketing. This view appears to be unsupported, as the majority of researchers perceive this matter completely differently. Philip Kotler [1999: 11], using the notion "marketing management" understands: "a process of planning and implementation of ideas, shaping prices, commodity bargains and distribution, services and ideas leading to a swap meeting the expectations of target groups of clients and organizations."

This diversity in understanding the term "management" with reference to media, and their basic product being "information," therefore requires a precise defining of what really should be understood by the term "management" in the context of information, and more widely, in the context of media. Still, it can be declared that information management is neither "control" nor "exerting pressure," not "managing" and much less "manipulating."

4.2.3. New technologies in information society

It seems that it is possible and with some likelihood, to predict that a great revolution in social and economic life of the world will be comprised of new technologies, progressing processes of digitization and convergence. Media digitization in particular will be of key importance. With great confidence it is stated that the common introduction of digital broadcasting and receiving will revolutionize the world of media. Even nowadays two different systems of terrestrial digital television, European Digital Video Broadcasting and Terrestrial (DVB-T) and American Advanced Television Systems Committee (ATSC), mark a new line of world division. The Americans emphasized the quality of transfer, whereas the Europeans recognized that the amount of transmitted information is more important than its quality. The DVB-T system has a twin specification of Digital Video Broadcasting: Satellite (DVB-S). The system is the basis of operation of satellite platforms in America, Africa, Asia and Australia. The specification of Digital Video Broadcasting, Cable (DVB-C), apart from European countries is used by operators of cable networks in Argentina, Brazil and Australia. It is possible that European DVB standards will be applied worldwide [Kindler-Jaworska 2000: 13].

In 1998, the first terrestrial digital television network was launched in Great Britain. The two prime multiplexes cover 90% of Great Britain. The office of Telecommunications (OFTEL) allocated one multiplex to public television BBC and the second to its rivals ITV (*Independent Television*) and Channel 4. The BBC, as a public broadcaster did not have to apply for an operator's license. In 2010, analog transmitters were shut down in 10 EU countries. Holland was the first to do so. Poland turned its transmitters off in 2013.

At this point, the question of specific profits from applying digital technology should be considered. There are more and more consumers willing to accept and pay for new forms of TV services, and new digital technology opens up various opportunities for commercial functioning which brings out an understandable interest in producers. Digital technology means not only more TV channels of better quality, but also interactive television, faster Internet access, online shopping, services such as Video On Demand, (i.e. payable television on demand, Pay Per View services, and purchasing of particular programs by the viewer such as films, sports coverage, concerts, etc.), Electronic Program Guide (EPG), but also a multitude of new services which are paid for by the consumer.

The digitization process is inseparable from the phenomenon of convergence. By this notion one should understand the blurring of boundaries among different sectors of telecommunication, media, and computers. Thanks to technological progress, the same services (images, sounds, and data) may be delivered via various network structures. This demands investments both in the broadcasting and receiving sectors. Many companies already manufacture integrated digital receivers which are a combination of a TV set and a computer. Digital television provides many more services than just TV programs. It transforms a passive customer into an active one by giving the customer the possibility of controlling and interfering with the content available to them.

4.3. Informational exclusion – a postulate about continuous education

One of the most serious challenges facing the contemporary world is that of teaching media language to society at large. Gabriel M. Nissim captured it in this way: "If your child lives at the seaside it is better to teach him or her to swim than to build a wall on the beach [www.krrit.gov.pl/stronykrrit/aktopraedumed2.htm]." Provided that the media are supposed to be the tools of public communication, it is necessary to teach future users how to speak media's language.

In the course of the Vienna conference "Media Education vs. Digital Age," a definition was formulated which outlined the spheres of action within media education. This was recognized that it is necessary to educate people about the scope of the printed word, graphics, sound and moving and motionless pictures conveyed by any technical means. Moreover, it was emphasized that media education not only enables people to understand media functioning in their countries, but also teaches how to use these media. The aim of this education should be [Schretter 2000]:

- analyzing how to evaluate and create media texts critically;
- identifying the media texts' sources, their context and political, social, commercial and cultural significance;
- interpreting of the news and values offered by the media;
- selecting appropriate media adjusted to convey one's own news and reports;
- demanding access to media.

At the beginning of the 21st century, a team was created at the request of the National Council of Radio Broadcasting and Television, who developed a report entitled "Media Education." The description of Polish reality in this respect is appalling. In the report we read, "…the issue of media education in our country is neglected and marginalized, and a consequence of this juncture is a badly prepared core curriculum, chaos at the decision-making level, lack of modern benchmarks and adequate scientific aids... [www.krrit.gov.pl/ stronykrrit/aktopraedumed2.htm]."

Apart from the opinion, the report contains suggestions concerning the repair of the current state. Its authors offer to reach to the patterns of critical media pedagogy which ought to comprise learning and teaching others how to decode media messages critically and how to trace a complex dimension of their interaction. Researchers claim that there is no other way to learn "proper" or "desirable" media behaviors but through a critical analysis of the so-called natural presence of the media in the social environment. The report's authors direct plenty of critical words towards the teachers. In their opinion, scholastic educators, trying to protect young people against negative influence of the media, encourage youngsters to take advantage of high culture patterns. According to the authors of the report, one ought to reject such mentorship. The basis of media education should be an active partnership based on the teacher's knowledge of topics that are of the teenagers' interest, and not something "desired" from a curricula point of view. The authors recognized that the basic matter of media education in Poland should be the politicians' and teachers' conviction that media education constitutes an indispensable and very important fragment of general education of the whole society [ibid.]. Such a subject has even been introduced into schools in some Western European countries.

The need of a media education also imposes additional tasks on the public media in this scope. Perhaps in all European countries following the British *Voice of listener & Viewer*, there is demand for an organization that would influence broadcasters and politicians regarding program content. Such an organization could play a significant role regarding media education. It could, for example, monitor adverse media phenomena.

It would be advisable to consider the issue of whether the public media ought to bear the responsibility for the media education of society. The answer to this question is not as obvious as it might seem, as private media organizations are generally shaped as companies and are therefore profit-oriented. On the other hand, media institutions as organizations of special significance, particularly from a social point of view, have obligations to society. Nobody has to be convinced of the power of the media, especially electronic media in this contemporary world. Taking these conditions into account on February 25, 1999, nine Polish TV broadcasters signed the "Friendly Media" agreement ("Przyjazne media"); the aim of this agreement was to undertake efficient actions aiming to protect children and teenagers from programs that may threaten their physical, mental and moral development. Guided by ethical, social, international and legal premises, the signatories pledged to voluntarily obey rules and regulations included in the document:

In accordance with ethical rules, the document stated that physical, mental and moral well-being of children and teenagers is a common good, therefore it is advisable to respect and strengthen this good.

The negative influence of some TV programs regarding the upbringing of the younger generation has become the basis and social prerequisite of the document. After all, its authors indicated a correlation between TV scenes of rape and violence and an increase in deviant behaviors among youngsters.

The international prerequisite concerning the coordination of legislative regulations in the scope of television programs in member states of the European Union results from entry 22 of Directive No. 97/36 of European Council and European Parliament on June 17, 1997. The document states that "Member States shall take appropriate measures to ensure that television broadcasts by broadcasters under their jurisdiction do not include any programmers which might seriously impair the physical, mental or moral development of minors, in particular programs that involve pornography or gratuitous violence."

The legal basis for the agreement made by broadcasting companies is deemed the Broadcasting Act of December 29, 1992, whose Articles 1 and 3 say: "broadcast cannot propagate activities contrary to law, Polish national interest and attitudes and opinions contrary to morality and social welfare" and "content which can endanger mental or physical development of children and youth cannot be broadcast between 6:00 a.m. and 11:00 p.m.," respectively.

The Understanding of Polish Television Broadcasters "Przyjazne Media" ("Friendly Media") contains three cardinal principles:

1. The broadcaster acceding to the agreement is obliged to do everything possible in order to prevent children and teenagers from being exposed to programs inappropriate for them;
2. Elimination of programs propagating violence and programs violating generally accepted moral norms requires an introduction of efficient supervisory mechanisms by the broadcasters themselves;
3. The necessity to introduce a uniform system of alerting viewers, particularly parents and teenagers concerning the potential harmfulness of programs for various age groups.

The implementation of these rules should be run with concern regarding the cooperation of broadcasters and viewers, and aim to primarily foster the creation of forms of consistent public dialogue on this topic with viewers. This should be done, in particular, with parents of children and teenagers, teachers and counsellors as well as with organizations expressing the viewers' opinion.

The signatories of the "Friendly Media" document undertook to tag its programs with symbolic colors: green: program destined for children; yellow: requiring parents' consent; and red: intended solely for adult viewers.

During the conference *Media Education – the Need and Challenge of the Future*, Didier Schretter [2000], the chairman of the European Association for Audiovisual Media Education (AEEMA), stated that modern data storage technique facilitates and its processing into information, which indicates a new type of wealth transition. By the following he meant that several ages ago richness was connected with land ownership, later on with the possession of capital goods and subsequently with services and in our times with the possession of information.

It appears that an understanding of contemporary media channels and their importance in the process of communication is determined by an appropriate level of education. Just as every piece of equipment requires getting acquainted with its manual, in a similar way, media tools require adequate instruction. It seems that in relation to communication instruments, it is education that ought to be such an instruction.

The contemporary, technically advanced world strives toward extending areas of social exclusion. It seems that all human beings at some point in their lives reach their own level of incompetence. My late mother-in-law, being of advanced age, used to call us on average once a month asking for help with her broken TV. My sons quickly discovered that their grandmother was unable to remember all functions of the remote control. My mother-in-law would usually accidentally press the AV button and as a result the image or sound disappeared. If this anecdote triggered a smile on anyone's face then they should think that he or she will eventually have their own symbolic "remote control," a device they will not be able to master.

The anecdote mentioned above leads us to the conclusion that the information management process requires both individuals as well as organizations to be entities which have mastered the craft of continuous learning. A permanent supplementation of information as a basic resource of the 21st century seems to be the *sine qua non* of normal functioning in an information society. In this case "normal" is defined as: someone who is knowingly able to benefit from information and devices used for receiving and processing this information. In short, someone who knows how to manage information.

Discussion questions:

1. What does the essence of digital exclusion consist of?
2. Wars used to be waged mainly about basic resources. What are the forms of "war" over information being the resource?
3. What forms should media education take on in the contemporary world?

Chapter 5. Economic Aspects of Media Management

Alan B. Albarran primarily [1996: 5] defined 'media economics' as a discipline investigating the way in which media industries use rare goods to create and distribute media contents among consumers in order to fulfill various needs and expectations. A few years later the same author defined "media economics" as a discipline which investigates the way organizations and media industries operate on different levels of their activity (e.g. global. national, household, individual) alongside other forces (e.g. global, regulatory, technological and social), by making use of theories, notions and rules resulting from both macro- and microeconomic perspectives [Albarran 2010: 3].

Both of the mentioned definitions refer to the fulfillment of social needs by means of a rare good (resource). A.B. Albarran does not define this good by providing just a general statement. According to the author of these considerations, this good stands for information, as the basic ingredient of media content.

5.1. Media economics as an area of research

Robert Picard [2006: 23] claims that media economics is a discipline which deals with examining how economic and financial factors influence a variety of communicative media systems' activities as well as individual organizations and enterprises, including telecommunications entities. R. Picard, considered to be the father of "media economics," claims that from a technical point of view a thing like "media economics," in the case that such a thing existed, would mean that the laws of economics applied to different domains do not have any application for the media. It could seem that R. Picard holds completely different views in this scope compared to P. Drucker, who – let us remember – claims that information as a resource does not undergo the laws of classic economics. However, R. Picard notices the distinctness of media markets writing: "media economics is a specific translation of theory and economy to the media industry." The word "specific" is key in this case. Therefore, both scholars see the distinctness and the economic specificity of the media sphere, yet they differ as to the level of this "specificity." Is it a distinctness large enough so as to consider it a new quality (as claimed by P. Drucker); or is it a mere dissimilarity within the frameworks of the same research current (as claimed by R. Picard)? Arguments included in this monograph refer to the output of both scientists; however, their conclusions place them closer to the way of thinking presented by P. Drucker [2000] and D. McQuail [2007: 227] who referred to the media as a "business like no other." Yet, this reference does not do any harm to the meaning of the output and the scientific thought of R. Picard, which has previously been represented and will continue to be in the following studies:

Media economics derives from the current of research done on social communication initiated in the first half of the 20th century. In their initial period, media enterprises were previously treated more like social organizations than subjects of the market. This approach should not be surprising, as in the early period scientists coming from sociology, political science, legislative sciences, linguistics and technical sciences studied the communication processes. Studying the economic aspects of communication processes was overlooked for a long time. The influence on neglecting the aspects connected with management and media economics found its basis in the attitude of the media entrepreneurs themselves. Many owners of small publishing houses, radio or TV stations in the initial period were more contented with the roles played by their enterprises and they did not personally pay attention to the economic aspects of the activities they conducted. By contrast, great media concerns in general belonged to and were funded by the state. Therefore, they were functioning beyond the economic realm. The case is similar to those huge concerns that used to function on the basis of a concession or a license, which generally gave them a monopolistic position. This was not conducive for paying due attention to economic calculations while carrying out business activities [Picard 2006: 24].

It was only the second half of the 20th century which granted the media a much stronger commercial nature and caused people to pay more attention to advertising. This, in turn, led to a massive growth in advertising expenditures. Public broadcasters also began to perceive advertising as a source to increase their revenues. These radical changes seemed to be a superb research field for scientists dealing with the media. Anticipating an increased research interest on these issues was expected. However, nothing like that happened. Picard writes that university departments that used to deal with the communication processes and the media, which in a natural way should be interested in the scope of research and education, did not offer courses in the area of media economics. Only a very narrow group of scientists carried out modest research of this scope, whereas didactic activity was limited only to occasional courses managed by individuals already employed in the media industry.

Consequently, as written by Picard [2006: 24–25], both scholars dealing with the media and the managers controlling the media, had even a dim idea about the basic economic aspects influencing their businesses.

The first works in the area of media economics appeared only in the 1950s. Alan B. Albarran [1996: 291–307] points out to: the works of R.H. Raya [1951: 444–456] – concerning competitors and concentration in the press market; W. B. Reddaway [1963] – analyzing newspapers as enterprises; P.O. Steiner [1952] – researching competitors in the radio broadcasting market or H.J. Levin [1958] – referring to the structure of an early television market.

In the 1960s and 1970s the economic approach to research concerning the media was related to the political economy. Contemporary researchers analyze how power influences the media and its market structure. Characteristic works of that period include those of: D. W. Smythe [1963], H. Schiller [1969], A. Mattelart and S. Sigelaub [1979].

The first known textbook that provided a detailed analysis of the media industry from an economic perspective was written in France in 1978 by Nadine Toussaint Desmoulins [1978]. Works concerning economic aspects by Alfons Nieto Tamarago that appeared in Spanish periodicals were written slightly earlier [1973]. In the 1970s the output of American researchers working on media economics was equally modest as the European ones. At the end of the 1970s, Benjamin Compaine published his works on the economic aspects of book distribution and freedom in the American media [1978, 1979].

A proper rank of problems connected with media economics began to be recognized only in the 1980s, but researchers still rarely dealt with media economics. The key monograph for the development of the discipline by Robert Picard entitled *Media Economics: Concepts and Issues* [1989] appeared at the end of the 1980s. The following year welcomed an extensive work by Nicolas Granham [1990] *Capitalism and Communications: Global Culture and Information Economics*. In the following years, new positions that consolidated the significance of media economics in learning came into existence. It would be advisable to mention the works of: Bruce M. Owen, Steven S. Wildman [1992], Alan B. Albarran [1996] and Sylvie Chan-Olmsted [1998], as well as the author of this monograph. A growing number of researchers dealing with media economics and, later on, with media management led to the pioneering of MBA (Master of Business Administration) courses being offered at European and American universities. By the beginning of 1990s, such type of education was introduced at the University of Turku in Finland and the University of St. Gallen (Switzerland) as well as at two American institutes, Northwestern and Fordham Universities. The University of Navarra in Spain, the University of Stirling in Scotland and the University of Southern California in the U.S. offer master's degree courses in the field of media economics. New doctoral studies in this field will be offered at these universities as well. An International School of Business managed by R.G. Picard leads this field and operates within the University of Jönköping in Sweden. Similar doctorate courses are also offered by several European universities (e.g., the University of Cologne and the Technical University of Dortmund) and American ones (e.g., the University of South Carolina).

One notices the growing importance of media economics in various parts of the world. This is proven by the number of books about media economics translated into different languages. The key monograph for this discipline, *Media Economics: Concepts and Issues*, has been translated into Chinese and Korean, for example. Moreover, original works from this domain appear in various languages, such as: French, German, Russian, Hungarian and Polish.

Researchers of different groups specialize in diverse domains of media management. Among these various streams R.G. Picard distinguishes three research areas: theoretical, applied and critical (Table 9: Research areas of media economics).

According to R.G. Picard, the theoretical approach in media economics derives from non-classical economics. By the means of applied tools, he tries to explain the influence of forces on media systems and markets. Researchers who represent this conceptualization often deal with the development and forecasting of the future of media organizations and also with the choice of optimum strategies for development.

The systemic approach is nowadays applied most frequently by researchers in the area of media economics. Its genesis is found in the cooperation between the media industry representatives and university employees dealing with these issues. Thus, research and the results are both scientific and utilitarian in nature. The representatives of this trend most frequently investigated the

Table 9. Research areas of media economics

Levels of analysis	Theoretical and applied approach		Critical approach
	Micro level	Macro level	Meta level
Scientific discipline	Business economics, management	Economics, political economics	Communication, media, political economy
Scope of research	Media enterprises, media consumers	Policies of governments, economy, media enterprises	Communication systems, culture, policy of governments
Issues under research	Cash transfers, cost structure, rate of return	Competition, consumption, efficiency, output	Social, political and cultural communication systems

Source: Picard 2006: 28.

structure of media markets in order to distinguish the changes and tendencies taking place within them. The utilitarian nature of the research made it possible for media organizations to adapt the offer to pending market changes at the right time.

Researchers representing this scientific conceptualization most frequently dealt with an analysis of consumer behaviors, trends in advertising, and the specification of media organizations.

The critical conceptualization in media economics emerged from the works of economists investigating the economic aspects of the communication processes. The scholars representing this scientific current generally used the cultural and social perspectives which enabled them to address the essence of such problems as the concentration or the monopolization of media markets, along with the consequences of shifting from an economy based on raw materials into one based on information. The influence of scholars studying these issues in the British market has been strongly incorporated in this approach, including those representing the neo-Marxist approach.

R.G. Picard points out that the microeconomic approach directs researchers towards analyzing individual players in media markets, but also towards the mechanisms which govern these markets as well. This approach concerns the media enterprises and the consumers of media products and services as well as the specification of the media markets. In this conceptualization the essence of the research lies in cash transfers, prices of products and media services, cost structure, return of investment, etc. It is necessary to remember that media markets differ from other markets due to their dual nature. Media enterprises provide their consumers with particular media goods and services but, due to their ability to focus "customers' attention" on their products and services (a rare good), they can sell this 'attention' to advertisers.

The macroeconomic approach is typical for researchers dealing with the influence of large market aggregates on media systems. In this approach, the analysis on national levels declines in importance in the context of the phenomenon of globalization. In order to comprehend the range of interactions, it is enough to refer to comparing the media enterprises that broadcast their own programs by means of satellites and transmitters.

Both practitioners as well as media theoreticians in each of these conceptualizations move beyond the appointed framework. While it may lead to tensions among researchers, R.G. Picard [2006: 30] points out that they are unnecessary as the variety of descriptions enhances, not weakens media economics.

It seems that the future of media economics as a research and didactic area shall be appointed by savage technological transformations coming along in media markets. The convergence of digitization and the media will not only enforce new ways of market competition but also new perspectives on the economic issues inside media companies. Undoubtedly, globalization will have implications which are not yet completely clear and have an effect on the economic aspects of media organizations. However, there is no doubt that the phenomena indicated here will lead to the disappearance of traditional media markets and the creation of brand new ones. Media alliances are also going to be new, along with directions of expansion. The demand for new media products and services will require a new description and indication of developmental trends. These are research areas that need to be explored but they also require didactic activities and the formation of new areas of education, especially in the fields of media economics and media management.

After the three decades during which media economics as a scientific discipline was being born, it turned out that a multitude of conceptualizations and research approaches are not obstacles when explaining key phenomena and trends in media markets. The discipline was employed to deliver usable knowledge to the media's governing bodies which made it possible to shape the offer and increase the quality of provided products and services. It appears that the utilitarian aspect of media economics might predestine its dynamic growth in the forthcoming years.

5.2. Media markets

In Chapters 3 and 4, it was indicated that the properties of a good (a previously defined information) offered in media markets can cause the said good to avoid the basic laws of economics. The distinctness of media markets results not only from the otherness of the offered good and the dual nature of media markets, but also from the means which these markets have for the shaping of the consciousness and opinions of customers on different issues and topics. Nevertheless, it does not mean that the media is not directed by the logic of the classical market. Media enterprises, while competing against one another, aim at monopolizing particular media sectors in order to gain a dominating position. As already demonstrated, the electronic media market is a regulated one; however, the press market does not report to such regulations. The characteristic which assigns the range of a press market is (still) paper. There is enough paper in the market to publish all newspapers. The case is similar for editorial, film, music markets, etc. In contrast, in the electronic media market, there are more people willing to run radio and television enterprises than there are available frequencies. Hence, the necessity to regulate this market arises.

The market in economic conceptualization is broadly defined as a generality of relations between the sellers who offer particular services or goods and the purchasers. The most essential condition of a free market is the right to an unlimited choice of partners in finalizing economic transactions. Due to the type and nature of finalized transactions, the market is divided into branch markets. The case is similar to the media market where one distinguishes the following branches: press, radio, publishing, television, film, etc.

The media market varies from all other markets and each branch has its specification. The film production cycle differs from that of a book or a feature film. The return of investment in the radio market is different from the one in the television market. The basis of a media market lies in the media enterprise that functions within it. The literature on the subject states that enterprises underlie the same cycles as in other trades. Therefore, the life cycle of a media organization has four phases [Kranenburg, Hogenbirk 2006: 325]:

1. introduction,
2. growth,
3. maturity,
4. decline.

The introductory phase depends on the size of the company, the capital, and the media sector a given enterprise is willing to enter. A small publishing house entering the market should overcome completely different problems in comparison to a huge media corporation which is expanding its activity within some other media sector. In one case, the scale effect might be decisive, and in another, defeat may be caused by the rule of declining revenues. Nonetheless, in the media sector, as previously discussed, by the means of information being the new resource, laws of economics become undermined. In the introductory phase the aim of a company is to struggle to survive and maintain its position in the market.

The growth phase in a media business is marked by a low financial liquidity and a large fluctuation in production. Hans van Kranenburg and Annelies Hogenbirk [2006: 326–327] claim that satellite TV and online media are located exactly in such a phase.

The stabilization of enterprise turnover takes place in the maturity phase. It is during this phase that companies have the most clients and reach the highest profits. Innovativeness in this phase consists in moving the product itself into the production process.

The decline phase, which is the last phase, consists in accumulating many negative phenomena which impair the competitive position of a given company and thus decrease its ability to generate profit. The reasons for this situation

Table 10. Life phases of media enterprises including characteristic factors for media markets

Market characteristics

company's life phase	sales	profits	clients	barriers		competitors	media industries
				entrances	exits		
introduction	low	negative	innovators	low	low	several ones	streaming; video online
increase	rapidly growing	growing	taken over early	moderate	moderate	rapid growth	satellite television; media online
maturity	peak	high	majority	high	high	relatively stable, later decline	music industry books; magazines, radio; television
decline	declining	declining	laggard	high	high	decline	newspapers

Source: Kranenburg, Hogenbirk 2006: 327.

may be both external (e.g. poor communication, decline in demand for a given good), or internal (e.g. mistakes in management). The previously mentioned researchers H. van Kranenburg and A. Hogenbirk [2006, 328–329] say that the publishing industry is currently in the decline phase as demonstrated by its history in Holland. The same authors, making use of research by R.G. Picard, devised a table showing the life cycle of media enterprises to account for the intensity of various factors characteristic of the media market: sales volume, profit, entrance and exit barriers, and clients' characteristics (Table 10: Life phases of media enterprises including characteristic factors of media markets).

There are no rules on how long a given enterprise is allowed to remain in a given phase. One notices a large number of companies which have never managed to go beyond the introductory phase and continually strive for survival in the market.

There are numerous models that describe the market. For many years the SCP model (*Structure-Conduct-Performance*) which describes dependencies among market structure, enterprise strategy and its results was considered to be one of key models in describing the mechanisms of an enterprise in the market. This model was presented in 1956 by Joseph S. Bain [after: Kranenburg, Hogenbirk 2006: 333]. In his opinion, the dependency among market structure, enterprise strategy and the effects is characteristically a one-way relationship. Most of the research affirms that the market structure is shaped under the influence of particular market behaviors, whereas an analysis ought to be carried out in four types characteristic for the markets: perfect competition, monopolistic competition (has features of both monopoly and competition), monopoly and oligopoly [Tirole 1990: 18].

Many companies in the media market, particularly the small ones, work in conditions of (nearly) perfect competition. They make use of the same technologies, their products and services are (nearly) identical, customers have (nearly) all information about the offered products and services. Because customers know their value, individual decisions of buyers and sellers have (nearly) no influence on the price of a given product. One deals with a monopoly when there is only one producer or service provider in the market. For example, there is only one cinema in a given city. In this situation, the product or service supplier determines a price (in general) aimed at profit maximization which is limited only by the size of purchasers' demand. The supplier's aim is to balance the final cost with the final income. In conditions of monopolistic competition many enterprises offer similar, yet homogeneous products or services. H. van Kranenburg and A. Hogenbirk [2006: 333] provide an example of the TV producers' market in Great Britain as a monopolist competition. There are about one thousands of them and each one is making efforts to differentiate its products from those of competitors. We come across an oligopoly when there are several large, mutually dependent enterprises operating in the market. A characteristic feature of this market structure is the lack of price competition. Provided one enterprise changes its market behaviors, the other ones also modify theirs. Wiliam J. Merriles gives such an example of two Australian newspapers: *The Sun* and *The Daily Mirror*. Both of them, in the scope of content and form, were substitutions for each other. For a long time, *The Sun* was the price leader. Each alteration in price elicited a similar reaction from its competitors. However, when *The Daily Mirror* did not react similarly to its competitor's rise, it was the one to gain more readers and become the price leader [Merriles 1983: 291–311]. In the case of an oligopoly, its crucial roles are played by its entrance and exit barriers. The former ones, in particular, limit competition to a great extent and are unfavorable from the consumers' point of view. While observing the entrance and exit barriers, many researchers are able to analyze changes that take place in media markets. Such studies were carried out by Hans van Kranenburg, Franz Palm, Gerard Pfann [Kranenburg, Palm, Pfann 2002: 282–303]. Their calculations concerned the Dutch press and included the period from the second half of the 19th century until the end of the 20th century. Their research confirmed that the higher entrance barriers meant the smallest opportunities of entering a given media market and the largest difficulties getting out of this market. This is related to the problem of "sunk costs". They are costs which cannot be recovered and must be sustained while entering the market. The costs of research and development, marketing and advertising are generally "sunk costs" no matter whether the offered products are popular among consumers or not. Producers of audio and multimedia recordings and film producers have to face the problem of high risk while offering a new CD, computer game or feature film.

Researchers emphasize the fact that media markets are also "contestable markets," i.e. ones that in oligopoly conditions behave similarly to competitive conditions, yet remain under the strong influence of potential entrants. The "contestability" results in low entrance barriers and low "sunk costs." A low level of "sunk costs" leads to an increase in competition. In media markets, one may distinguish four attitudes towards the problem of "sunk costs" [Stiglitz 1987: 883–947]: 1. media enterprises are not willing to enter a given market, even though leaders gain profits; 2. subsequent entrances do not lead to an increase in competitiveness (the entrance of one leads to the exit of another one); 3. market leaders undertake strategic actions in order to prevent further entrances; 4. enterprises are inefficient; they do not gain profits even though the market is competitive.

The model offered by Boyan Jovanocic [1982: 649–670] was also crucial for the media industry. The author suggested that media enterprises enter the market in a particular order. This succession is appointed by a company's efficiency determined by its costs.

Another interesting concept referring to media markets was proposed by Chris Anderson. In 2004, he published the framework of *Long Tail Economics Concept*. It is one of the most interesting ways of looking at the issue of media economics as a direct effect of shifting from traditional media to post network cultures based on broadband connections. Such an alteration leads to market diversification on a grand scale. In Anderson's opinion, network means of communication cause media contents to reach many of our niche markets and may bring bidders a satisfactory profit [Lister, Dovey, Giddings, Grant, Kelly 2009: 296–300]. According to Anderson [2006: 52] our culture and economy less frequently focus on a relatively small number of hits (products and markets of the mainstream of great customer interest) on the peak of the demand curve and rather transfer attention to numerous niches situated in their tail.

Many market opinions can be divided into two conceptualizations. According to the first conceptualization, media markets are driven by hits. That is, before a hit emerges in a media market that would support a media undertaking, very often creations of poor or average quality are formed. Secondly, there is a notion of the "first copy cost" that exists in media economics. Its essence comes down to the fact that the cost of producing the first copy of a media product is very high and only the sales of some threshold number of newspapers can generate profit. A newspaper or a feature film available only in one or several copies would be horrendously expensive. Only a specific number of copies makes an undertaking profitable. Therefore, the traditional media were dependent on large capital investments without which any enterprise was impossible to accomplish. According to traditional media economics, products with high manufacturing costs and low circulation found themselves in a "long tail" of the demand curve that was ignored by the producers. As a result, only a small number of hits would generate very large profits. Traditional sellers of media contents were unable to lift the weight of "long tail" products as they generated revenues that were too small. The new media changed this situation dramatically [Lister et al. 2009: 296–297].

Research concerning media markets, barriers of entrance and exit, analysis of operation costs, prices of offered products etc. is one of the most substantial research fields that may yield the data necessary for making the right media enterprise decisions? It appears that the forthcoming years should bring concentration of research on the market effects related to digitization and convergence in the media business, including opportunities provided by "long tail" products.

5.3. Management of finances in media organizations

In regards to finances, the media business features similar processes of financial engineering as the other sectors. Hence, we are dealing with dividends, monetary flows, return of investment, fusions, takeovers, bankruptcies, etc. However, it should be noted that the European and American experience in this field is distinct. For example, mergers and takeovers in the American market are much more frequent than in the European market. Ronald J. Rizzuto [2006: 155] indicated three areas which were of interest to American researchers:

1. Analysis of return on investment on capital before and after the merger,
2. Evaluation of company value that can be brought by a merger,
3. Case studies in relation to individual mergers.

Douglas Shapiro [2004: 1–21], while analyzing some of the greatest media mergers of recent years (e.g.: AOL/Time Warner – USD 165.9 billion; Vodafone/Air Touché – USD 62.8 billion; AT&T/MediaOne – USD 55.8 billion), reached the conclusion that the mergers did not lead to any increase in value. In his opinion, the shareholders lost out as a result of these mergers. Time Warner stock, for example, was sold at USD 43 before the merger with AOL, while their value dropped to USD 16 after the merger.

R.J. Rizzuto [2006: 157] draws attention to the fact that one of the most important research areas related to the management of media organizations is the investigation of areas connected with winning new sources of financing and the structure analysis of previous measures. Convergence and digitization processes cause readers' withdrawal from traditional paper editions of newspapers and an increase in the use of Internet editions. However, the loss of advertisement in traditional paper versions is not compensated by the increasing revenues from advertisements placed on the Internet.

Jeff Kaye and Stephen Quinn [2010; pl.ejo-online.eu/?cat=4], in their monograph titled *Funding Journalism in the Digital Age. Business Models, Strategies, Issues and Trends,* carried out a review of new sources of media financing. The first of the two authors is an experienced journalist and media consultant and the latter is a professor of journalism from Australia. The authors indicated several new methods that can serve as solutions to the financial difficulties facing the media industry:

1. formation of companies by media enterprises and Internet giants, such as Google or Yahoo;
2. adjustment of the content of news services to the requirements of browsers and not the readers' needs (it concerns placing such words in the offered information so as to make them highly positioned in browsers);

3. reference to "hyperfocality";
4. "dayparting" – adjusting the media offer to the rhythm of the day of current and potential customers;
5. micro payments for individual media services;
6. voluntary contributions supporting particular kinds of journalism or media;
7. helping out financially individual titles from commercial and public sources.

One shortcoming of J. Kaye's and S. Quinn's monograph is its focus on an English-speaking market. However, one has to admit that the crisis of printed media in this market has been noticeable. Nevertheless, it is worth pointing out that Europe, including Poland, is seeking new ways for additional press financing. Such new ways include adding music or film CDs to magazines, as well as books that comprise a source of additional financial revenues. In some Scandinavian countries the press market is subsidized by resources coming from TV advertisements.

The lack of financial means is also visible in the public media market. Some European countries are abandoning the subscription method – the traditional form of public media financing – or are combining it with other financing sources. In Holland, for example, the government increased the personal income tax to devote a portion to financing the public media. In Belgium, Estonia and Hungary, public broadcasters are financed by budgetary subventions. In Iceland and the Czech Republic, representatives are planning to completely abolish subscriptions and replace them with some other form of financing the public media, for instance budgetary means, as is the case in Estonia. One European country where the public media is financed from commercial sources is Luxembourg [Jędrzejewski 2010: 121–123].

The only two European countries which have been maintaining a stable and safe level of public media financing from subscriptions are Germany and Great Britain. Stanisław Jędrzejewski rightly emphasized this while describing the work of the BBC: "The mechanism of a subscription has up to now been a basic guarantee for these broadcasters to be free from political pressures, being market-dependent and economic pressure [ibid.]."

Media organizations have several sources of financing. Generally, these are revenues derived from advertisers, customers and the state. It is assumed that the commercial media at the prevailing level are provided for by advertising revenues, whereas the public and social media are provided for by tributes (voluntary or compulsory) from media customers. Both the public and commercial media gain profits from the turnover of copyright and related laws.

The situation of the media in Poland when considering sources of financing is similar to that of other European countries. The printed media are intensively seeking to increase revenues as the income from advertisements placed in traditional paper editions has decreased. An increase of revenues from advertising placed on the Internet does not compensate for this loss. However, the situation of the public media is particularly dramatic when it comes to financing. In the legal sense, financing the public media is governed by the Broadcasting Act as of 1992 and on Subscription Fees as of 2005. Article 31 of the Broadcasting Act of December 29, 1992 states that public income of radio and television companies in Poland are:

1. subscription fees,
2. sources deriving from eligibility to broadcasting turnover,
3. revenues from advertising and sponsored auditions,
4. revenues from other sources.

However, the Act on Subscription Fees lists many categories of people who are legally exempt from paying the subscription. Furthermore, the weakness of the state as an institution and the attitude of some politicians (exhorting not to pay the subscription) means that levying the subscription is on a dramatically low level. In recent years the amount of charged subscription fees in Poland has dropped to almost half of what it used to be (Table 11: Distribution of subscription incomings within 2009–2011).

The National Broadcasting Council for Radio Broadcasting worked out a new algorithm of division of subscription means which favored the radio and which also reclaimed means of the public television. The regional stations of the Polish radio for 2010 (despite low subscriptions) generated a profit. In contrast, regional branches of public television presented almost all reruns. The only first-run programs were mainly news services. It is worth noticing that there were not enough subscription resources in order to even finance a decent amount of activity of regional branches of public TV. In 2010, the management at TVP devoted all of its subscription resources to the purpose of their branches' activities and was forced to contribute from advertising

Table 11. Distribution of subscription revenues within 2009–2011

Year	Total	TVP SA	PR SA	Regional broadcasting stations of PR
2009	628	301	172	155
2010	537	221	157	159
2011 (forecast)	389	144	122.5	122.2

Source: own study by the National Council of Radio Broadcasting and Television.

revenues. Through these means commercial public television continues to subsist in Poland. A few years ago the author of these reflections, while describing the situation of the public media, pointed out the growing dangers in this respect [Nierenberg 2007: 60]: Should this phenomenon intensify, there will be two solutions: 1. public media will be soliciting resources in the advertising market more intensively; 2. the state will activate mechanisms that will enable the increase in collection rate to the level noted in Western European countries. Since that time the collection rate of subscriptions has dropped by almost half. It was acknowledged that increasing the subscription collection rate is unnecessary as the public media ought to be supported from the budget. Meanwhile, the subscription fee was brought back in two European countries: in Portugal and Hungary. Also, in France, Greece and Cyprus the subscription fee is collected along with other public fees, an act that in Poland was considered illegal.

In line with recommendations set by the European Union, the incomes of the public media can be diversified. Along with the subscription fee, it can be diversified through advertising revenues, sponsorship, turnover of copyrights to broadcasting, or other sources, such as grants or subventions. However, pursuant to union directives, extra subscription revenues should not be excessive and ought to be adapted to the needs of broadcasters and suitably registered.

It is also worth keeping in mind the case of New Zealand, a country which in 1989 began experiencing deregulations in the media market, on the basis of which public television was appointed to maximize profit and consign as much dividend as possible to the main shareholder, the government of New Zealand. Requirements concerning types and quality of programs as well as the size of national production of auditions broadcasted in total were eliminated for public broadcasters. One measure cancelled any limitations in the field of advertising, sponsorship and the size of foreign investments in the media market. The government appointed an agency which carried out tenders for the production and transmission of missionary broadcasting. After ten years, the New Zealanders concluded that they have become poorer. In 2003, the New Zealand Television Charter was adopted to include all missionary aims of public television along with a guarantee of an increase in budgetary measures. The final decision was made by the minister responsible for issues concerning radio and television in New Zealand:

> For much too long we have allowed for purely commercial respects to decide what is happening in the institution that ought to be the foundation of our culture. We are going to return to the group of developed countries which acknowledge the meaning of public television as a cultural medium and a source of information needful for us as citizens [Jędrzejewski 2010: 123].

In Chapter 3 of this monograph R.G. Picard's observation was noted [1989: 17], that all media, under any circumstances concerning their nature and media, have two primary functions:

1. social mission,
2. commercial.

One recalls this thought as many researchers repeat untrue statements concerning the nature of the conflict between public and commercial media [Misiak 2003]. In their opinion the basis of this conflict is the participation of the former ones in the market of advertisement as well as the fact that it deprives the broadcaster independence in programming. However, this diagnosis is not entirely true. Let us recall the instance of the BBC and R. Picard's idea that all forms of media perform a double function: that of a social mission as well as a commercial one. Even though the BBC does not broadcast any commercials within the area of Great Britain, it still performs a commercial function.

An example of a program presented by the BBC and watched by three million viewers was mentioned in Chapter 4. Is it possible for these three million to watch a program on commercial television? Of course, it is. Therefore, provided such a program and the BBC did not exist, most likely some portion of the viewers – perhaps a considerable one – would watch a program on commercial television. At the same time its audience would have increased, as well as the CPT index (*cost per thousand* – one of the basic indexes of advertising effectiveness). This is particularly appealing to advertisers. Hence, the BBC, despite not broadcasting advertisements, fulfills a commercial role in the market. It is thus unjust to claim that the conflict between commercial and public media comes down entirely to the fact that the latter ones transmit commercials. This is only a superficial description of the economic aspects of media management that does not penetrate the essence of this issue.

Discussion questions:

1. Characterize media markets.
2. Indicate and discuss sources of income in media organizations.
3. Solve the essence of the conflict between commercial and public media in the financial context.

Chapter 6. Management of Advertising

Advertising is one on the most essential elements of the media market. For commercial media, it is the most significant, as advertising revenues constitute the basis of many organizations' upkeep. They have become an essential agent between producers or service providers and their consumers. The contemporary media landscape does not exist without commercials. Therefore, the ability to manage advertisements is one of the crucial elements of general media management.

Similar to any other innovation, media organizations that enter the market are characterized by a course of diffusion. In the initial course period only a few people make use of a given medium. Yet, as it becomes widespread, it enters a period of profitability to become a mass medium in its third stage. This diffusion period then undergoes a continuous shortening. Let us make use of figures from the United States as an example. The first nation-wide newspaper was published in 1672 and needed 160 years in order to become a mass medium. For magazines it took 110 years, 30 years for radio, and just 10 years for television.

John M. Lavine, Daniel B. Wackman [1988: 22–24] accentuate three major reasons for an accelerated diffusion:

1. Curtailment of working hours resulting in the extension of time-off which in turn led to an increase in media consumption, especially when electronic media became widespread;
2. Electronic media required more minor skills from viewers than printed media, e.g. the ability to read (J.M. Lavine, D.B. Wackman point out that the diffusing of media connected with computers was slower than that of television);
3. Technological changes in media accelerate the diffusion process.

Such a multitude of competitive media is highly importance for media management. It means that it is essential to use every competitive advantage in order to defeat competitors and acquire new consumers. Secondly, rapid changes taking place inside the media should make managers focus primarily on the management of changes in the realms of technology, employees and media consumers. The aforementioned authors emphasize that the last 50 years of the 20th century stood for stable expenditures on media consumption. It was about 4% of the American GDP. On the other hand, expenditures on advertising accounted for about 2% of the GDP at the time [Lavine, Wackman 1988: 25]. Inside this constant GDP percentage, flows from one type of media to another within the same branch take place, as well as flows between the "old" to the "new media." Such processes are relatively permanent and their nature necessitates learning their governing principles.

6.1. Origins of advertising

To comprehend the mechanisms that govern advertising, one must define it, invoke its origins and describe the advertising market. It demands a vast knowledge of advertising specifics, media forms and institutions that create advertising campaigns. It simply requires advertising management. It would be difficult to understand the complex questions regarding advertising without knowledge of its history.

The heritage of advertising aligns with the history of civilization. The oldest documented examples of advertising date back to the Babylonian earthenware plates from over 5 thousand years ago, containing advertisements by shoemakers, scriveners and balm tradesmen. The ancient Phoenicians also made drawings of different products on rocks along roads where parades were held [Doliński 2001: 7]. Similar illustrations and inscriptions were found in Ancient Egypt, Greece and Rome describing slave fairs and gladiators' fights. The British Museum holds the oldest advertisement in world history. This piece is a papyrus dated ca. 3000 BC found in the area of Thebes, illustrating a reward for finding a runaway slave [Bajka 1994]. In the book entitled *The Last Days of Pompeii*, we find a story of a pharmacist living next to a brothel who became disturbed at night by others looking for the prostitutes. Annoyed, he placed a sign on his house informing potential customers that the place they sought was next door and that later they could visit him for medical reasons if necessary [Lytton 2004: 43].

Pictograms were designed for the illiterate. For example, an image of a goat denoted dairy whereas one of a mule swivelling mill wheels meant a bakery. Ancient Greece, apart from many other arts, perfected the art of rhetoric in advertising. It was Aristotle in his *Politics* who described various ways of winning supporters, rules that are applied in advertising even today [Aristotle 2002: 263–347]. In contrast, Cicero describes a merchant who, "annonas clamavit" (expertly) recommends figs. Intellectual elites of ancient times (Cicero,

Horace), however, claimed that mercantile actions such as advertising were oftentimes "immoral" and recommended that one should advise the application of the "caveat emptor" rule towards these practices (known as "may the customer beware") [Bajka 1994].

The word "commercial" derives from the Latin word *clamo, clamare*, which stands for "shouting," "calling loudly." This was the primary function of advertising in ancient markets because the more a given merchant praised his goods, the greater the chance he would lure potential purchasers to his stall. This mechanism is still applied today, particularly by many salesmen in the Middle East.

It was in the 18th century when promotion started to be defined as *advertising*. It derives from the Latin word *advertere* and has a close semantic meaning to the word *clamo*, putting the emphasis rather on the act of drawing close attention to something.

The 20th century's immense mass media development and the processes connected with digitalization that followed brought about notably rare advertising functions. The world – as written by McLuhan – has become a global village [McLuhan 2001: 12]. Media globalization led to global needs and, in turn, powered the globalization processes in the economy. Advertising needed to react somehow to such phenomena as well. The global world in the dimension of media culture has become spaceless and one directional [Smith 1990: 177]. Many contemporary researchers point to the fact that advertising is a business investment as well as an element of contemporary culture [Leiss 1990: 5]. In the age of *online* communication that has been developing extremely quickly, global marketing has become a necessity. Each company is not only able, but should be functioning in a global dimension. Costs of telecommunication services are decreasing which to a large extent influences the lower costs of global activity, allowing small companies to develop their activity globally. The example provided herein is highly characteristic of this trend.

Anthony Rex used to run a small bistro in New York. While his clients were pleased with his pasta and pizzas, the baguettes were their favorites and were bought by a large number of people as takeaway. Rex's Baguettes (he called them T-Rex) soon gained so much popularity that the owner developed an ambitious plan to allow the whole world to eat T-Rex baguettes. To begin, Rex made a list of the most interesting (in his view) ten most economically developed countries and researched the Internet addresses of potential business partners. He next subcontracted the creation of a website under the name *Bread Stick World*. There, one could find baked goods trivia along with reviews by notable personalities. Afterwards, he sent emails to his potential partners, encouraging them to visit his website and fill out a survey on baked goods. In return, he offered to deliver a free batch of baguettes. The effects were visible after several months as orders began pouring in from different parts of the world. Three years later, with an incredibility efficient website, T. Rex became the most popular producer of baguettes in the world [Bishop 2001: 18–22].

Advertising is defined in many ways. Tens, if not hundreds of definitions are scattered throughout professional literature. For the purpose of these speculations three definitions have been offered. The first of them belongs to the oldest ones in Polish territory and its author, going by Alias (it is hard to predicate who hid behind this pseudonym), wrote the following at the beginning of the 20th century:

> Advertising – in the most general sense of the word – is used to inform the public on the existing state, private and charity enterprises; it encourages the use of these enterprises. The particular objective of trade advertising is to familiarize the public with commodities on the market and encourage them to purchase those commodities [Aljas 1907].

The definition of an advertisement that has binding power in Poland is the one included in the Broadcasting Act. This sates that, through advertisements, one understands every transfer which does not derive from the sender, aiming at promoting and making use of goods or services, supporting particular issues and ideas or for the purpose of achieving some other effect desired by the advertiser, yielded by means of payment or some other form of remuneration.

However, provided we look into advertising using a systemic approach, we would have to define it slightly differently. Advertising is an element of the communication process where the sender intimates something to the receiver with a view of reaching the intended result. This result does not have to stand for, for instance, higher sales. In the case of social advertising against cigarette smoking, the goal is to make people buy as few of them as possible, if not none. It is worth noticing that efficiency and efficacy are seemingly identical notions, as T. Kotarbiński clearly indicates differences between them [Kotarbiński 1965].

Advertisement is therefore an act of communication characterized by teleologicality (purposefulness), unilateralism of media, multimedia condition, being mass and commercial (although social advertising is becoming as important in the contemporary world as a commercial means). An advertisement has its aim and serves particular functions.

6.2. Advertising agencies and their duties

The creation of advertising campaigns is generally a domain of highly specialized agencies, yet it is possible to perform an advertising campaign on one's own, making use of specialized services, which shall be discussed further in this chapter.

Advertising agencies were formed in the United States at the end of the 19th century. Brokers of payable publishing space were the first agents and helped their customers with creating advertisements. In this way a new type of business activity arose, which with time, turned into the advertising business [White 1997: 46]. Until now advertising agencies have existed in order to prepare advertising campaigns for their clients and place them in the appropriate media. One of the definitions of an advertising agency states that it is an "independent organizational unit, comprising of business people and creative personnel who prepare, elaborate and locate the advertisement in mass media for salesmen looking for clients interested in their products and services [Russell, Lane 2000: 131]." It was right in the initial period when the division of media advertising took place – ATL and non-media one – BTL. This division is of prosaic origin. Advertising agencies, billing their clients, used to divide a sheet of paper with a horizontal line. One placed media related costs *above the line*, hence ATL. In the initial period it meant checks for the purchase of advertising area in newspapers. But *below the line*, hence, BTL, the costs were related to non-media advertising. This stood, for instance, for costs of presentation, shows, conferences, etc.

The essence of advertising agencies' activities is a creative elaboration of ideas. With a high degree of probability it may be ascertained that the success of any efficient agency depends on its artfulness in helping its clients. This ingenuity, also known as creativity, is verified by the relative efficiency of an advertising campaign.

In practice, we distinguish three ways of conducting an advertising campaign [White 1997: 48]:

1. campaign contracted out to an agency,
2. campaign prepared with the help of specialists,
3. campaign carried out on one's own.

There are several elements that conjoin in an advertising campaign, yet its basic component is a single advertising communication. The entire campaign ought to be subdued for the aim of this campaign. Everything depends on whether its aim is to introduce a new product onto the market or if it stands for a social campaign to combat a particular addiction, such as cigarette smoking.

Obviously, in order to create an efficient mass media it is inevitable to consider the complexity of perceptions. As shown by research, any further expositions of messages elicit both an alteration in consumer attitudes and changes in the quality of their perception. From the standpoint of a broadcaster, the recipient of the first advertising releases in a campaign is completely different from someone who has already been convinced of the necessity of fulfilling their need in a given way, even if unaware of the means to achieve it. In practice, it means a question about the scale of domination of rational and emotional factors in a campaign's particular moment.

A plan stands as a useful tool when creating advertising campaigns. It is possible to create it in numerous ways. One of them is the so-called plan of "6M," being an acronym of the first letters of words which contribute to this plan [Budzyński 1999: 32]:

1. mission – selection of advertising aims,
2. market – selection of market addressees of an advertisement,
3. money – determination of the company's budget,
4. message – selection of advertising contents,
5. media – selection of advertising media,
6. measurement – examination of advertising efficiency.

In professional literature one may come across various advertising models (AIDA, DIPADA, DAGMAR etc.); however, the circular model of Stephen King appears to be particularly useful while planning an advertising campaign, as such planning is not a one-time act. One distinguishes three phases in an advertising campaign: 1. introductory; 2. informative-coaxing; 3. resembling.

The first issues of advertising communicators are received fragmentarily and processed on a shallow level. In the initial stage of an advertising campaign the broadcasting service competes with challengers for consumers' attention. Therefore, the introductory stage consists of channelling the state of information processing included in an advertisement to a level that would allow for its reception in accordance with the broadcaster's will. An informative-coaxing phase begins, in the course of which the recipient aligns the obtained information with his or her own experiences. A need to act may be born under the influence of this process, if not right away, then with the passage of time, which is served by the reminder function. Further stages of the campaign do not have to succeed one by one, nor does the effectiveness of one stage have to condition the efficiency of the following one. Nevertheless, from the perspective of effectiveness related to advertising communication, factors such as the receiver's preferences, the structure release itself, and the manner of its broadcasting along with its reception conditions matter. The influence of these factors is, to a large extent, determined by the efficacy of previous expositions. The decisive factors for the effectiveness of an advertising campaign therefore depend on a combination of these elements. Its essence lies in the difference between the perception of persuasive pieces of information processed on both semantic and non-semantic levels at the beginning and at the end of an advertising campaign. Research proves that in the primary stage of an advertising campaign recipients tend to prefer information based on graphic codes, and in the final one – on semantic forms [Albin 2000: 120].

The preparation of almost every advertising campaign begins with a *brief*, i.e. an indispensable compendium necessary to create the said campaign. It rarely happens that the person ordering is able to create the *brief* on his or her own. Generally, such a brief is prepared in collaboration with an advertising agency or specialists. The basic elements of a brief are as follows [Kall 1999: 39]:

1. Introduction – a description of the market situation in which a company operates, its competitors and their advertisements, along with the way in which clients purchase things;
2. Target group of recipients – a versatile description of consumers, concerning their knowledge about a product, and their habits and ways of product application;
3. The aim of an advertisement – what the advertiser wants to accomplish thanks to an advertisement (e.g. sales increase, increase in market share, building of an image, etc.);
4. Promise – a sentence that shall include content that is most motivating for clients to act;
5. Support – all kinds of activities proving a given promise (e.g. test results, consumer opinions concerning a given product, etc.);
6. Desired consumer reaction – what a consumer should think and do under the influence of an advertisement;
7. Executive indicators – what is worth emphasizing and what should be displayed in an advertisement to a smaller extent;
8. Indispensable components – what is to be placed in an advertisement and what should be given up;
9. Possible limitations – generally, restraints of a legal nature, e.g., a ban on presenting situations associated with leisure or sex in beer advertisements;
10. Media – generally, the media plan, indicating the type of media and the frequency of advertisement broadcasting;
11. Efficiency evaluation – studying whether the established aims have been fulfilled.

The aforementioned speculations indicate that advertising is a complicated and costly domain. Services provided by advertising agencies are generally expensive, yet their professionalism to a much larger extent guarantees efficacy of an advertising campaign compared to the work of independent actions. Regrettably, large companies in Poland generally make use of advertising agencies' services and they are the ones that examine the efficiency of their own adverts. The majority of companies frequently advertise themselves independently or do not see any point in advertising as such. The author's own research entitles him to draw such conclusions.

6.3. Advertising campaigns

An advertising campaign, as mentioned previously, is built on the basis of single advertising releases. This enterprise is complicated, requiring an amalgamation of artistry, invention, creation, vast knowledge concerning the market of advertising and thorough knowledge of media operation, particularly focusing on communicative efficiency. This kind of knowledge makes it possible to obtain an effect of synergy, i.e., a reinforcement of advertising transmissions by disposing them skilfully throughout individual forms of media.

The Internet enabled the use of completely new, unprecedented advertising techniques. Specialists in the field of marketing and advertising began using a mechanism of searching for help on the web for whenever we "have a problem." Such a "problem" may be finding the address of a good plumber or where to best purchase a new refrigerator. It is when people usually tend to look for people who have had a similar "problem" to find out how they managed to deal with it. This mechanism is used by word-of-mouth propaganda or whisper marketing [Kirby, Mardsen 2005]. While marvelling at something gratuitously, people "enthuse" other web users to a particular product.

In the United States, on a portal on weddings and wedding receptions, a person who was too eager in encouraging others to purchase particular household goods as a wedding gift "caught in the act". There was also a teenager unduly delighted by a PlayStation game. There are more and more such cases and it seems that such a way of advertising is ethically questionable. More on these issues will be discussed in Chapter 9, titled *Legal and Ethical Aspects of Media Management.*

An efficient management is one that fulfils its aims to the utmost extent. Numerous examples of both successful and abortive cases of advertising campaigns have taken place throughout history. The case of the Ford Edsel is widely cited a classic instance of an unsuccessful advertising campaign. While the producer was expecting great success, two years later it was necessary to stop the production of this car altogether. In the advertising business, the notion of "Edsel" became a synonym for an advertising campaign defeat. Examples that have been used for the purpose of this monograph have been drawn from the author's previous publications [Nierenberg 2004].

Ford Edsel

This advertising campaign stands as an example of the most spectacular catastrophe. The Ford Edsel was presented with a flourish in August 1957. The producer was anticipating sales of 200,000 vehicles already in the first year, yet, two years later when the production of Edsel was suspended, it turned out that combined sales amounted to barely 109,000 units.

The disaster was so great that up to this day it has been a subject of analyses of advertisement researchers. D. Doliński discerns its sources in the fact that Ford believed in the success of this model by engaging large sums of money in the product itself, but not much in the advertising. However, in the period of 1920–1957, only a few brands had managed to conquer the American automotive market. Generally, success was achieved by modernizing already existing models. The instance of the Edsel proves what has been known in marketing for a long time; the new breaks through with difficulty. Researchers of the advertising market seek reasons of this defeat in the fact that in the second part of the 1950s, along with a recession in the United States, one noticed a rapidly declining interest in vehicles for the middle-class. It is equally probable that the defeat was caused by a lack of connection between the advertising ideas with the real nature of the Ford Edsel. When following individual stages of this campaign it seems that nothing had been neglected. A document titled "Procedure of selecting an advertising agency for the Special Products Department" was several hundred pages long. In the end, out of 12 competing advertising companies, Foote, Cone & Belding (FCB) was chosen. They prepared an advertising campaign with a military-like precision. The first television commercials announced: "Here is the Edsel." Printed advertisements featured an additional remark: "new member of the Ford family of fine cars." Posters advertising the Edsel claimed that it was a car of the future. Nonetheless, the only noticeable differences between the "car of the future" and other models of this class manufactured by Ford were a vertically embedded inlet grate and the pushbutton placed in the middle of a steering wheel. The disappointment was immense, and a huge amount of money was wasted. The causes of this gigantic failure are to be found both in the product itself and its advertising campaign. The FCB agency did not manage to coordinate an advertising campaign with information that appeared about the Edsel in the media, with the press in particular [Advertising Age 1996].

Absolut Vodka

Professional literature considers the campaign for this alcoholic beverage as one of the most successful. It was in 1980 when the Carillon Company was importing a Swedish vodka called *Absolut* (not well known at the time) to the United States. Michel Roux, the company's boss then, decided to invest USD

65,000 in market research, the results of which were not encouraging. The interviewees considered the vodka's name as excessively intricate, and the shape of the bottle as quite ugly. According to bartenders, it was uncomfortable to pour the drink and the bottle also did not stand out on the shelf. The individuals surveyed also claimed that they did not trust Swedish vodka. The conclusion should have been obvious – that it is necessary to give up importing a good which barely sold 12,000 units per year. Meanwhile, Roux recognized that the vodka diverged from consumer perceptions to such an extent that it was impossible for the results of the research to be trustworthy. He was convinced of the need for an intensive advertising campaign. The TBWA Company won the order out of the competing advertising agencies. The company's artistic director Geoff Hayes offered something which explicitly diverged from the offerings of other agencies, who invoked typically Swedish pictures with a sauna in the background. What others considered to be Absolut's disadvantage, Hayes recognized as a virtue. What he offered was a poster depicting merely a bottle with the inscription: "Absolut perfection."

Michel Roux managed to appreciate the brilliance of this idea and fleshed it out for the campaign. In 1982, the cost of advertising calculated per single bottle sold was a cost of USD 10.69 for Carillon. During that time, Stolichnaya's analogical index amounted to USD 3.09 whereas for Smirnoff it was USD 1.08. The effectiveness of the Absolut advertising campaign was so immense that sales started to grow rapidly, as in 1983 160,000 cartons were sold. In the following years Absolut's advertising campaigns featured drawings of well-known artist Andy Warhol, yet each time in the characteristic shape of a bottle of vodka [Nierenberg 2004: 109–110].

6.4. Selected methods of researching advertisement

Researching an advertisement is difficult because in many cases artists deal with its creation (and it is hard to measure a piece of art). Nevertheless many aspects of an advertisement, such as its efficiency or effectiveness, belong to well-researched and easily measurable processes. Generally, the research consists of issuing the advertisement to customers and determining the level of its reaching customers' consciousness to convince them of its persuasive message. Nonetheless, some researchers warn against being too trustful towards the research results. The previous Absolut vodka example campaign proves that being mistrustful towards research may at times be profitable. However, it must be noted that the author of this monograph is preoccupied with the notion that the research was carried out incorrectly. Hence, the results turned out to be negative for the advertising campaign, whereas it should have been the inverse considering that the vodka an unknown brand in the United States. As a result of an advertising campaign, Absolut placed itself in third place (right after Stolichnaya and Smirnoff). Therefore, while an advertisement must undergo preliminary research, it should be done properly.

The following methods stand for the easiest ways of researching advertising frequency and range [Nierenberg 2004: 116–118]:

- journal,
- telephone interviews,
- radiometry,
- telemetry.

Journal interviews are an archaic research method that consists of the respondents noting in their journal their own activity concerning the media. They were carried out in the past by OBOP (Center for Public Opinion Research) research facilities. To conduct telephone interviews, interviewers call a randomly chosen group of people. Thanks to these people, it is possible to determine audience ratings of particular programs. Both radiometry and telemetry demand installing suitable measuring devices that examine time and frequency of accessing radio or television programs. By means of this method one measures indicators applied for determining the efficiency and effectiveness of an advertisement: size of the audience, effective reach, ratings (percentage number of individual viewers out of the entire population or target group, watching a specific advertising band of a particular TV station), GRP (*gross rating points* – a sum of ratings obtained throughout the entire advertising campaign), CPT and CPM (*cost per thousand; cost per million* – the average cost of reaching 1000 receivers with an advertising message).

The previously described methods of examining the efficiency of advertisements assumed a priori that mere watching or hearing a release brings a desired result. In contrast, an advertisement is almost never displayed in a dissected way. Research shows that as many as 85% of all advertisements are ignored by viewers. It is estimated that every American comes across about 1,600 advertising messages every single day. Only 5% of them attract their attention and only 1.33% elicit some reaction which not always leads to a purchase of some good or service [Sztucki 1997: 171].

Methods to have an advertisement effectively reach consumer consciousness' are as follows [Nierenberg 2004: 118–121]:

- the "eye-camera" method,
- examination of advertisement legibility,
- consumers' evaluation,

- playback method,
- recognition method,
- program analyser,
- examination of voice pitch,
- penetration method.

The eye-camera method consists of presenting a given advertisement to a randomly chosen group of people. Movements of eyeballs are registered at the same time. It makes it possible to determine which elements of an advertisement the eyesight stops for a longer period of time, and which it runs through faster.

The examination of advertisement legibility consists in examining the level on which the recipient has been acquainted with a given advertisement. The so-called Flesh formula has been formulated based on empirical studies. According to this iteration, messages built up of short sentences comprised of 11 words maximum are adopted easiest by consumers. The entire announcement should not use more than 100 words.

Consumers' evaluation consists of showing several advertising messages to a group of consumers. Participants in this study do not have to stick rigidly to only one advertisement. Research shows that such examination tends to be analogous to the evaluation of the entire group of consumers of a given product.

The playback method refers mainly to press advertisements by means of the so-called pre-tests. A specially printed copy of a newspaper is delivered to selected respondents. Interviews are carried out after 24 hours. The people being tested are given a sheet of paper with names of all products advertised in the paper. Respondents mark products whose advertisement was remembered by them. A similar method of studying advertisements is the *recognition method*. The study is carried out among readers of newspapers and magazines. One determines on which level they are capable of connecting the indicated advertisement with appropriate products or companies. As many as 200 to 400 participants selected at random take part in the tests.

Program analyser is a method in which a selected group of people are shown radio or TV advertisements. The respondents express their opinion on the advertisements by pressing buttons.

Examination of voice pitch consists of measuring the voice pitch delivered by people watching or listening to advertisements. It is based on the assumption that pleasant emotions increase voice pitch whereas unpleasant ones decrease it.

Penetration method was expanded on by Rooser Reeves according to whom the receiver of an advertisement has tendencies to remember only one idea from the shown advertisement. The method uses the assumption that only every fifth person who managed to remember the basic idea of an advertisement and identifies with its broadcaster buys the advertised product or service. After six months, half of these people are going to forget the product featured in the advertisement: however, the second half are likely to remember it, provided they are under the constant influence of the advertisement. Assuming the campaign is carried out continuously, per every thousand people, there will be more or less the same number of receivers who are going to remember the main idea of the advert. This exact number expressed in a percentage is known as the penetration index. According to this method the advertising efficiency may be calculated by means of the following formula:

$$e = \frac{pc}{100}$$

where:
e – advertising efficiency,
p – index of penetration,
c – constant index of 20%.

The constant "c" index (effectiveness of an advertisement can be 20% max) is considered to be a drawback of this method. On the other hand, its advantage lies in a high level of eliminating other factors (apart from the advertisement itself) that influence the purchase bulk of a particular product [Łodziana-Grabowska 1996: 102].

Models are one of the most useful research tools. Through models one can examine changes in the receivers' attitudes. At the turn of 19th and 20th centuries the first model based on a simple formula called SLB – *Stay, Look, Buy* came into existence. Other, even more complicated models that accounted for even more factors started appearing in the course of the following years.

The simplest models of examining changes in advertisement receivers are as follows:

• *AIDA* model,
• *AIDCAS* model,
• *DIPADA* model,
• *DAGMAR* model.

The presented models of advertising are hierarchical in nature. For instance, in the case of the *DAGMAR* model, in order for a purchase to take place the buyer needs to go from being unaware to being conscious of the product as existing. To do this, he or she must understand its characteristic features that distinguish the product from other ones. Finally, the buyer should become convinced by the product's excellence in comparison to others [Czarnecki 1996: 13].

One distinguishes many other models depicting various aspects of advertisement operations that are to be found by the reader in the abundant professional literature. They include psychological, econometric models, study of external advertising effectiveness, etc. For people making decisions concerning media management, the effectiveness of undertaken actions, such as the relationship between achieved results and the costs, ought to be of particular importance. As already mentioned, examining efficiency requires verifying whether the aim of the advertisement has been successfully achieved. However, it frequently happens that an enterprise has a certain amount for advertising at its disposal and searched for more effective ways to use them (Fig. 5: Dependency between advertising effects and costs). Point P in the graph stands for an "awareness point" and its responsive level of expenses. Provided an enterprise fails to dispose of at least such resources that enable it to exceed this threshold, one should not begin an advertising campaign at all. Only after having exceeded this "threshold," the effects grow faster than the expenditure up to the moment of saturation (point B). The "boomerang effect" begins after crossing the point B, which means that expenses on the advertisement grow and the effects decrease.

At the beginning of the 1990s in Poland, the advertising awareness point was relatively low at an estimated amount equalling emissions. Within the subsequent period it increased to 12 emissions. It was in 1993 when the boomerang effect began to be noticeable. According to research, the awareness point has constantly been increasing. Exceeding this point is an important goal for a company, but without reaching the boomerang effect. Therefore, carrying out research on advertising campaigns is very essential. As previously stated, in Poland only about 10% of all enterprises have regularly carried out research on their advertising campaigns. The effectiveness of an advertisement is in most cases measured by means of such indexes as: CPT (*cost per thousand*) – the cost of reaching a thousand people in a target group or CPP (*cost per point*) – the cost of reaching one percent of the target group.

Perhaps the most effective method of testing advertising campaigns is examining them through a mini-market. The basis of this method lies in the thought that an inefficient advertising campaign costs as much as a successful one. Hence, already by the first half of the 1970s in the United States and a decade later in Europe as well, a mini-market was convened as the most effective tool of examining advertisement. In essence, the mini-market stands for nothing but a particular country. Just as a primary election sample survey is carried out in some regions of a country with the goal of investigating the result of the real ones, the consumers' market and the market of advertising also started being

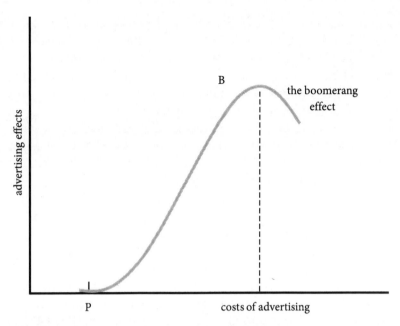

Figure 5. Dependency between advertising effects and costs

Source: Sznajder 1993: 79.

investigated. A special method of research in this mini-market was elaborated. In Europe it is used only in Haßloch, Germany, the place where the author of this monograph used to carry out his research. This small town possesses just over 20 thousand people inhabiting about 10 thousand households. Some of the residents work in nearby Ludwigshafen. The experimental mini-market is comprised of two thousand households. Its complement is a monitoring panel made up of one thousand households. This mini-market is a diminutive model of Germany's real market and it is possible to carry out all kinds of consumer research quite accurately. The research program applied in Haßloch is called GfK BehaviorScan® and was developed on an American license, whereas its application began in 1986.

The entire panel which includes two thousand households is connected to cable TV by means of a special TV studio and each participant in the experiment is equipped with a special device connected with their TV. Also, they receive *The Hörzu* magazine containing the TV program guide, oddities from the world of film and television, as well as advertisements (the magazine provides an opportunity for publishing press advertisements).

Let us make use of an imaginary example in order to illustrate how the mini-market operates. If a producer of beverages wants to check whether their new product will be accepted in the market, they prepare an advertising spot for this drink and bring it to the TV studio in Haßloch. A worker at the studio looks among ad blocks of various TV stations (GfK signed proper agreements with sundry TV stations) for a suitable place to "paste" the beverage advertisement. The ad becomes emitted the moment they find such a place, in a way nobody is able to notice any change in the program.

Each household participating in the test holds one or several special cards (they are similar to credit cards) that are shown at the checkout while purchasing. Every participant's acquisition is registered through a special scanner. Based on the shopping structure of people participating in the test, it is possible to extrapolate the consumer behaviors nationally and examine market opportunities for new products. *The Hörzu* magazine offers additional possibilities to study the combination of television and press advertisements. By the means of this magazine, it is possible to explore distinct types of press insertions. A share of households entering the test are confronted with an ordinary advertisement, whereas the rest are confronted with the one being tested. The success of an ad is measured directly at shopping checkouts. The data derived from the scanners is retained and processed in the GfK statistical center in Nuremberg. The center has real data at its disposal. It can assess precisely the reaction of people who watched and who did not watch a test ad while shopping. The authors of compilations prepared to order parties are capable of ascertaining, almost to one Euro, the influence of a test advertisement on the consumer. It is possible to measure not only the efficiency of TV or press advertisement but also to assess which of the advertisements tested had a greater influence on consumers. Furthermore, the system allows for the collateral testing of different variants of advertising campaigns and selecting a better advertising spot and determining the most optimal advertising budget (Chart 5: Mode of looming a better advertising spot and determining the most optimal budget).

The test and monitoring groups are identical; however, the TV hook-up varies. It is the customer at the shop checkout who decides whether a given ad spot works better. The Targetable TV technique allows practically for direct cause and effect analyses. The study refers to a direct influence of TV advertisement on real behaviours of consumers while shopping. By the means of an optimization program the total number of households under observation might be divided. For instance, based on previously defined criteria specific for each project, they can be divided into identical test and monitoring groups, or groups characterized by the same social demography and identical behavior while shopping, or otherwise. The benefits from these studies are evident. Any success or defeat in the mini-market – alike in reality – is measured at shop checkouts.

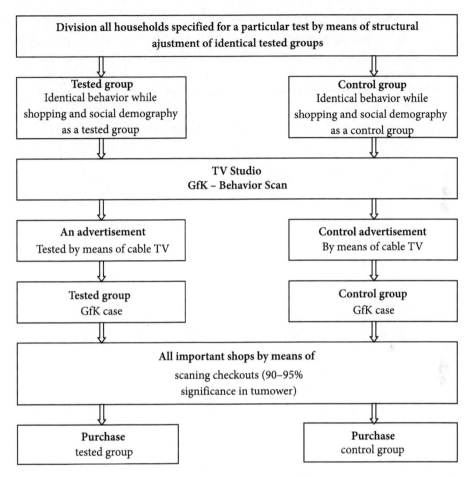

Chart 5. Mode of looming a better advertising spot and determining the most optimal budget

Source: own study on the basis of the conveyed research in Haßloch.

Studies carried out in the mini-market presume that obtaining realistic answers to many questions is critical for advertisers. Here are some of these queries:

1. How many consumers will a company gain when they purchase a given product for the first time, and how many of them are going to buy it again and finally, how many new customers will the company gain?
2. What kinds and sizes of products sell the best?
3. What benefits will a particular promotion and household testing going to bring?

4. How will the TV and press advertisements work? Where is the best location to place advertisements? What should the correlation of individual
   advertising forms of media be like? What media-mix shall bring the best
   results?
5. What market share is the new product going to have? Which competitors represent the biggest threat for the product undergoing research
   and who will emerge the victor in the struggle for clients?

The list of companies willing to test their products in the Haβloch mini-
market is long. This research is not cheap, yet undoubtedly less expensive than
an unsuccessful advertising campaign. The tests carried out in the mini-market allow for an almost total certainty in evaluating market chances of a new
product and the selection of the most efficient tools for its market promotion.
The mini-market is undoubtedly a very credible research tool, yet available
only for large and wealthy companies.

Discussion questions:

1. Indicate the meaning of advertising for media organizations.
2. Explain the meaning of the boomerang effect.
3. Indicate methods of studying advertisement.

Part 3

Chapter 7. Managers and Journalists

This chapter will deal with people who manage the media (quartermasters and managers) and media workers, primarily journalists who for many decades exemplified the essence of the media. In the 19th century and for a good part of the 20th century, journalism was perceived as a public service. In the 19th century it was even thought that a journalist performing his or her duty should not receive any monetary compensation so as not to be dependent on the cash buyer. The notion of the "journalist" today has been increasingly superseded by the notion of a "media worker" and not only and not primarily in its semantic meaning. In turn, distinction into media quartermasters and managers is significant as every manager on a level suitable for their competences is a media quartermaster as well. On the other hand, not every media quartermaster is a manager. For instance, it is hard to call Zygmunt Solorz a manager who deals with direct management of a media organization. In fact he is a media quartermaster who profoundly influences TV Polsat as the major shareholder. His decisions or lack of them also predestines the situation within the entire business. Thus, an analysis of cases of chosen media careers, both quartermasters as well as managers and journalists, will be included in this chapter.

7.1. Human resources in media

In the monograph *Media Management. In the Age of Giants* one finds an interesting anecdote that can serve as a great starting point for discussing motivation and productivity in the media. Professor Bob Gassaway of University of New Mexico recalls his job interview which he had many years before with the publisher of a journal from Missouri. While looking around the office, Gassaway asked his prospective boss about the number of people working in the editorial office. "'Well' – the old editor said slowly, bending over the desk – 'as far as I know, more or less one in three [Herrick 2003: 67]." Human resources in the media along with their motivation to increase productivity have always posed a major challenge for managers, but a substantial research field as well.

From a historical point of view on management, it would be possible to point out various ways of motivating workers. The scientific approach to management deals with motivating mainly by means of material resources. Managers tended to believe that the higher the pay, the greater the performance. This was so in the early days, after which performance stopped increasing. In the behavioral stream of management, it was discerned that humans are social beings and material resources are not necessarily the only things that motivate them to do better work. Oftentimes, good treatment is enough. Management techniques referring to human resources (HR) would work only when employees were used according to their knowledge and skills. The Y theory appealed to the human needs of creativity and self-actualization, whereas the Z theory appealed to a dialogue where managers talk to workers about an organization mission and aims. It appears that theories of motivation attempt to elucidate why some workers put in more effort than others while completing some tasks.

The essence of Abraham Maslow's studies has already been discussed in Chapter 1. Let us remember that Maslow perceived human needs in a form of a ladder (a pyramid) that a human being climbs in order to achieve self-actualization at its peak. Maslow conceptualized it in the following way: "Clear appearance of their (need of self-actualization) is possible after fulfilling physiological needs, safety, belongingness and appreciation [Maslow 1954: 80–81]."

Kenneth Starck applied this research perspective in order to explain problems concerning the ethical attitudes of journalists in Romania in the 1990s. Those journalists – as written by K. Starck – take bribes, fetch and carry for the governing ones. In a word, they do things that would be perceived as unethical by American journalists. However, it is difficult to care about ethics – says K. Starck – as making a living for the family brings serious grief [Starck 1998: 28–41].

One may agree with this evaluation or not, nevertheless for many companies Maslow's attitude was the basis of perceiving workers as human beings having their own needs and motivations, instead of thoughtless peons. Such a vision of human resources is particularly supported in media organizations. These premises seem to form one of the most popular methodologies of media management: *management by objectives* – MBO.

Its essence consists in [Herrick 2003: 92]:

1. setting clearly formulated, realistic goals;
2. arranging an activity plan by means of which the plan is to be carried out;
3. regular appraisals of employees who realize this goal;
4. modifying an action plan, if necessary.

The originator of this management concept is P.F. Drucker [1954]. He articulated its rules in a book entitled *The Practice of Management*. He based his research on Harrington Emerson's previous projects, the first of which was a set of twelve rules of efficiency that emphasized a clearly determined objective. Basic MBO presumptions are as follows: indispensability of establishing an aim, monitoring progress in the course of its accomplishment and eliminating failures. It is the aim which matters the most. Being deprived of clearly specified objectives, the company veers in an unknown direction. The ideas of P.F. Drucker were artfully developed in a later period, adding the element of the workers' involvement in determining a company's objectives, but also a facet of evaluating one's own performance. The basic rule of MBO is for both managers and workers to clearly and identically understand aims of an organization. In the same way they should be aware of their roles in completing these aims. Everyone's effort, both that of an executive manager, and that of a worker filling the lowest post ought to be measured by successes and failures while achieving the goals of an organization. P.F. Drucker even claimed that "effective management must direct vision and efforts of every manager for a common objective, for the result I expect" [Drucker 1954]. For this purpose a manager should undertake five basic pro-MBO actions:

1. establish the aim or aims of an organization,
2. organize a working group in order to achieve them,
3. motivate workers and take proper care of communication within the group,
4. measure performance,
5. care about workers' development (upon common agreement).

Dennis F. Herrick notices that many managers, while executing MBO-related tasks have a tendency of praising employees for issues not concerning areas of their employment or behaving like a judge who utters a verdict for a worker. That the fact that each of us prefers to be spoiled by praises rather than perfected by criticism is obvious. The employees are better inclined towards tasks in the first case than in the second one. Herrick asserts that as far as he is concerned workers who are praised achieve better results in comparison to the ones who are continuously criticized. Criticism that is too frequent leads to a decline in self-appraisal, an increase in resentment, and thus a decline in efficiency [Herrick 2003: 94]. It appears that many other managers tend to have observations of this type. The author of this monograph is in favor of such insights as well. Excessive criticism may result from a manager's lack of empathy and interpersonal skills. A shortcoming in these qualities makes it impossible to carry out an assessment of an employee in a constructive and acceptable way. What is even more critical is that the assessment should be constructed as an improvement opportunity, not a reason to degrade his or her self-appraisal. Moreover, the supervisor should adopt an open attitude oriented towards two-way communication. The success of MBO is contingent upon whether or not every employee in an organization participates in meeting its objectives.

One of the most essential problems of managers who are in charge of media organizations and who use MBO as a management tool is the fact that as a rule such organizations employ highly creative people. In effect, in comparison to workers of other professions, they are more independent, more certain about their opinions as they succeed from their skills. As a result, they are proud of the executed work. Unfortunately, these types of employees cope very badly with criticism and they are the ones who tend to accuse their managers of lacking interpersonal skills. A manager characterized by special qualifications is necessary in order to manage such workers. Such a person needs to be callous at times, sometimes very emphatic and yet also a good psychologist able to identify variable moods of their media stars. Robert H. Giles [1988: 360] even writes: "Editors who introduce the MBO process for the first time are usually surprised how much time you need to devote to do it right. Discussing ideas, documenting objectives, coordinating roles and appointing realistic deadlines is a complicated and challenging task."

There are situations when an agreement cannot be reached between an employee and the employer. Laying off an employee belongs to one of the least pleasurable tasks of a manager, and not only the media one. Harvey Mackay [1988: 167] once wrote, "It isn't the people you fire who make your life miserable, it's the people you don't." Herrick advised several potential and current media managers who were forced to make a worker redundant. While not all of his pieces of advice can be applied in European reality, many of his observations are critical and may be of practical value for media managers. Making people redundant, including disciplinary leave, should not be a surprise for an employee. It should not take place until the worker receives a formal word of warning and opportunity to work out mistakes for which he or she is supposed to be made redundant. This situation is known as "progressive discipline." All further steps of the employer should be well-documented and in accordance with legal regulations in a given country. A dismissal which is carried out in a wrong way may be threatened with legal action. A manager should make sure that his or her conduct is in compliance with company policy and labor laws. According to Herrick after a worker is made redundant, he or she should be asked to leave company premises immediately, and if the employee needs to go to his or her office or other workplace it is to be done under rigid supervision. While this seems strict, being treated too nicely may end up in the theft of documents or some other form of sabotage. "If an employee threatens you with court, answer simply that they are allowed to do everything they consider suitable and do not go into discussion" – claims Herrick [2003: 82]. Providing a worker with severance pay may serve as a form of placating the parting and minimizing the risk of the employer being taken to court. It may result from a contract signed by an employee or may serve as a form of voluntary compensation for broken-off work post. Herrick writes that in the United States, most states apply the "employment-at-will" rule according to which the employer is entitled to fire a worker on the grounds of any legal reason. He also adds that during this extremely stressful moment the manager should comply with the following rules [ibid.]:

- Firstly, prior to any redundancy procedure a manager is to make sure that he/she knows his/her own rights as well the employee's rights in scope of state and federal labor laws.
- The meeting with the worker being made redundant should take place discreetly, yet in the presence of at least one witness (preferably from the HR department – in the case of large companies), whereas in a small firm it should be the next person on the management hierarchy.
- The employer should inform the employee about redundancy. The information should be as desultory as possible. Provided the employee insists on receiving the exemption in writing, it should be assumed that the employee is going to enter legal action.
- During the conversation concerning redundancy one should neither apologize nor discuss reasons of dismissal. It is a good moment to offer possible severance payment.
- On informing about redundancy one should order the employee to leave company premises and send his/her private things. Alternatively, the manager or some security worker, in case of a large company, walks the employee to his/her desk to collect his/her personal belongings. Allowing the employee to take his/her things on their own might increase the risk of causing some damage to the company, e.g., deletion of computer data.

An employee who is being dismissed is not completely vulnerable facing the employer. The employee might enter into legal action or count on the protection of trade unions. In their book entitled *Managing Media Organizations*, John M. Lavine and Daniel B. Wackman [1988] indicate how to cooperate with trade unions in media organizations. The said authors affirm that "some media managers are intent on driving unions out of their organizations." Others believe that unions serve a valuable function and they are able to work effectively with their union employees. These managers view unions as just one of many methods for employee/employer decision-making; as having pluses and minuses, just as other arrangements do [Lavine, Wackman 1988: 214]." Trade unions tend to be described by means of economic terms, both by workers and management. However, the main reason for company management's objection to trade unions (which usually is not discussed) is the matter of control. A trade union is placed somewhere between the supervisor and the supervised. Managers claim that trade unions menace prerogatives attributed to the management, repudiating its role in an organization.

Herrick points out that trade unions in media business (in the United States there are a few unions that matter) have a long history. The strongest unions operate in production and newspaper distribution departments; however, employees in newsrooms are not affiliated with them. Similarly, trade unions were formed at many TV and radio stations but this trend did not concern newsrooms. Such a situation existed in the initial period of media industry development in the United States. Afterwards, trade unions started emerging in newsrooms as well. "The Newspaper Guild" was the best-known trade union representing the employees of newsrooms and sales departments. In 1933, a group of independent reporters, dissatisfied with their pay, set up the first trade union of this kind with "The Newspaper Guild" under the leadership of the columnist Heywood Brown [Herrick 2003: 70].

In publications from the 1980s and 1990s, one could find that the number of trade union members in American media was dropping drastically. However, latest data does not confirm it. In 1987 there were almost 35,000 members in "The Newspaper Guild." The number had dropped to 26,000 in 1993, but already by 2001, the number of members in the United States, Canada and Puerto Rico had risen again to 34,000. The union's president Linda Foley confirmed in 2003 that the number of trade unionists has been on the same level. And the Graphic Communications International Union stands as the greatest trade union in the media business, representing 150,000 active and retired employees of newspapers and other media. Among broadcasting stations the most prominent trade unions are the National Association of Broadcast Employees and Technicians (NABET), the International Brotherhood of Electrical Workers (IBEW) and the Writers Guild of America (WGA).

Striking is the most effective, but not the only weapon of trade unionists. Media employees might square off against the management, eliminating the holding of a strike. For instance, in 2002 the printing house of "The

Washington Post" did not include notes about the authors. Presenters also refused to appear in front of cameras. The basic task of managers during every strike is maintaining the continuity of issuing a newspaper or broadcasting a TV or radio program. The workers are referred to as "blacklegs" by those on strike. In the United States, there are many law firms that specialize in breaking strikes and advising how to win a face-off with trade unions. It happens frequently that strikers issue a "strike paper" which is supposed to be a kind of competition for their native paper and a voice of objection towards its further publication without the ones on strike. The majority of "newspapers" of this kind conclude their activity the moment an agreement is reached. One of the most notorious strikes of this kind took place in New York in 1963 and lasted 114 days [Herrick 2003: 70–72].

The legal basis of strikes in American media is section 7 of The National Labor Relations Act (NRLA) of 1935, also known as the Wagner Act that states: "Employees shall have the right to self-organization, to form, join, or assist labor organizations, to bargain collectively through representatives of their own choosing, and to engage in other concerted activities for the purpose of collective bargaining or other mutual aid or protection [www.newsguild.org/mission/today.php]."

It appears that the best method of avoiding conflicts with trade unions is fair treatment of employees and the provision of acceptable working conditions. A large number of American media companies managed to prevent formation of trade unions by using services provided by employees via the Internet. These "computer workers" had a less demanding attitude in comparison to workers employed directly in the newspaper office [Herrick 2003: 73].

Drucker [1942: 295], one of the world's most distinguished management processes researchers, had an ambivalent attitude to trade unions. In 1942, he wrote about the role of trade unions: "It is an antidote to social toxins. However it is not creative institution, nor designed as such." In his opinion, their constitutional and social aims were frequently discredited by their operational methods. Trade union leaders oftentimes would settle their own business, facing their members with a situation of swapping one tyrant in a president's suit with another in the union's seat. John E. Flaherty [1999: 43] wrote that Ducker was anxious that, similar to corporation management, leaders of unions had turned into lawless, selfish bureaucracies, dealing more with execution of power than with needs and aspirations of their members.

Descriptions of trade unions' operations in the USA, as previously mentioned, are not always useful in European realities. Undoubtedly they may serve as great comparative data, rather theoretical, as strikes in European media enterprises are much less common than in the United States.

7.2. Managers (media steersmen)

Management science was born out of a need to search for ways to motivate employees to work more efficiently. The management of employees in media companies most often consists of appreciating their skills and leaving a large margin of freedom in the realization of given tasks. Ardyth Sohn [1999: 69] and co-authors in the monograph *Media Management. A Casebook Approach* make the convincing argument that media employees, and their employers as well, "crave their ability to create, react constructively, and see the meaning of their work."

A manager can achieve a fair share of success the moment he or she employs the best workers while helping them become even better. Harvey Mackay [1988: 155–156] provides advice on how to recognize the most valuable workers for the media industry. H. Mackay noticed that winners tend to surround themselves with winners. Winners are aware of being who they have become. Winners do not need any flattery. Winners are self-confident and know that they will achieve a lot provided they cooperate with people who not only are capable of keeping pace but who themselves are going to prompt good ideas. Mackay also advises that while networking one should look not only at their opposite number in the second company but also at their subordinates. Does he or she trust them? Does he or she confide tasks to them? Do his or her immediate subordinates support their boss with their skills? Or perhaps they are just his or her clones?

Collin L. Powell [1995: 355], an exceptional American general and the Secretary of State in George W. Bush's cabinet, gave an account of his own rules of selecting coworkers: "Look for intelligence and judgment and, most critically, a capacity to anticipate and to see around the corners. Also look for loyalty, integrity, a high-energy drive, a balanced ego, and a drive to get things done."

Without any doubt, these pieces of advice are essential for managers and media steersmen, though describing their role in functioning of media organizations is not an easy task as. In general, every person responsible for media management has a strong personality and people he or she manages (as a rule) tend to have such a personality as well. For the purpose of the analysis two distinct cases were chosen. The first of them is Greg Dyke, a former chief executive officer of the BBC who, in the public eye, achieved success by saving the BBC's independence. The second case revolves around Kamil Durczok, executive editor of the *Fakty* news program on TVN, the success of which enhanced his position in the TV station itself as someone who defeated the news broadcast of the public television channel TVP. In the case of both managers, one distinguishes some common features: a strong success orientation, team diligence, achievement of goals that are possible here and now for a price that is payable as well as a strong personality.

Greg Dyke – case study

The case of the former CEO of the BBC Greg Dyke is highly characteristic of managers employed in the public media, who in one form or another are endangered with political pressures. Oftentimes it is a kind of direct attempt of "controlling the media manually," influencing its content, while also an influence concealed by concern about the public trust or an equal access to the public medium. Every manager who manages the public medium can be charged with not fulfilling the "mission," regardless whatever may be understood by this notion.

It is widely and justifiably believed that the BBC is a role model of public media organizations. And rightfully so, one should bear in mind that nothing lasts forever and nothing falls out of the skies. The BBC was forced to fight for its independence. The first serious attempt for independence began in 1926 during a nine-day general strike. On the strength of the Wireless Broadcasting License of 1923, the British government had the right to directly intervene in programming. The Minister of Treasury at the time, Winston Churchill, was an adherent of the BBC's subordination to the government. However, Prime Minister Stanley Baldwin did not decide to undertake such a step. No British newspaper was issued in the course of the strike (except "The British Gazette" belonging to Churchill), and the BBC became the only source of information for the English. It was the first serious test of objectivity and impartiality. Subsequent ones appeared during World War II, the Suez Crisis in 1956, during the Falklands War in 1982 and in 2003 when Great Britain joined the war in Iraq. The latter issue is connected with the dismissal of Gavyn Davis, the then president of the BBC, Dyke, the CEO [Jędrzejewski 2010: 75–77].

A piece by Andrew Gilligan marked the beginnings of the whole case. In his work the BBC journalist formulated accusations towards the British government regarding a governmental report which stated that Iraq disposed of weapons of mass destruction. Gilligan claimed that the threat of Iraq was being bumped up and that the whole report was counterfeited. It is worth remembering that the report was a justification for Great Britain's entrance into the Iraq war. When it came to light that Gilligan's informer was Dr. David Kelly, a United Nations inspector in Iraq, Kelly committed suicide. Hutton's commission convened by the British Parliament indicated numerous mistakes by the BBC and the government's innocence in this case. However, the public opinion was different. As a result, contrary to government's expectations, there was an increase in trust for the BBC and a decline in trust for Tony Blair's government.

G. Dyke, who used to be the CEO of the BBC between 2000 and 2004, after handing in his dismissal, published a book entitled "Inside Story" in which he accused Prime Minister Blair of incompetence and lies related to the Iraq war. It was in April 2006 when the Polish trade journal "Press" published an interview with G. Dyke where he shared his reflections on his work for the BBC [Dominiak 2006: 57–59]. His considerations are even more significant as they not only refer to the case of Gilligan and the war in Iraq, but also address problems connected with public media management. In this case, the analysis referring to G. Dyke should be divided into several subjects: 1. media vs. politics; 2. employees; 3. the BBC as a brand; 4. management; 5. future.

Media vs. politics. At some point in the past, Dyke was on friendly terms with Prime Minister T. Blair and was a frequent visitor to Downing Street. His political beliefs were close to left wing. However, it does not mean that G. Dyke was prone to break standards of the BBC's independence for his view as exemplified by the case of Gilligan. Dyke was charged with breaking standards in this matter, as one of the BBC's binding rules is that content broadcasted should be confirmed by some other source. Meanwhile, Gilligan's material was broadcasted on the BBC's "Today" and was based only on one source. From the cases beginning to the end, Dyke defended the author, arguing that in the case of leakages there is little probability that one would get more than one source. Gilligan's work was rigorously examined in the BBC's editing system. Moreover, the report of Lord Rupert Butler (evaluating activities of British intelligence within the period preceding Iraq invasion in July, 2004) confirmed information gained by Gilligan. When the journalist asked Dyke about the legendary impartiality of the BBC, he stated: "I honestly believed just as the president of the BBC at the time, Gavyn Davies, that the BBC is independent from the government. However, compared to other public media in Europe, the BBC is still quite independent. I know the bosses of Spanish public media who used to receive calls from ministers every day [ibid.]."

In another interview given by Dyke at the time, referring to the case of Gilligan, he declared: "My sole aim has been to defend the BBC's editorial independence and act in the public interest [http://news.bbc.co.uk/2/hi/uk_news/politics/3441181.stm]."

Employees. As previously mentioned, Dyke defended the BBC journalist Gilligan. However, his defense was substantiated as he was convinced that his employee met all possible journalistic standards. For these rights, Dyke parted with his existing political environment supporting it in the following way: "…I have my own political views but I have always been more into journalistic independence than political one. Unfortunately, in this country the manner of leading politics for several years has been defined by people acting in the style of Richard Nixon or George W. Bush style – you are either with or against us. When Blair was sending me a letter criticizing our way of reporting the Iraq war I replied: 'I am sorry but you are not the one to evaluate our impartiality,' as Blair perceived impartiality as supporting his version of events." Such a relationship among the BBC's Chief Executive Officer, employees and politicians was defined probably most accurately by John Simpson, one of the BBC's best war correspondents: "…it is not a problem if the government extorts influence on the BBC. Difficulties begin the moment the broadcaster bends under their pressure." G. Dyke did not falter under a massive pressure of the ones in power. He handed in his own resignation. No wonder that after his leaving the BBC employees wrote in a notice published in the Daily Telegraph that they were saying goodbye to a boss who had always stood up on journalism and was not afraid of looking for the truth [Dominiak 2006: 57–59]."

The BBC as a brand. The BBC is one of the most well recognized brands in the world. The company built its brand over several decades. The standards accepted at the BBC are a benchmark for many media organizations all over the world. When asked about this myth of the BBC's uniqueness, Dyke replied: "What is striking, politicians who feel panic towards the BBC believe in this myth. They consider this TV station to be much more powerful than in reality. However, it concerns media in general. Mind you, notice how they support Murdoch as they are afraid of his newspapers, with "The Sun" tabloid in particular, however this journal sells currently a million copies fewer compared to the 1990's" [ibid.].

Dyke is aware that changes are inevitable, as forced upon the BBC by a fiercely changing world of media. Nonetheless, as claimed by Dyke, one must not abandon the BBC being a strong and recognized brand. In his opinion, the thing that is going to defend the BBC from attempts by politicians are voters who love their "Auntie" (that is how the Brits refer to the BBC – "Auntie" or "Auntie Beeb"). Dyke recalls the case of Margaret Thatcher who used to fight fiercely against institutions financed by public means, yet never did she attempt to impair the BBC in any way. It was the fear of her voters from the south of England rather than the fright of the BBC that was stopping the *Iron Lady*.

Management. Dyke was perceived in Great Britain as one of the best media managers. He began his career in the commercial media and later joined the public media. The beginning of his career is connected with LWT (*London Weekend Television*). It was estimated that at the moment of the LWT takeover by the media concern Granada, Dyke earned about GBP 7 million. Therefore, he chose the BBC not because of the money but in order to prove what kind of manager he was. Four years of his governance marked a great time for the BBC. His coworkers referred to him as a risk-taker in the most positive sense. He became courageous while making decisions due to his financial independence but also the experience he gained from commercial media management. Dyke did not fear challenging Ruper Murdoch, a media giant. *Freeview*, the digital platform he created on the basis of the BBC, turned out to be one of the most successful media ventures in the course of past years in Great Britain. Dyke did not give into accusations by his critics stating that he used a public logo for the sake of promoting a very commercial enterprise. In his opinion, creating Freeview was dedicated in the utmost of the public interest. His assertion emphasizes this *experssis verbis*: "Assuming that the free market is a reply for everything is in my opinion completely fake and does not stack up in the economy. We have a vast number of regulations in health service, education, why not have regulations in media? [ibid.]." Another of Dyke's accomplishments was corporate decentralization. He moved some parts of production from London to Manchester, to the north of England. His idea for the residents of the northern part of the country was to feel an equally strong bond with the BBC as the ones from the south.

Dyke was aware that the BBC had a lot to make up for regarding management. As an instance of such an incompetent body, he pointed out the BBC's Board of Governors (an equivalent of a supervisory board operating in Polish public media; The Board of Governors has 12 members). In Dyke's opinion most of the 12 governors had neither the managerial qualifications nor the proper knowledge concerning journalism for them to occupy a spot in this prestigious body [ibid.].

Future. Dyke claims that the greatest revolution is about to strike the BBC in the area of news programs as "…the aim of the BBC is to enable the viewers to watch the news on demand, any time they want. The entire problem is that continuous reporting is reminiscent of factory work and requires alterations in the way of thinking even of someone who until now used to work on the BBC news at 10 p.m." The force behind these changes is the Internet, as in the era of widespread access, "people can get the news from everywhere, whenever they want and how they want [ibid.]." From Dyke's point of view, the Internet is going to become even more important than 24-hour news channels within several years.

Kamil Durczok – case study

The example of Kamil Durczok is the absorbing case of a man who became the chief editor of *Fakty* TVN editorial office right after Tomasz Lis. W. Godzic [2010: 308] defined Durczok as an uncertain celebrity. However, the subject of this analysis is not Kamil Durczok the celebrity but Kamil Durczok the manager. In order to make both these figures (Dyke and Durczok) at least a bit comparable, a similar perspective of analysis was applied: 1. media vs politics; 2. employees; 3. media organization as a brand; 4. management; 5. future.

Media vs. politics. Before transferring to TVN, Durczok spent 12 years working in public television (TVP). As the host of the main news *Wiadomości* and journalistic programs such as *Forum* and *Centrum Uwagi*, he gained a large popularity among his viewers. Nonetheless, working in public media can be compared to standing in a minefield. One never knows which political powers shall take control over TV and introduce their own people in place of the previous ones. It is a highly uncomfortable situation for journalists who treat their job seriously along with assigned standards of impartiality. It must have been for this reason as well as a battle with a serious illness that made Durczok decide to go over to his competitors who, to a smaller extent, were endangered by political conjecture. When he took over the flagship news program of TVN on May 1, 2006, Durczok received assurances that no one would "furnish" his program politically. He had a free hand, especially right after he revealed his primary aim to the station's bosses – namely, to outperform TVP's flagship program "Wiadomości" in market share.

Employees. The team that Durczok manages has been of great importance. Specifically, he was taking over the team of *Fakty* after Tomasz Lis who shaped the program in accordance with his own vision. At present – Durczok declares – there are only two people from his predecessor who are still working for *Fakty*: Grzegorz Jędrzejowski and Grzegorz Kajdanowicz. However, Durczok emphasizes that the kindness of Tomasz Sekielski and Grzegorz Jędrzejowski enabled him to join the team of *Fakty* relatively peacefully. He highlights that he was overtaking a team consisting of strong personalities that worked well together. "'The worst thing I could do' – says Durczok – 'was trying to carry out some personal revolution. I was aware that if there were any changes to be made, they would have to be rather of evolutionary rather than revolutionary character. I was joining a team of strong individuals, well-known names, efficient and success-oriented ones' [all statements by Durczok are derived from an interview conducted by the author in March 2011]."

Durczok noticed that the team was deprived of a clearly defined goal. Recognizing this is what convinced them that they could "hunt Wiadomości down, defeat them and take over the kingdom in ruling." By setting a clear goal, he managed to convince the team. Durczok became the kind of a headman who leads his soldiers to victory. They soon found a common language.

Durczok says: "The team I have currently been managing is nowadays the best on the market. At some point I was considering one or maybe two transfers to other TV stations, but I abandoned this idea. Today, the team at *Fakty* is the best in the Polish news market. Obviously, provided I spotted some star in the media market I could persuade the concern management to sign a contract with him or her, yet currently I see no need of this kind."

TVN as a brand. For Durczok TVN stands for one of the greatest media brands in Poland and *Fakty* belongs to one of the pillars of this brand. The strategy undertaken by Durczok consisted of and still consists of efforts to strengthen this brand. The bosses of the station equipped him with "tools" thanks to which he was able to execute his plan. His contract enabled him to conduct his own programming concept. As a rule, he can discuss neither this concept nor the strategy as they are industry secrets along with the terms of his contract.

The strategy of *Fakty* does not contain its mission, yet the very works related to it lasted relatively long. "Though, we reached a conclusion that developing it the course of everyday work, in specific cases stands for the best action. We have at our disposal an internal code which is concurrent with majority of large media and electronic corporations in the world. To a large extent it is based on rules binding in the BBC, partly on Reuters, but for example Reuters' records concerning the image were unacceptable for us, as they assumed that any treatment of footage is punished by sacking the employee. We, except for disasters and other incidents of this kind, tend to play with images which makes *Fakty* recognizable. It is simply inscribed in the reporters' workshop and way of thinking. An image addresses the viewer and we are able to do anything with it (apart from its deformation), in order to make it even more convincing for the viewer." – concludes Durczok.

One of his original program achievements was inventing the "*Fakty* po faktach" program. It appeared that the show, as a "post scriptum" to the main program of *Fakty* had little chance of being successful. The time of its broadcasting was the same as that of the most serious competitor "Wiadomości" of TVP. However, the program eventually "grabbed the chance" and its ratings are constantly rising. It has become another brick in building the TVN brand.

Management. Durczok has managed various teams and has vast experience in this field. However, he is aware of his own weaknesses that result from his lack of theoretical knowledge in this scope. His managerial talent results from not being afraid to admit that he is influenced by the management styles of other people as well as being able to distance himself from his own actions and reflect upon his own operations.

The moment Durczok appeared on the *Fakty* team, he offered a partnership-based model on management. "However, there were several things to be laid on the line. Yet, I made attempts to minimize these tensions right from the very beginning. I was aware of what they were thinking about me 'there comes a new guy, from a different backyard who had already been fighting against us, and now he is supposed to manage us.' Things must be made clear: I am not going to make a step backwards, but we are playing on the same team." – adds Durczok.

On the topic of things that are characteristic for his management style of the *Fakty* team, he indicates three sets:

1. the state of possession – it is about people and tools disposed of by TVN,
2. program strategy – established for program and people of *Fakty*,
3. intuitive realm – according to Durczok, this is the most difficult to describe. In his opinion, it is a collection of decisions which were undertaken by him as a result of what is referred to as a "nose," intuition, ability to react or predict certain things which he is unable to define, yet

things that were undertaken on the basis of experienced gained by him in over 22 years of practice.

Being asked about his management priorities, Durczok points out several diverse ways of management, motivating, motivating especially in critical situations, and solving conflicts. "The thing which in other branches stands for a primer for managers, is a new, receptive domain for the media. Only a few people in Poland have dealt with it before, namely, treating the editorial office as a business which has to be managed and that is exactly the thing I have been learning to do." – Durczok asserts.

Future. As regards the future Durczok once more appeals to the necessity of learning. "The thing I have currently been dealing with and what I have been learning are ways of management, particularly in the context of transferring to the web: How is a brand like *Fakty* supposed to function on the web?" – asks Durczok. Nevertheless, in his opinion such notions of program formats or "prime time" will not be eradicated in Poland for some time, as Poland is a country where TV consumption is a cultural phenomenon deeply rooted in Polish customs. While the transfer of news broadcast to the web is inevitable, it is not likely to happen very soon.

7.3. Journalists

Over the course of many decades journalism was a kind of mission, yet not a profession performed by the employees of media organizations. It was still in the 19th century when an editor's lack of "professionalism" was a substantial premise of his or her credibility, and which (the said editor) "…should have some specific, fixed, adequate livelihood," as "spiritual independence along with civil courage cannot exist without material independence [Grzelewska et al. 2001: 57]."

The notion of the profession referred to as a «journalist» in the contemporary world is becoming more and vaguer. Even experienced researchers like Peter J. Anderson and Geoff Ward [2010] have difficulties defining this profession and, despite many objections, keep using the 19th and 20th century formula according to which "journalism is about collecting and widely spreading information [Anderson, Ward 2010: 24–25]." However, the problem is that the contemporary world keeps on "flooding" its recipients with information. The essence of the problem does not consist of deciding "where to take information from?," but of "how to select information to have a useful character for the recipient?." The aforementioned authors seem to ignore this basic problem and focus on the division of the news into "hard" – concerning politics and economy, that exert crucial influence on people's lives and "soft"– concerning sports, music, pop culture, etc. [Anderson, Ward 2010: 24–25]. Admittedly, the authors themselves spot some kind of anachronism in this perception of the world, saying that for representatives of the middle class below the age of 30, the »hard« news might be a synonym for things which are read in boring papers by their parents. It is a direct journalistic style that is more convincing for many recipients of this generation (…), where things that matter include comprehensive language, gaudy format and a mixture of attractive topics, celebrities, lifestyle, music, and et cetera [ibid.]. However, it seems that simplifying the journalistic profession and dividing it into "serious and hard" journalism and "soft infotainment" is merely an epidermal description of events. The most essential question is the following: Will there be a profession of journalism at all in the future?

In 2010 the Institute of Media Monitoring along with the Association of Polish Journalists carried out research concerning the condition of the journalistic profession in Poland. A survey conducted on a group of 500 people showed that the things journalists tend to be worried about are declining earnings, politicization and manipulation as well as the increasing influx of people without appropriate background into the profession. Even then, as much as 76% of those surveyed were pleased with performed work [http://www.press.pl/newsy/pokaz.php?id=24491; 2011]. Results of this research indicate a peculiar ambivalence on the part of journalists, characteristic not only in Poland. This survey seems to be a good starting point for an analysis of a journalistic professional group. Looking into the past and describing the present state might serve as a solid basis for anticipating the future of this incredibly substantial media professional group.

Journalism ought to behave as a "watchdog" in a democracy. It is in the interest of the entire society that journalists closely monitor the authorities. Frequently, politicians tend to undermine media legitimacy to perform the function of the so-called fourth authority, accusing the media or individual journalists of lacking objectivity. Not getting into details of these accusations it should be recalled that the canon of impartiality concerns informational journalistic genres. A journalist has the right to express his or her own views. In the meantime, even many distinguished journalists strive to convince us at any cost that they maintain high standards of objectivity. In contrast, according to the Hutchins Committee the media not only ought to provide reliable and objective information and check up on authority, but also introduce and explain "social aims and values [McQuail 1994: 184]." This latter sentence seems to be "neglected" by the media. One reason might be responsibility for declaimed beliefs that would have to be taken on by media steersmen, publishers, and also authors of particular programs. In the meantime a common practice not only in the Polish media is the following: the author of a journalistic program that tackles a sensitive topic, e.g., abortion due to social reasons, invites advocates of such practice together with its opponents. The program comes to an end and in fact the viewers do not hear the opinion of the author of this program. My late mother used to watch a program of this type. After the program finished she would turn to me and ask, "So, what is it supposed to be like, in fact?" The media, or rather the people in the media do much to avoid answering this question. Journalism is in decline because it frequently escapes from answering sensitive questions. There is also a second reason. The development of new communication technologies has meant that the prestige and the significance of the journalistic profession have substantially decreased. Thanks to the incredible possibilities offered by the Internet, classical journalism has found itself falling behind. One even started speculating upon an absolute decline of this profession in its classical meaning. In such a view born in the 19th century and cultivated in the 20th century – a journalist was the only person to collect and elaborate information that is publicized by means of the mass media. Meanwhile, it is unnecessary to look for information in the contemporary world. Information, in an overwhelming majority of cases, is in public circulation mainly by means of the Internet.

One might acknowledge that the turning point which marked the end of the classic type of journalism as well as the beginning of a new journalism (which requires a description and definition) was caused by two events. The first of them was in the year 2004 when the two major American parties – the Democrats and Republicans – both conceded that bloggers perform the same role as classical journalists and accredited first bloggers during their conventions. The second symptomatic event was when the United Nations accredited its first blogger, Matthew Lee [http://www.nytimes.com/2007/04/30/business/media/30blog.html?_r=3&hp&oref=slogin&oref=slogin; 2010].

Ryszard Kapuściński was one of the most outstanding realists who clearly perceived the commercialization of the journalistic profession. He indicated that the mission of the journalistic profession was terminated the moment businesspeople understood that information is a commodity that one can profit from. Kapuściński was probably one of the last classical journalists. On the other hand, in the contemporary world one notices the rising demand for media workers and not journalists. This case requires separate coverage as it is of particular importance. The case of Kapuściński is – as it seems – its best exemplification.

Ryszard Kapuściński – case study

The 20th century was an age of revolutions, great wars, and fights for freedom and independence. The oppressed fought for their rights by means of rifles or patient obstinacy, just like Ghandi or Martin Luther King. In both cases there was a lot of bloodshed and many died. However, in his own description of the world, Kapuściński does not include great battle scenes or events of pomp and circumstance. The author searched for things, objects, people, and phenomena that were of little interest to others. The contemporary world values encyclopedic information, preferably useful and practical. Meanwhile, Kapuściński wrote: "…it was the description of a shadow casted by a tree, the description of river's silence going through the Sahara Desert which posed so much difficulty for me. But critics do not pay attention to such images. All they are interested in is politics, sociology, economy" [Kapuściński 2007: 13]. For Kapuściński, the world was divided into the one inside and the one outside of one's self. He was uninterested in a Confucian journey without leaving one's own house, a journey into one's inside. He was rather enamored by the world in its fullest diversity [Kapuściński 2003: 12–13]. Kapuściński experienced his first journey as a reporter in 1956 in India and Afghanistan. Most probably, this was when Kapuściński the reporter was born. "As soon as I began writing about all those places where most of the people live in poverty, I realized that it was exactly the topic I wanted to devote myself to. I also used to write for ethical reasons, because the poor are silent. Poverty does not cry, poverty has no voice. Poverty suffers, but suffers in silence. Poverty does not rebel. You come across a revolt of the poor only when they cherish some hopes – they defy when believing that they are able to improve something. Generally, they are wrong but only hope is able to motivate people to act [ibid.]." Only a man deeply imbued with humanism, ideas of Christianity and close to left-wing ideals could have written these words.

Kapuściński oftentimes perceived things not noticed by others. In his "Lapidarium IV" he wrote that power in the world of media was overtaken by business people who have nothing to do with journalism as the media tend to "trade in" information which is a commodity one can profit from. Moreover, it is the media that – according to Kapuściński – have become the centers of actual authority [Kapuściński 2000: 89–90]. Perhaps it was a drastic opinion, yet not without rationale and rudiments. During various revolutions, rebels would first try to get control over the TV studio, and only later on would they attack the parliament.

This transition was taking place before Kapuściński's eyes. He was disgusted by it and objected to any possible monopolies. His objection was especially brought forth by the phenomenon of the monopolization of information sources accompanying the information revolution: "…once there was a central committee of the central communist party, whereas now there is a «central committee» of information. The centralization of a great media network is taking place and more and more information is in possession of a fewer number of hands. Tendencies of large capital in order to purchase information sources, to join communication networks are visible [Kapuściński 2003: 130]."

Kapuściński indicates two sources of such a situation here. The first one resulted from properties of business entities operating in any market in order to monopolize the said market. Unfortunately, it also concerns the information market, or even the market of ideas. The common opportunism is the second source. In this respect the contemporary world resembles the communist one almost in its pure form.

It was in 1997 when the author of this monograph participated in a meeting with the writer. When asked what features a good reporter should possess, Kapuściński said that he or she should be like a good mother. When she prepares dinner and hears noises of a child playing in the next room, the mother does not react. However, when there is silence the mother instantly hurries to other room as it may signify that the child might do something rash, like setting the house on fire. The case is similar with classically trained reporters. They should pass off to the region of the world that is suspiciously quiet. That is exactly what R. Kapuściński was like. At the same time he perpetually took care of his journalistic workbench. "While writing about contemporary times we have to therefore be aware of imperfectness of our journalistic instruments, we have to continually wonder how to enrich our workshop, so that it is able to bring out the actual sense of history happening right now." There was one more, very meaningful defining feature of this profession: "In order to practice journalism, one has to be a good man. Bad people cannot make good journalists. For it is only a good person who attempts to understand others, their intentions, their faith, interests, their difficulties and tragedies. And at once, right from the very first moment, to become a part of their fate [ibid., 18–21]."

Journeys into flammable regions of the world as a reporter exposed R. Kapuściński to many dangers. His playing with death resembled playing with fire. Just like at the time when Lumumba had been murdered in the Republic of Congo. Death was for R. Kapuściński like fire. It brought out fear and terror, but at the same time it fascinated the author. In his "Wojna fulbolowa" he described the passing away of a young soldier: "Everyone was curious of this fight as they wanted to know how much strength there is in life and how much strength there is in death. Everyone wanted to know how long they are able to strive with death and if a young life which still exists and does not want to surrender will be capable of surviving the death [ibid., 187–188]."

In the contemporary world, war does not take place in the battleground, but on television screens. NATO planes in Yugoslavia were bombarding TV stations. It was – according to Kapuściński – additional evidence that "authority has moved from the edifices of parliament and government to facilities of television." It brings forth a feeling of power, strength and superiority in the media, particularly in the people in the media. Kapuściński describes a landing operation of a NBC television work group onto a village in Kosovo that was at war in 1999. They unload plenty of equipment from the helicopter after which they "rip off some poor woman (…) from the crowd. The woman cries, nervously rearranges her shawl, shakes her infant, sobs something obscurely, they are filming it all, the entire scene lasts for a few seconds. Next, they drag one more poor woman, right after some toothless chap (he must be toothless, they do not film the ones with teeth). They finish the picture and immediately pack their cases in a hurry (…). They did not even care to ask whether they are allowed to be there and do anything. No gestures of sincerity, no signs of understanding. Only contempt. New majesties. New colonialists [Kapuściński 2000: 95]."

Kapuściński knew how important it is for a reporter to be independent, especially for a writer who captures and not reinvents reality. In 2002, during a conversation with Maria Nadotti he said that of course complete independence is the ideal, but the reality is distant from this goal. Journalists must report to many pressures in order to write according to their employee's wishes. "Our lineage is a continuous fight among dreams, desire of independence and actual situations that force us to respect business, views and expectations of our publisher" [Nadotti 2002].

Objectivity has been raised almost to the rank of a holy relic in contemporary journalism. The worst allegation a journalist might encounter is a lack of objectivity. Kapuściński – not without reason – frequently claimed that: "A thing like objectivity does not exist. Objectivity is a matter of conscience of the one who is writing. And this person alone should answer whether the things they write about is nearly true or not. But these things are very individual, and impossible to be generalized [Kapuściński 2003: 40]."

Kapuściński did not want to be a "media worker;" he was willing to be a "journalist." He knew that it was becoming more and more difficult in this contemporary, commercialized world where "information is a commodity that brings exorbitant profits," as it stopped "underlying traditional criteria of the truth and lies [Kapuściński 2000: 90]," and to a larger extent to the laws of the market, the basis of which is to strive for even larger profit and monopoly. In this world journalists stop being "journalists" and become "media workers" for whom the mission is only an empty slogan.

Matthew Lee – Case Study
Matthew Lee works thirteen hours a day. He is an accredited United Nations (UN) journalist. There would be nothing strange about this except for the fact that Lee does not work for any editorial office. He is a blogger. In 2007, the New York Times printed an article by Maria Aspen, "As Blogs Proliferate, a Gadfly with Accreditation at the U.N.," in which she described Lee's work. Calling Lee a gadfly may not be polite but brings out the essence of a blogger's nature of

someone who works hard to share his opinions with others. Every month over 90 thousand people read his blog. He set up a website innercitypress.org, which has almost 300 thousand viewers [http://www.nytimes.com/2007/04/30/business/media/30blog.html?_r=3&hp&oref=slogin&oref=slogin; 2010].

Lee is neither nice nor amiable. He treats his job very seriously like many Internet journalists. He investigates the substance of things during numerous press conferences. And it is of no importance whether it be another boring resolution, a fire drill in the edifice of the UN or a misappropriation of funds.

Until recently he had a companion for his actions. He was a 73-year old blogger named Pincas Jawetz who lost his accreditation in the United Nations as a result of asking too many questions not connected with the topic of a conference [http://www.pardon.pl/artykul/1496/ciezkie_zycie_nadwornego_blogera_onz; 2010]. Lee frequently notices what has been "missed out" by the larger entities in the media. For example, he used to write how the Ukrainian delegation "honored" the casualties of Chernobyl by trading vodka in the halls of the UN.

Bloggers were no longer treated as harmless note-takers. Tuyet Nguyen, a correspondent in a German agency says that "bloggers, serious ones, do contribute to the spread of information, I don't see any difference in what he [Mr. Lee] is doing and what we are doing." Not everyone is as kind regarding Lee's activities as Nguyen. "Mr. Lee is a bit like a bull in the carefully diplomatic china shop of the United Nations press corps. He has broken a few stories and irritated more than one senior official. He has printed gossip, rumors and what several officials called lies, and was once called a «jerk» by Mark Malloch Brown, the deputy secretary-general under Kofi Annan [http://www.nytimes.com/2007/04/30/business/media/30blog.html?_r=3&hp&oref=slogin&oref=slogin; 2010]."

Still, Lee's credibility was not as jeopardized as in December 2006, he was elected to the authorities of the Accredited Journalists Association at the United Nations. Lee himself says that he minds his own duties: "I am a supplement, addition to the main informational trend." He deals with cases that remain unnoticed by others, enabling him to predominate over even the greatest media.

Making a comparison of the attitudes of Kapuściński and of Lee one may say that it is technology that differentiates them, but they share a sensibility towards the damages done to the world described. Kapuściński travelled to developing nations in order to describe poverty, despair and adversity of the people inhabiting those regions. While Lee does not travel away from New York, he reports on similar sentiments. He set up two web portals where he calls for the rights of the poor in their fight with the giants of the commercial world – banks. By means of his own blog, he makes efforts to defend human rights. Lee highlights those regions of the world where such rights are constantly violated.

He reports on the appalling fate of refugees from areas under military actions. The tools that were used by Kapuściński in defense of disadvantaged people were his reportages and books. For Lee it means his blog entries as well as press conferences at the UN where the same, inconvenient questions for the powerful of this world are still being asked.

This sensitivity to problems of the world is exactly what makes the most essential determinant differentiating a journalist form a "media-worker." In this context, both Kapuściński and Lee are journalists in the best sense of the word. However, this ascertainment does not nullify the question concerning the future of the journalistic profession.

Researchers cited in this chapter, i.e., P.J. Anderson and G. Ward [2010: 83], while analyzing the future of journalistic profession are aware that economic and technological factors will have a negative effect on information "meeting democratic needs." In fact, they explicitly write: "We do not have irrefutable proof yet whether the so-called civic journalism (e.g. in a form of independent blogs) shall be a sufficiently reliable and substantial source of information for the «consumers» of the news to be willing to use it, in order to fill gaps in their knowledge being the result of inadequate functioning of major news providers [ibid.]." In this case, the diagnosis of the aforementioned researchers seems to be equitable. Nevertheless, the key matter concerning the future of the journalistic profession remains open nowadays: what and who is going to be considered "the main news provider" tomorrow? The answer will predestine the future of the journalistic profession and assuredly resolve the dilemma: journalist or media worker?

Discussion questions:

1. What is the role of human resources in media organizations?
2. Show the differences between the notions of a journalist and a media worker.
3. Solve the question of the future of journalism as a profession.

Chapter 8. Strategies of Media Organizations. Value for Consumers

8.1. Strategy vs. marketing communication

Peter Doyle [2003: 6] indicates that the history of economic changes until now might be examined through the lens of three subsequent epochs. The first of them, being the agricultural period, began 10 thousand years ago and ended in the first half of the 18th century. After that, the industrial period lasted until the 1960s when the information age began. Two antecedent epochs had exhausted their developmental capabilities. The agricultural period in its decadent stage lowered the standard of life. A new developmental impulse accompanied industrialization which started using up its developmental capabilities in the second half of the 20th century. At this point, entering the informational epoch served as a countermeasure to the lowering of the standard of living. Determinants that ought to be considered in this new informational epoch while building the strategy of operation are as follows:

1. Globalization of markets,
2. Change in the structure of industry,
3. Informational revolution,
4. Growing expectations of customers.

One distinguishes many definitions referring to strategy. For the purpose of these considerations the following one seems to be of great use: "Strategy can be defined as the determination of the basic long-term goals and objectives of an enterprise, and the adoption of courses of action and the allocation of resources necessary for carrying out there goals [Chandler 1978: 13]." In other words, a strategy is a plan to make use of enterprise resources in order to obtain a competitive advantage [Doyle 2003: 12]. The cited definitions also seems to be useful in analyzing the strategy of media organizations.

The media in the contemporary world are subject to numerous processes that determine the strategy of their operations. These include above all processes of convergence, digitization. In the case of the electronic media the process of moving from an analog to a digital signal is not merely a simple change in technology. It is an immense transformation, the final results of which are hard to judge as of now. It is primarily an ability to use properties of information as the new resource (as previously mentioned repeatedly). Convergence, being in a way a derivative of the digitization process, causes a violent media transformation, the final shape of which is impossible to predict at this time. Another factor which must be considered by the managers of media organizations is the rising requirement of consumers. It is creating values that are expected by the consumers. Every time it requires undertaking decisions – one must be aware of the consequences which will predestine the present and future fate of an organization, as decision-making is one of the most important and most responsible human activities. Market participants, while permanently making decisions, find themselves in a field of development appointed by opportunities and threats. This in turn directs the manager towards strategic study. One of the most popular techniques of strategic analysis is SWOT, i.e. the examination of the strong and weak points of an organization as well as opportunities and threats it faces. The basis of comprehending what is going to happen in the future is the knowledge of what is happening today. The aim of a SWOT analysis is "collecting and presenting in an organized way the entirety of information which will have decisive influence on future strategic choices [Kowal 1997: 161]."

On the other hand, Drucker [2000: 7] claims that 90% of problems an organization deals with is of general nature. Only 10% make up the specifics of a given organization. These specifics determine what aims and what mission are superordinate in a given organization as they shall decide upon espousing the strategy of operations. On the other hand the strategy shall determine the shape of a particular organization, its structure and tasks. Drucker [1954: 17] claims directly that strategy is about analyzing the current situation and changing it if necessary. His way of thinking about strategy contains a characteristic systemic approach.

In turn, Józef Penc [1996: 19] remarks that "in systemic approach, the enterprise tries to match marketing and technological, ecological and humanistic needs, as fulfilling those needs in a way as complex and as full as possible conditions its internal efficiency, market efficiency and positive image." Before appointing any strategies that media organizations tend to refer to, it is crucial to understand mutual dependencies between management and strategy.

For quite a long time the dominant approach in issues concerning management was the marketing approach, according to which management stands for "process of planning and execution of ideas for pricing, promotion and distribution of goods, services and ideas, which is to lead to trade meeting requirements of target groups of customers and organizations [Kotler 1999: 11]." The general concept of marketing says that marketing management is a specialized domain of enterprise management that encompasses the whole of decisions and actions connected with shaping and utilization of a market as a basic source of a company's revenues.

Sooner or later every company has to deal with two key problems:

1. even higher requirements of consumers,
2. excessive operation costs of an enterprise.

Marketing based on partnership may be one of the tools that are useful when solving these problems [Przybyłowski 1998: 237]. This notion is much more complex than maintaining good relations with customers. By this idea we understand operations of an enterprise that are aiming at creating sustainable, cost-effective relations with individual clients, that lead to mutual benefits [Shani, Chalasani 1992: 32–42]. The imperative motto of this kind of marketing seems to be: it is not about selling, it is about holding a client by a given brand so that he or she does not leave for competitors. A model that describes such an action is a "win-win situation," i.e. a situation where both parties (the buyer and the seller) after making a transaction are convinced that they have made a good deal.

Information technologies play a fundamental role in partnership-based marketing; since profound changes in relations between enterprises and their customers were possible only due to a revolution in the field of cumulating marketing data. Currently, both consumers and entrepreneurs participate in two types of markets: the traditional market that hosts physical salesmen and purchasers, and in the so-called market space based on an electronic information flow. At present, a customer is able to go to a bank and make a money transfer or take advantage of the same service provided online. Independent of the type of market, behaviors of its participants require a detailed system of marketing information. On the other hand, such a system determines the process of enterprise management.

In turn, the Integrated Marketing Communication (IMC) – stands for managing the dialogue between the companies with its surrounding market [Fill 1999: 13]. Thus, it is a notion more complex than advertising. The marketing communication is a coherent, homogeneous, coordinated image of a company and its offer that is presented to the environment. Many companies have been interested in introducing IMC. However, as shown by research carried out in the mid-nineties of the 20th century in the United States – only the efforts of one-third of the companies turned out to be successful. Lack of knowledge was the main reason for introducing IMC.

One marketing "weaknesses" is an over-instrumental treatment of the very concept of marketing, i.e., basing the whole thing solely on investigating the market and target consumer behaviors while forgetting about people who execute these operations without whom the economic enterprise would be impossible. It appears that the "managers of tomorrow" shall be working in organizations of a new type, "lean ones," which to a greater extent are based on teams having a stronger bond with customers and suppliers. They will be of a flat structure with a flexible, quality-focused global operation. The problem is that although everyone has an inkling of upcoming organizational structures, nobody in fact knows what these organizations are going to look like. Therefore, contemporary academies ought to teach future managers how to answer questions that have not even come into existence yet. Nevertheless, elements of this future image seem to be quite clear:

1. Organizations of post-hierarchical type shall be dominant, of horizontal structure consisting of task forces. Middle management supervisors will be distributing resources and knowledge among independent employees who define their own tasks. Consequently, entirely new professions such as: organization processes supervisor or chief specialist for knowledge will come into existence.
2. Such false dilemmas of "yesterday's" management and managerial education are going to become meaningless. Such notions are staff or line, centralization, tasks or people, cost or quality, specialization or integration, and etc.
3. There will be a "mass customizing" revolution spreading in the market that will abolish traditional divisions into mass products and prepared to order, whereas "company's congeniality" will become a significant fifth element of marketing mix.
4. The economic and organizational world will vigorously create and develop a completely new level of its functioning – the virtual level. Moving on this level will require abilities of thinking in cyberspace categories. For instance, in France, Bishop Gaillot was suspended by the Pope created the first parish with virtual faithful ones.

Drucker [1992: 39] claims that innovativeness is the basic condition of development of every enterprise as innovations produce completely new possibilities of using resources (more extensively discussed in Chapter 3) and in order to create wealth. Innovativeness in an organization should be inscribed in its structures and processes, and not only be an indication of a spontaneous activity. Values are created only then and they can give an advantage to a particular organization over its market competitors.

8.2. Media value chain

The conception of the "value chain" was developed by Michael E. Porter who referred to the "value" as a sum of company's revenues, being the function of a price of a given product and the amount of products sold. The analysis is based on values, not costs. According to this concept the source of a company's competitive advantage is not so much its efficiency as a whole, but the synergic sum of respective techniques undertaken by an organization. Each action undertaken by an organization has its contribution to the company's position in the market.

Tadeusz Kowalski [2006: 44], taking as a starting point M.E. Porter's chain, proposed the "value chain" in the media, considering it as useful for an analysis of media organizations. T. Kowalski distinguished three stages of fabricating a media product: 1. production; 2. creation of packages; 3. distribution (Figure 6: Value chain in media).

Production means creating media content. It is an effect of the joint work of journalists, directors, script writers, stenographers, producers; in brief, people who are referred to as creative professionals. At this stage basic media functions, both informative and entertaining, are implemented. The aim of creative actions in this phase is the transformation of work and intellectual property into some good (broadcast, article, coverage, etc.) that will be accepted by consumers.

The next stage is putting together individual elements (media goods) into packages (individual broadcasts concur to a radio or TV program, articles concur to a magazine, etc.). Kowalski [2006: 44–45] indicates that at this stage one notices the effect of synergy, i.e. obtaining a larger value than it would result after a simple addition of elements. Distribution takes place in the last phase, i.e., delivering of ready-made products and media services to media customers. The market offers a multitude of ways and distribution channels of media goods.

Kowalski emphasizes that it is the last element that determines the strength of a media value chain. In his opinion: "Media content has no market value until it is place in distribution channel, in turn broadcasting network has no value without content which can be published and offered to the audience [ibid.]."

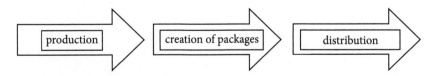

Figure 6. Value chain in the media

Source: Kowalski 2006: 44.

The author points out that from an economic point of view none of the phases described here can be of superior value which may appear shocking, for content makers in particular.

Allan B. Albarran [2010: 35] points out that the traditional value chain in the media consisted of four elements: 1. content creation; 2. production; 3. distribution; 3. exhibition (Figure 16: A traditional media chain).

According to A.B. Albarran [2010: 35], content creation, in the case of television or film, generally has its beginnings in writing a script. Production of "media content" takes place in newspapers, magazines, radio, TV, or film campaigns. Distribution is held through various networks (radio, television, a chain of newsagent's, distributors, etc.). Traditional media presentations used to take place in theaters and cinemas, later by means of radio or TV sets. The development of the new media has developed this presentation and broadcasting spectrum to a large extent.

In turn, Lucy Küng [2010: 143] claims that the media industry is not a monolith, and therefore it is impossible to create one common strategy for all media businesses. Therefore, L. Küng proposed diverse value chains for different media branches. For the magazine branch it consists of six elements (Fig. 8: Value chain in the branch of periodicals).

On the other hand, the value chain in the television industry consists merely of three links and is characterized by a large level of vertical integration. It was a chain that went through many decades virtually unchanged. The reason for this state of affairs was a dominant role of national media and a relatively firm technical base [Küng 2010: 78] (Figure 9: A traditional value chain in TV industry).

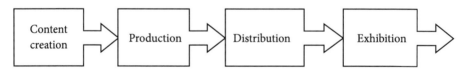

Figure 7. Traditional value chain in media

Source: Albarran 2010: 35.

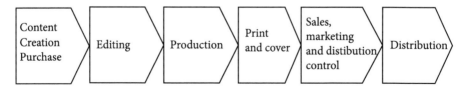

Figure 8. Value chain in the branch of periodicals

Source: Küng 2010: 67.

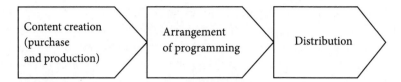

Figure 9. A traditional value chain in the TV industry

Source: Küng 2010: 78.

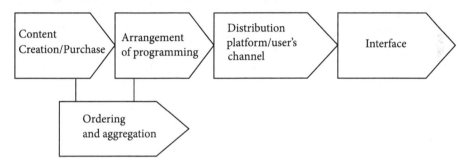

Figure 10. Value chain shaped in the TV industry

Source: Küng 2010: 79.

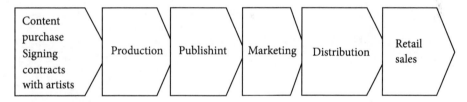

Figure 11. Value chain in the phonographic industry

Source: Küng 2010: 109.

The proceeding liberalization of the TV market and technological advances has led to an increase in available channels. Subscribed services have come into existence and their management has contributed to the formation of a more user-friendly communication. Viewers' preferences have changed as well. These factors led to a fragmentation of the audience and an increased diversification of financing which had its effect on the chain value in TV industry [ibid., 79] (Figure 10: Value chain shaped in TV industry).

In the phonographic industry, the value chain created by Küng, similar to that for periodicals, consists of six elements (Figure 11: Value chain in the phonographic industry), though in the case of many elements it is identical to the book publishing industry.

It is worth remembering that the added value in the media is not merely an effect of phases appointed by individual elements of the value chain but also of other different legal and market processes. In previous chapters it was indicated that the electronic media market is a regulated one due to a scarcity of the good that constitutes its basis – broadcasting frequencies. As an example, Polsat TV at the time of obtaining a license to broadcast TV signal via terrestrial way (October 5, 1993), notably increased its value. The growth of company value always provides new opportunities for a given enterprise, especially possibilities of development that generally are the reaction to new customer's needs.

Drucker [2000: 29] emphasizes that the basis of a "…wider notion of management should be customers' values and needs." It has its roots in a rule according to which potential customers who have not yet been convinced by the services and goods offered are as important, if not more important than current ones [ibid., 28]. In Drucker's opinion [2002: 192], management based on setting goals and self-control may be called a management "philosophy."

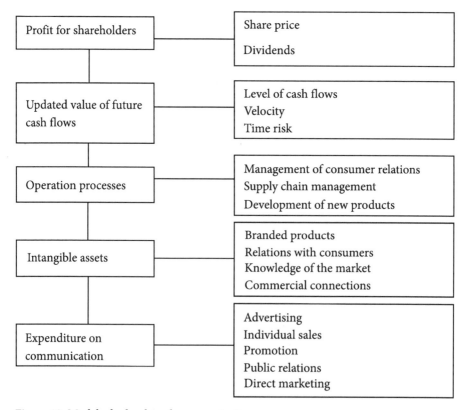

Figure 12. Model of value-based communication

Source: Doyle 2003: 347.

P. Doyle [2003: 347] suggests to make use of theoretical assumptions of value-based communication. Doyle relates his concept to business ventures but it seems that this idea could be adapted for non-profit organizations or public enterprises. Figure 12 shows a model of value-based communication.

The monograph *Public Media Enterprise. Determinants, Systems, Models* [Nierenberg 2007: 114–121] indicated costs of delivering the value, particularly in the case of public media organizations, especially in public media organizations, where five efficiency indicators, useful for strategic management would have their application:

1. Key Performance Indicators – KPI,
2. Balanced Scorecard – BSC,
3. Activity Based Costing – ABC,
4. Measuring of effectiveness by means of target management (applied by the BBC).

The second and fourth indicators have been discussed for the purpose of these considerations.

A Balanced Scorecard (BSC) is based on determining strategic directions of management in the public media and a system of managerial controlling [ibid., 8–31] (Strategic directions of management in the public media – Figure 13 and system of managerial controlling – strategic management – Figure 14). In the case of using the BSC indicator, the control of effectiveness is carried out on two levels: strategic and operational. In the first case, effectiveness is examined on a level appointed by the company mission and its strategy. In the second case, the process of planning and control is analyzed by means of effectiveness indicators.

The BBC is considered (not without reason) a specific benchmark of a public broadcaster. To a large extent such a corporation owes its high quality to procedures which accurately describe formation and course of particular processes in an organization itself.

The BBC has three main aims [http://www.bbc.co.uk/]:

1. Management of enterprise operations,
2. Implementation and execution of a strategy,
3. Responsibility and reporting.

Under the term "management of enterprise activity" we understand quarterly and annual evaluations of achievements, analysis and defining of basic problems, appointing and monitoring annual targets, as well as yearly inspections of staff, which results in promotions, rewards and possible sacks [ibid.].

At the BBC, a strategy is elaborated once every five years but the level of implementation of the adopted strategy and the SWOT analysis are carried out every year. In case of adverse phenomena the strategy is updated. The proper course of described processes increases the company's value.

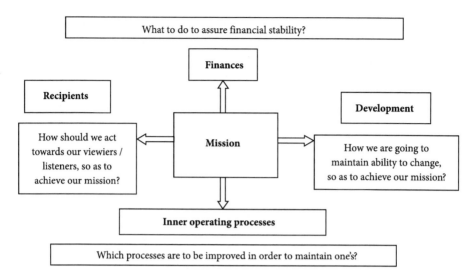

Figure 13. Strategic directions of management in the public media

Source: Bochenek 2006: 12.

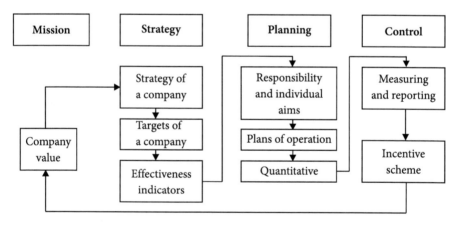

Figure 14. System of managerial controlling – strategic management

Source: Bochenek 2006: 13.

In compliance with the third basic aim, every year the BBC management submits a report of annual activity to the Board of Supervisors and British Parliament. The document is basically a settlement of adopted program strategy and a reliable settlement of the received subscription.

In the case of the BBC, the algorithm of assumed operations is as follows: the mission appoints aims and strategic challenges which in turn appoint key

Figure 15. Mission of the BBC connected with strategic aims

Source: Bochenek 2006: 21–22.

areas that are analyzed by means of indicators. In the case of effective target management in a public media enterprise its essence is connecting a mission with strategic aims. It is depicted by Figure 15, Mission of the BBC connected with strategic aims.

It appears that from the management point of view, or virtually its effectiveness, it is essential to treat high costs of enterprise functioning as a consequence, not the cause of low effectiveness. Increasing effectiveness means an alteration of processes, functioning and finally the mindset of the managerial staff and the whole personnel. Operation strategies of media enterprises are applied for such purposes.

8.3. Value creation in media organizations

Recent years have brought changes in the way of evaluating managers' performance. Many companies have applied the criterion of value increase for shareholders as a superordinate criterion of strategy and managerial staff evaluation. It is based on an assumption that strategies ought to be evaluated through the lens of investment return for shareholders. A tool applied for this purpose is the shareholder value analysis – SVA [Doyle 2003: 23]. By all means, in the era of information the analysis referring only to material values is of no importance, as the main values are intangible assets. Value is created by an idea, invention, or the information owned. In order to illustrate it is enough to refer to an example of Dell Computer Corporation that was established in 1984 by Michael Dell, a nineteen-year old university dropout. In 2000, the value of his company amounted to USD 20 billion. While his computers were not outstanding, Dell made up a new way of selling. One gave up a costly dealership network in favor of direct sales which resulted in bringing the company a considerable competitive advantage [Magretta 1998: 72–85]. The Internet provides particular opportunities in this domain of money accumulation. At the end of the 1990s, the Charles Schwab brokerage made global dealership services available. Thanks to this courageous step the company tripled its value within one year.

Although the Internet bookstore Amazon.com was set up in 1995 and did not note any profit in its first five years of operation, its value in 2000 was evaluated at the level of USD 20 billion, i.e. larger than of all other American booksellers [Doyle 2003: 18].

An extremely interesting monograph by Robert G. Picard [2010] entitled *Value Creation and the Future of News Organizations* was published in 2010. To make the study clear, it was assumed that media organizations that deliver products or informational services would be referred to as "news organizations." Other things that need be made more precise are methods of value creation, especially in news organizations.

Most works of research concerning value-created strategy indicates four approaches that a strategy can be based on [Wernerfelt 1985: 171–180]:

1. Resources,
2. Organization,
3. Transactions,
4. Innovativeness.

Resources that a company possesses creates a value the moment customer satisfaction is obtained while the prices of offered products are lower than competitors or the products offered are perceived by consumers as distinct [Picard 2010: 65]. However, not all companies compete on equal terms, as market positioning depends on both the company's own resources as well as the size of the company itself. In Poland, the dominating position still belongs to public television exactly due to access to archives of programs that were created in times of real socialism (various TV series, TV films, TV theater, cabarets, etc.)

or due to its size. Larger companies can afford to formulate more general strategies and adopt more objectives. Smaller companies have to implement more oriented strategies [Wright 1987: 93–101].

Moreover, it is worth highlighting that skills of managerial staff are central to value creation, as it is their decisions that highly influence the formation of a product that will be satisfactory for customers [Bowman, Ambrosini 2000: 1–15]. In media companies it is frequently HR that decides upon the appointed strategy. Media personalities turn out to be the most valuable, attracted to a given company by managers. Journalists who are more successful create better texts and broadcasts. Their "superiority" will consist of creating an improved value useful for customers. To a great extent it determines the actions of media managers, which were discussed in the previous chapter.

An organizational approach is another type of creating strategy, according to which value creation is understood as the function of market power and increases in efficiency. Value creation might also be an effect of controlling costs [Williamson 1979: 233–261].

Innovation, being the basic premise of another strategic attitude is predominantly understood as a factor that causes a change. Any alteration alters the existing order in a company and replaces it with a new one. Innovation might refer both to technology as well as structures and processes. An innovative change usually favors savings that, in turn, foster the generation of a greater value than competitors [Besanko, Dranove, Shanley 2001: 221–235]. In literature of the subject, divagations concerning strategy usually focus on creating heterogenic products – frequently protected by patents – which are characterized by advantages that are difficult for competitors to copy. For the time being, the news media seldom refer to strategies applied by companies that create values based on heterogenic products. The media tend to introduce similar technologies at one time. As an effect, the news media find it difficult to create one-of-a-kind products that would be outstanding (in the sense of value creation) from those offered by competitors. Therefore, it seems that the pace of delivery is a thing that is decisive in the case of the news media. However, all news media have their own strategy that is oriented towards the pace of delivery. Hence, none of the media organizations that deal with news delivery can recognize the "speed" factor as a crucial condition that contributes to increasing its value. This has also been proven by research practice. In conclusion, general rules concerning the creation of business strategies are of little usefulness. Information services makers should first answer a key question: for whom do they create the value? In Picard's opinion [2010: 66–67] the value is created for media customers (readers, viewers, listeners) as well as stakeholders, which requires forming values, especially for the news media.

It should be noted that the method referring to the value creation of a company exceeds standard approaches to a strategy. According to this method one should not make an artificial division between a company and its stakeholders, but investigate all possible relations among them as it is the key to success which may result in higher revenues, greater market share or distinguishing the offer of one company from competitors' proposals. The method of value creation should also take into account the fact that interactions that occur only between the company's stakeholders as a stable value is the result of the cooperation of all participants in this process. Picard [ibid.] emphasizes that a market approach to journalism, based on the belief of "offer anything and people will buy it," is oversimplified. The value does not derive from the product itself offered to customers but is rather a result of many factors: experience, common relations, personal experiences, individually perceived profits, etc. Therefore, it can be stated that the company value is created by a vast circle of participants who form the company value chain. This approach assumes a long-term method of thinking, not only for the here and now. At the same time it does not mean neglecting short and midterm aims. It poses great challenges for managers maintaining the balance between the needs of company itself and its stakeholders as well as pursuing the greatest value at all times, and not only within some short period. It requires a detailed investigation of relations that take place between a company and its customers, carried out by the managers. It means a continuous monitoring of changes occurring in attitudes of customers and their transmuting needs. It also requires providing for customers' points of view by the managers. A media organization (the news media in particular) should implicitly investigate the activity of a company from the consumers' standpoint. This approach derives from research concerning customer satisfaction, the effect of which was an assertion that the said satisfaction (value perceived by the consumer) derives not only from supplied goods or services but also from the relation between their supplier and customers as it may lead to customers' loyalty towards a given brand. [Ravald, Grönross 1996: 19–30]. It is worth recalling that value for the client was defined primarily as benefits arising from consumption in relation to the price. However, currently it is thought that the said value is rather an outcome of product perception through the prism of its attractiveness and usefulness as well as the general context of relations proceeding between the seller and the buyer. Robert B. Woodruff and Susan Gardial [1996] claim that achieving the state desired by customers by means of offered products or services constitutes the value of customers. In this approach the added value is the surplus over what is offered by the basic product itself. An example of such a case was the behavior of cable TV in the United States in areas where it was possible to receive terrestrial uncoded TV. Cable television companies were stressing additional virtues of their services: a better quality of picture, greater choice of film, sport and children's channels as well as news services. The cable TV's offer also included local live channels, foreign news services and private channels. Actions undertaken were aimed at improving provided services and, subsequently, increasing customers' value and satisfaction. The moment when increasing the value becomes an essential and even perhaps the major aim of the news media, it should become the main component of the said media's strategy. Value management differs considerably from other conceptions of management. That is, operations of managers ought to focus on improving products and services by means of understanding the way customer needs are fulfilled while searching for other innovative changes. This, in turn, leads to the increase in value of a given company's products and services. However, it is essential to bear in mind that in the short run there is a risk of excessive financial input in a company's value that may result in staggering the short-term company profitability. As a result, it would make the managers perform actions aimed at lowering the offered value so as to restore profitability immediately. However, in the case of the news media, which also results from the very essence of journalism, it is always advisable to consider the relations among profits, non-cash aims, real delivered value and social values [Picard 2010: 60–70].

Picard indicated several categories of stakeholders for whom the informational media creates the content. They are as follows [ibid.]:

1. society as a whole,
2. customers,
3. investors,
4. journalists,
5. advertisers.

Each of these groups of stakeholders might have (and usually does) distinct businesses and diverse aims. Therefore, the primary aim of the news media should be balancing these businesses. At the same time, it must not take place at the expense of losing basic functions (tasks) of the news media. Experiences from recent years have shown that this balance has been unsettled. The weight was shifted towards investors and advertisers. Consequently, in order to be successful, media organizations should continually maintain this balance in relation to all their stakeholders. These decisions ought to be attributed to top management of information organizations.

Value changes might be depicted by means of a pentagon, the vertices of which indicate particular groups of stakeholders: society, consumers, investors, journalists, advertisers (Figure 16: Value conceptualization for information media).

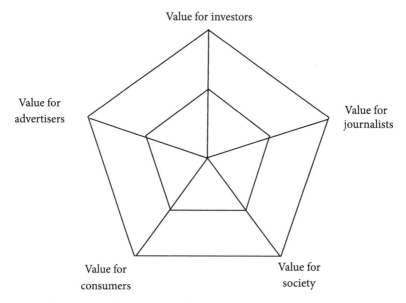

Figure 16. Value conceptualization for information media

Source: Picard 2010: 71.

Picard [2010: 72] begins his analysis of informational media from the "golden age" of the said media. However, it strikes one as whether something like this has ever existed. Nevertheless, provided the answer to this question was positive, then such a "golden age" would have to be characterized by creating some high value for society and media workers, mainly journalists (Figure 17: Value creation in the "golden age" of informational media). This epoch would have also created value of the informational media and for advertisers. However, due to the relatively low pressure on operations imposing high profitability, contribution of these factors when creating the value would be relatively low as well. Therefore, it would be an epoch with an appreciation of a high level of journalism, in which journalists would be respected and highly rewarded. The very journalists who write for newspapers indicate that in their case such a period would have been the 1960s and 1970s. For electronic media (this concerns American and Western European media) it would be the 1950s and 1960s. Many journalists, especially the older ones, recall this period nostalgically.

Changes take place after this "golden period," in which the market becomes the superior determinant. The final 20 years of the 20th century represent an "explosion" of advertising expenditures. The flowing stream of money intensified pressure on the media market. One noticed a progressing pursuit after monopolization, to creating huge media corporations. Oligopolies were dominant

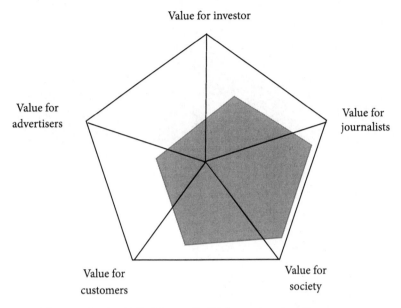

Figure 17. Value creation in the "golden age" of informational media

Source: Picard 2010: 71.

in many segments of the media market, as a result of concentrated activities. Monopolization increased profits of monopolists. A shift of accents connected with value creation towards investors and advertisers took place (Fig. 18: Value creation in the "corporate era" of informational media). Value reduction for customers, for society as a whole or for media employees, resulted in dissatisfaction of journalists and social criticism of informational media.

Social and economic changes, as well as changes in lifestyle have led to the alteration of information consumption and at the same time another imbalance in value creation. Here, by means of new technologies, classic ways of using information have landed on the scrap heap. The influx of financial resources from advertisers to classic media is becoming smaller. Declining income from advertisements printed in paper issues of newspapers are not re-compensated by greater revenues from Internet advertisements offered by e-versions of these newspapers. Informational media should offer their stakeholders some additional value they were deprived of during the "corporate era." This change is also inevitable in order to indicate to the news media the aims that are going to bring a long-term balance and increase the value offered to stakeholders (Figure 19. Value creation implicated by the future of informative media). It is a requirement of this imminent and not too distant future as only this kind of balance can force consumers to accept the higher price of a product resulting from a declining support from advertisers.

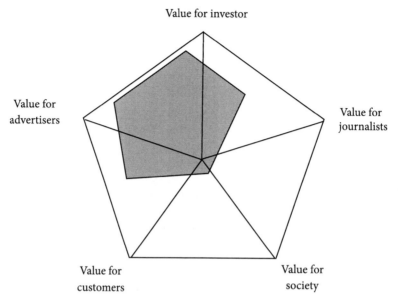

Figure 18. Value creation in "corporate era" of informational media

Source: Picard 2010: 72.

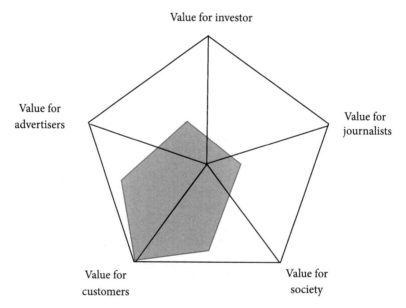

Figure 19. Value creation implicated by the future of informational media

Source: Picard 2010: 73.

In 2011, the National Broadcasting Council of Poland adopted a strategy for the following three years. As a priority for the Polish government, the following were recognized: freedom of speech, public media, transition from analog broadcasting into digital one and implementation of EU directive concerning audio-visual media services. The document also indicated current trends in the media market [http://www.press.pl/newsy/pokaz.php?id=25463/]. This document constitutes frameworks for the strategy that may be adopted by Polish media organizations to build the discussed values within its framework.

Discussion questions:

1. What should be understood by the notion of a media value chain?
2. How is the value chain created in media organizations?
3. Indicate and discuss the most substantial indicators of effectiveness in media organizations.

Chapter 9. Legal and Ethical Aspects of Media Management

9.1. Boundaries of media freedom

Media freedom is one of the pillars of a democratic country as it is connected with everyone's right to the freedom of speech. This right should be guaranteed. One of the first regulations of this type can be found in clause 12 of the Virginia Declaration of Rights of April 12, 1776: "That the freedom of the press is one of the great bulwarks of liberty, and can never be restrained but by despotic governments [Barta, Markiewicz, Matlak 2005: 15]."

Freedom of the media in the contemporary world is a key issue due to the fact that the mass media shape attitudes, views, and in a word, an image of the contemporary world in the minds of their customers. Will Rogers, one of the best-known American observers of public life of his times, used to begin his comments with the words: "I know only as much as in newspapers [Mallette 1996: 83]." D. McQuail [2007: 175] noticed that the "mass media not only wield some objective influence on society but are also used for social purposes."

It can be assumed that the basic determinants of media freedom are of three types:

- legal and ethical,
- socio-political,
- economical.

The legal norm which ensures media freedom is the basis. However, this freedom would be just an empty slogan, provided there is no political will or the will of the ones in power to respect this freedom. The media cannot operate without resources that are essential for its functioning, without economic resources. Therefore, it appears that media freedom should be guaranteed in these three dimensions. A shortage of any of them will cause media freedom to become deformed or even non-existent. Also the journalists themselves, concerned about high standards and the freedom of the performed profession, invoke used deontological codes. It seems that a breakthrough in this scope was the Hutchins Commission Report of 1947, the aim of which was "to examine areas and circumstances under which the press of the United States is succeeding or failing; to discover where free expression is or is not limited, whether by government censorship pressure from readers or advertisers or the unwisdom of its proprietors or the timidity of its management [ibid., 183]." The report became one of the most important documents, forming the basis of a democratic communication order, even more so in Europe than in the United States.

For the needs of this monograph one can assume that the freedom of the press and media freedom are identical notions. The basis of adopting such an establishment in Poland is Article 7 of the Press Law Act in effect as of January 26, 1984 with subsequent amendments, according to which by the term "press" one should understand not only journals, magazines, agency services, radio and TV programs, but also "all existing and arisen as a result of technical progress [Polish Press Law]."

In Europe, the guarantees concerning the freedom of the media were commenced by the French Declaration of the Rights of the Man and of the Citizen as of August 26, 1789: "The free communication of ideas and opinions is one of the most precious of the rights of man. Every citizen may, accordingly, speak, write, and print with freedom, but shall be responsible for such abuses of this freedom as shall be defined by law." Two years later, in 1791 the First Amendment to the United States Constitution was adopted stating that, "Congress shall make no law [...] abridging the freedom of speech, or of the press;" [Barta, Markiewicz, Matlak 2005: 15].

The Polish Constitution of May 3, 1791 was an unfinished work. Hence, it contains no references to freedom of media. However, after the regaining of independence by Poland in 1918, the enacted March Constitution, Article guaranteed freedom of speech, press and banning of censorship in Article 105: "Freedom of the press is guaranteed. Censorship, or the system of licensing printed matter, may not be introduced. Daily papers and other matter printed in the country may not be debarred from the mails, nor may their dissemination on the territory of the Republic be restricted."

In our times, the issue of freedom of the media in Poland is regulated primarily by the Constitution of the Republic of Poland as of April 2, 1997. The authors of the fundamental work "Media Law" – Janusz Barta, Ryszard Markiewicz and Andrzej Matlak – point out that "freedom of media" was adopted in the Polish Constitution as a system law. "Freedom of media" is an instrument of freedom realization described in Article 54.1 "The freedom to express opinions, to acquire and to disseminate information shall be ensured to everyone;" 54.2 "Preventive censorship of the means of social communication and the licensing of the press shall be prohibited. Statutes may require the receipt of a permit for the operation of a radio or television station." However, appropriate entries placed in the very first chapter of the Constitution of the Republic of Poland indicate the importance of media. Article 14 states: "The Republic of Poland shall ensure freedom of the press and other means of social communication." This entry explicitly establishes freedom of the media as one of institutional rules of Poland. This constitutional norm was discussed in detail in Chapter II of the Constitution, which concerns the freedom of human beings and citizens' rights and obligations, and in Chapter 9 concerning organs of state monitoring and legal protection of the National Council of Radio Broadcasting and Television. Article 213 says: "The National Council of Radio Broadcasting and Television shall safeguard the freedom of speech, the right to information as well as safeguard the public interest regarding radio broadcasting and television."

Confirmation of constitutional norms concerning media freedom has been introduced in two basic acts regulating the media order in Poland: the Public Service Broadcasting Act and the Press Law.

The article of the Press Law states: "The press, according to the Constitution of the Republic of Poland makes use of the freedom of speech and accomplishes the right of citizens to being informed earnestly, the quality of public life and social control and critic."

The Public Service Broadcasting Law refers to the Press Law. Article 3 states that the regulations of Press Legislature apply to radio and television broadcasting unless otherwise provided. By contrast, in Article 6 the preservation of freedom of speech was expressed *expressis verbis*: "The National Council of Radio Broadcasting and Television shall safeguard the freedom of speech in radio and television, independence of broadcasting companies and interests of audience and shall ensure open and pluralistic character of radio and television broadcasting."

The complement of norms included in the two aforementioned acts concerning freedom of speech is the Act on the Access to Public Information. In Article 2 one reads that "Everyone is entitled to public information, provided with the restriction of Article 5, the Law…"

Right after World War II, the Hutchins Commission Report was placed at the heart of the theory of social responsibility, the basic canons of which were as follows [McQuail 2005: 185]:

1. The media have obligations to society, and media ownership is a public trust,
2. News media should be truthful, accurate, fair, objective and relevant,
3. The media should be free, but self-regulated,
4. The media should follow agreed codes of ethics and professional conduct,

5. Under some circumstances, government may need to intervene to safeguard the public interest.

While the first four points do not seem to arouse any doubts, the last point
requires explanation. Rulers in many democratic countries, inclined towards
democratic presumptions, intervened in the media market in order to maintain
diversity and counteract the concentration of media property. When the radio
station KDKA began broadcasting in Pittsburgh in 1920, it was just a matter
of time before new stations were going to appear. The problem of overlapping
frequencies used by individual stations was a matter of time as well. When the
US government was trying to normalize this problem they were met with an
objection from the Supreme Court, in spite of the fact that citizens themselves
were claiming suitable solutions in this matter. Only an appropriate act enacted by the Congress in 1927 helped the Federal Radio Commission (FRC) solve
the problem. The FRC transformed in 1934 into the Federal Communications
Commission (FCC), and started to deal with distributing radio frequencies,
determining the range and power of transmitters. It stands for an instance of
state intervention into the media market on behalf of public interest.

After 1989 Poland was following the path of Western democracies. However, despite being comprised of institutions that are distinctive to democratic
countries, Poland is still an arena of attempts at appropriating different spheres
of public life by subsequent teams winning the elections. Whether it is the
right or left wing is without meaning. This concerns the media as well, especially the public media.

Attempts at appropriating the media is not unique to the Polish media market. Perhaps the first attempt of this nature was made in the 1920s in Great
Britain, as mentioned before. Nevertheless, the BBC under the reign of Sir
John Reith managed to deal with this problem, at the time and during subsequent years. Therefore, it is not without reason that the BBC is perceived as
a role model of independence.

Journalism, by nature, ought to behave like a "watchdog" of democracy. It is
of interest to the entire society that journalists keep an eye on the authorities.
Very frequently politicians undermine the media's legitimacy to perform the
function of the so-called fourth authority, accusing the media or individual
journalists of lacking in objectivity. It is essential to recall that the canon of
impartiality refers to informative journalistic genres. A publicist has the right
or even the obligation to express his or her own views.

Stefan Bratkowski, the doyen of Polish journalists and the honorable president of the SDP, referred to this notion in the following way: "It is the voter
who chooses a politician, journalists are voted every day by the audience – buy-
ing a newspaper, choosing a TV or radio channel. If they happen to mangle,

embellish something – they lose what is the essence of their profession; reliability, the right to perform their profession [Bratkowski 2006: A21]."

The media, or rather media institutions, became a part of market economy in Poland, with all possible arising consequences. It began the moment businesspeople discovered that information is a commodity on which one can earn from (already mentioned in Chapter 7 entitled *Managers and Journalists*). This very moment was accurately described by Ryszard Kapuściński [2000: 89–90]:

> Old, oftentimes idealistic truth-seekers have been replaced at the peaks of authority by the people of media, frequently having nothing to do with journalism at all. This transition shall be noticed easily by anyone who has been visiting different editorial offices and radio stations. In general, they were located in flimsy buildings, cramped, dirty, cluttered rooms swarmed with journalists, usually dressed sloppily, earning poor money.
>
> Nowadays it is enough to visit any of editorial offices of large TV stations: a man enters a luxurious palace, moves around marbles and mirrors, is led down quiet corridors by an extremely elegant hostesses. It is exactly where the real power has moved. For the power belongs to the one who has a TV studio, or more specifically – media in general.

The description by R. Kapuściński aligns with the words of Hermann Schlapp [2002: 13] who said that:

> there are many publishers who see sheer business in journalism [...], the success of which is conditioned entirely by supply and demand, the size of expenditures [...] there is a great temptation to use all possible stunts to come into being before competitors. It is possible to survive on for those who succeed. Advertising focuses only on the media of high expenditures in the market that experiences real struggle for the rate of expenditures and over amounts of the so-called radio and television inclusions.

The market dictatorship in the media has also led to a change in attitudes towards advertising by the journalists themselves. Many of them perceive advertising as a great source of extra earnings by the way of appearance fees. Generally, journalists do not approve of such a condition because it can result in differences in the material status of the ones employed in editorial offices with a lot of income coming from advertising in comparison to that of those in offices with a much smaller income coming from advertising. When evaluating this phenomenon, the journalistic environment is characterized by a peculiar ambivalence. On the one hand, it remains quiet because of the possibility of cashing in on this popularity, especially via TV. On the other hand, it actively supports the activities of the Media Ethics Council which criticizes famous journalists that they cash in on the public's trust by doing advertising for shopping chains, cosmetics, clothing, interior decoration, banks, etc.

This ambivalence concerns not only individual journalists but also entire media organizations. In Macedonia, many advertisers are influenced by political and not economic reasons while purchasing advertising space in newspapers. Oftentimes, the relationships of a given title with particular political forces are more decisive than the market needs of the ones who ordered the advertisement. In Moldavia, by means of sponsorships and acts of charity, sponsors may count on a favorable disposition of the subsidized media, all thanks to a statutory entry which permits the anonymity of sponsors [Hrvatin, Petkovič 2005: 25–27].

Perhaps the most glaring instance concerning how freedom of the media is influenced by political and market pressure is the Watergate scandal. Almost everyone is acquainted with the names of "The Washington Post" reporters, Carl Bernstein and Bob Woodward who in the 1970s worked with great determination to reveal the details of this scandal. Not many people know or remember that if not for the determination of Katherine Graham, the owner of the concern to which "The Washington Post" belonged, we most likely would have never found out who tried to influence the presidential election result in the United States through means of illegal methods. It was Katherine Graham who, in spite of political pressures coming from the highest governmental circles of the United States as well as economic pressures, decided to publish texts that divulged the affair. She was neither scared of the threats coming from the Attorney General of the United States who said that she's "going to get her tit caught in a big fat wringer if that's published," nor president Nixon who warned that the Federal Communications Commission (FCC) controlled by his people would not renew the contracts of two TV stations which belonged to Graham. Although the exchange value of The Washington Post Company dropped at the time from USD 36 to 16 per share, it was due to the consent of the owner that Woodward and Bernstein were able to publish their articles. It was two whole years before President Nixon handed in his resignation in 1974. It appears to be one of the most garish examples of constrained media freedom by means of illegal political and economic pressures. When the investigation revealed that "The Washington Post" was correct, the paper was awarded the Pulitzer, the most prestigious award in the journalistic field. However, one should bear in mind that in a free country such as the USA, "The Washington Post" published over 200 articles on the Watergate scandal within a two-year period. At the time not even one newspaper, radio or TV station mentioned the things that Woodward and Bernstein were writing about. One does not have to be a prophet to realize that the fear of losing legal action, concession, and lucrative advertisers were the driving factors. Each and every one of these facts could have led to the fall of a media organization. Not to mention a situation when all of them would occur simultaneously.

9.2. Journalistic deontological codes

The job of a journalist is one of high public trust. Even until now, in order to sound more reliable, people say: "I heard it on the radio, I read about it in a newspaper." Not all things can be settled legally. Many behaviors are protected by the law but are considered unethical. Environmental deontological codes are applied to weed out such attitudes. The participation of journalists in advertising campaigns is seen as an instance of a journalistic action that cannot be legally forbidden, yet is considered unethical. Magdalena Bajer, the President of Media Ethics Council emphatically asserted that the "job of a journalist is a public duty and should not lead to gaining reliability in order to turn it into cash."

Media institutions and journalistic associations established rules that were captured in appropriate legal frameworks marked out by the state and concerning borders of freedom. The canon of journalism was first issued in the United States by the American Association of Press Publishers in 1923. Similar documents appeared a bit later in Europe, France, Sweden and Finland [McQuail 2007: 186].

The purpose of journalistic ethical codes is mainly to reinforce media freedom by establishing high professional and ethical standards connected with performing the job of a journalist and professions inextricably connected with it. Concerning Poland, it mainly refers to:

- Ethical codes of journalistic associations and Newspaper Publishers' Association,
- Documents normalizing activity of courts of journalistic associations,
- Media Ethics Charter and activity of the Conference of Polish Media and Media Ethics Council,
- Ethical regulations and activity of the Ethics Committee in Polish Television Company and Polish Radio Company.

Institutions appointed by journalists for the purpose of protecting media freedom, and particularly providing help to "non-humble" journalists, most frequently examine issues concerning journalists' participation in various advertisements. The Press Freedom Monitoring Center did not register a single case of terminating a journalist on the basis of Article 10 of Press Law. Article 10 sec. 2 of Press Law states that a journalist, in the scope of employment relationship, is obliged to implement a certain general program line of this editorial board appointed in the statute or rules of an editorial board where he or she is employed. Furthermore, in sec. 3 of the same article we read that a "journalist's activity contrary to sec. 2 constitutes violation of an employee's obligation."

It seems that the only institutions that by definition are not allowed to appoint any program line are the public media. Their essence lies in a broadly defined pluralism of views and opinions. However, reality is oftentimes completely different.

On March 29, by the initiative of Association of Polish Journalists, representatives of the largest and most important media institutions in Poland signed the Media Ethics Charter. Their signatories: journalists, editors, producers and broadcasters declared that in their work they would be guided by the following rules:

The principle of truth – which means that journalists, editors, producers and broadcasters make every effort for information to be truthful, conscientious and without distortions, report the facts in their proper context and in cases of dissemination of incorrect information they promptly make a correction.

The principle of objectivity – which means that the author depicts reality independently of his or her opinions, reporting different points of view in a reliable fashion.

The principle of separating information from a comment – which means that a statement is supposed to enable the customer to differentiate facts from opinions and views.

The principle of honesty – which stands for acting according to one's conscience and the welfare of the consumer, non-compliance with influences, incorruptibility, and refusal to act inconsistently to one's beliefs.

The principle of respect and tolerance – which stands for regard towards human dignity, rights, personal rights, with privacy and goodwill.

The principle of priority of customers' welfare – which means that basic rights of readers, viewers and listeners are superior to the business interests of journalists, publishers, producers and broadcasters.

The principle of freedom and responsibility – which means that the freedom of media imposes responsibility for the content as well as all arising consequences and form on journalists, publishers, producers and broadcasters.

The aforementioned principles indicate the enormous responsibility of the journalistic profession, about which Max Weber wrote that it is greater than that of a scientist. For instance, journalists must not find employment in PR agencies and at the same time work in a journalistic profession and "not receive remuneration from institutions or private companies, provided their position as a journalist, their influences and relationships could be used in an inappropriate way [Rutkiewicz 2003: 83]." This entry in the Code of French Journalists appears in many similar documents across different countries. A similar entry can be found in the Journalistic Social Code of Social Democracy of the Republic of Poland: "A journalist is not allowed to accept any kind of benefits for themselves or their families in return for placing or not placing a journalistic work. It is unacceptable to place materials that are of an advertorial nature. Advertising in the press and electronic media which are prepared in cooperation with journalists ought to be clearly separated from information."

This tendency to work simultaneously as a journalist while receiving remuneration for activities in the field of PR derives from impoverishment of journalists. Jacek Sobczak [2003: 201–202] stated boldly that:

> journalists belong to a professional group which has greatly contributed to the existence of structural transformation in Poland. It is an occupational group that lost basically everything and probably gained nothing. They gained social recognition which is exceptionally elapsing [...] Journalists lost first of all social benefits which they used to have, which they used and which they now do not have anymore.

These words are particularly meaningful when taking into consideration that they were uttered by someone who is not only a university professor but also a judge of the Polish Supreme Court.

It appears that this pauperization is indeed a factor that leads to vulnerability in the journalistic environment to political and economic pressures that foster the breaking of ethical codes. Also one should track the sources of susceptibility and tendency to manipulation. This can be done in one's own interest, in the interest of an organization as the workplace of the journalist, and in the interest of the owner or political authority.

9.3. Media manipulations

In spite of the ethical codes of the field, individual journalists as well as media organizations are susceptible to manipulations. From time to time someone manipulates the media and sometimes the media manipulate their consumers. M. Iłowiecki [2009: 81] states that under the term "manipulation" we understand "some ways of influencing an individual or a group (even the whole society), changing beliefs and attitudes – and achieved beyond consciousness of these individuals or groups." The same author points out that there are various phenomena that constitute methods of obtaining influence on people and manipulating them (these two notions do not have to be identical):

1. agenda setting function,
2. spiral of silence theory,

3. third person effect;
4. the hidden persuasion;
5. effect of media production, i.e. media facts.

The essence of news programs lies in the selection and the assortment of topics and the presentation order of such information. Determining the order of presentation should take place according to a criterion of actual meaning, honesty, objectivity and adequate proportions. Unfortunately, these rules are broken and the bodies that decide on the shape of news programs (usually television broadcasts) follow two conditions: the ratings and the political interests of the broadcaster. In the 1960s, Bernard Cohen [1963] declared that although mass media "may not be successful much of the time in telling people what to think, but it is stunningly successful in telling its readers what to think about." Over the past fifty years not much has changed in this respect.

The spiral of silence theory was first described by Elisabeth Noelle-Neumann [1974: 43–51]. Based on research carried out in the 1960s, this German academic discovered that an essential engine of human behaviors is a fear of isolation. People whose views are not compliant with the opinion of the majority try to hide it, i.e., they fall into muteness. The media are of high importance in shaping this phenomenon. Provided an individual notices that his or her views are not reflected in media transfers, they leave the public realm and take refuge in the private sphere. The process requires one to adopt a systemic approach in order to comprehend its essence, but only a statistical examination. Maciej Iłowiecki [2009: 87] makes the assumption that "Media make use of this phenomenon (here: the spiral of silence), promoting by all possible means such views which in social judgment are perceived as the views of the majority." Unfortunately, while oftentimes views are considered as approved by the majority, sometimes they are not. And even if they were, it is not a justification for neglecting the views of the minority.

The spiral of silence theory is connected with the phenomenon of "pluralistic ignorance." It stands for a situation when, under an overwhelming influence of the media, customers pretend that a commonly popularized opinion is the opinion of majority. Stanisław Ossowski [1983: 256] warns that:

> empirical research in sociology, especially when relating to the participation of an individual in the social sphere, together constitutes a social activity; they reveal multiple eye-opening opportunities where they were unnoticed. They suggest the importance of some matters through the fact that they were included in a questionnaire, at least they vicariously enlighten some scales of values, and they indicate the necessity of making a choice.

Therefore, it is essential to place rules referring to the social mission of the media in deontological codes.

Susceptibility (unrealized) to media manipulations is illustrated by a phenomenon known as the third person effect. It is a belief overestimating the influence of the media on other people while the person in question minimizes its impact on oneself (advertising has no influence on me, other people buy under its influence).

The phenomenon of hidden persuasion is considered to be the most dangerous within the domain of media manipulation. It consists in presenting an opinion of some group (e.g. political or economic) as a most obvious truth, so evident that it does not require any proof. Hidden persuasion uses notions that are obscure, undefined yet are delivered with an absolute certainty of proclaimed opinions. This method of manipulation proves most efficient among ignorant social groups, the so-called functional illiterates. M. Iłowiecki [2009: 89–91] carries out an analysis of some statement (published by some high-outlay newspaper) from the standpoint of hidden manipulation. It sounds as follows: "It has been an open secret that with all his virtues John Paul II inhibited transformations of contemporary Catholicism." In this statement one assumed that transformations of Catholicism are always rightful and everyone agrees with it (an open secret). Hidden persuasion is achieved by inoculating the reader with the following convictions: 1. "Progressive Catholicism" is apparent for everyone; 2. the Pope and the church hierarchy should stand for "progressive Catholicism"; 3. it is not the Pope and the church hierarchy that are entitled to say what is good and bad for the Catholic Church.

Media staging of events stands for media facts or provocations. Bans on using media facts, i.e. events created by the media, are not found in all journalistic ethical codes. The domestic statute of Columbia Broadcasting System (CBS) television contains the following statement: "All putting events on stage is forbidden." The statute describes acceptable exceptions along with the manner of their presentation: "In some situations it is essential to reproduce some event (e.g. walking on the Moon) in order to use it in the program. In such a situation one should always explain to the viewer that the program contains events that have been recreated and it is an accurate reconstruction of some event. Such a measure should be used sparsely." The managers of CBS must remember very well what can be the results of staging. It was this station that broadcasted the radio drama *War of the Worlds* that was directed by Orson Welles and based on a novel by Herbert G. Wells. The drama was broadcasted the day before Halloween, October 30, 1938. It led to an outburst of panic among many residents of New Jersey who were convinced that the Martians really attacked the Earth.

The BBC, the best-known public media organization in the world, has its own ethical codes regulating the work of journalists in various realms concerning the news from areas of war, issues related to euthanasia or even sport [http://www.bbc.co.uk/ethics/]. These rules also address the acceptable limits of stage production: 1. it should be clearly marked; 2. one must not forget the facts; 3. drastic scenes and violence should be avoided in reconstructions.

According to the rules of the BBC it would be impossible to project the documentary movie entitled *Arizona* by Ewa Borzęcka. The author presented a grim picture of everyday life of people living in post state-owned collective farms where everyday entertainment consists in drinking cheap wine called "Arizona." Many scenes were staged in the movie. Perhaps such scenes could have taken place yet the viewers are unaware of it. The border between what is real and what was recreated was erased for the needs of the movie. It drew the ire of the TVP SA Commission of Ethics that in its decree of April 1999 stated that: "[…] the author treated heroes of her film subjectively. She used their naivety and abused trust by showing them almost entirely in the state of alcoholic inebriation and in drastic private situations, thus exceeding the limits of intimacy and stripping them of their dignity [Iłowiecki 2009: 97]."

These kinds of things happened not only in Poland. One of the most famous media facts was a series of reportages of Peter Arnett, one of the most gifted reporters at Cable News Network (CNN) television. P. Arnett specialized in reporting from regions under war. For one such coverage he received the Pulitzer. The coverage concerned the use of the deadly dangerous gas sarin by the American army in the Far East. The application of the chemical weapon was later confirmed on Arnett's program by Admiral Thomas Moorer. Afterwards, it turned out that the truth looked completely different. Indeed, the gas was used but it was CS gas, not sarin. Moreover, it was not applied against innocent villagers but rather the Vietnamese army. The greatest manipulation concerned Admiral Moorer who at the time of recording was 87 years old. A dishonest reporter made a 7-hour reportage with the aged admiral and cut out one sentence that did not match the thesis of his reportage. Peter Arnett was stripped of the Pulitzer and dismissed from CNN.

The deliberations included in this chapter contain three conclusions. First of all, the very letter of the law is not enough to protect journalistic liberty, and what follows, the freedom of citizens of a given country. Secondly, a strict observation of journalistic deontological codes is necessary, and should serve as a basis of defying all possible forms of manipulation. Both of the media and by the media. And finally, any activity in favor of social democratic harmony requires adequate measures. It is worth remembering that freedom is not only the courage to voice one's opinions but also the possibility of presenting them. This is generally related to money, and when money is lacking, freedom may be lacking as well.

Free press is not only a "watchdog of democracy," it is also the development of civil society where the scope of available freedom is spreading, with the free public debate with all the possible symptoms, along with cultural and social transformations taking place. Freedom of the press should be the foundation of democracy as it means being free of political and economic influences as well as resistance to manipulation.

The issue of moral responsibility of journalists, editors, and media owners in a world shaped by simulacra is of high importance. It is obvious that in the contemporary world the voter does not vote for trueborn politicians, but rather votes for their media image. Here, the area for possible abuses and manipulations is enormous. Therefore, the necessity of educating future journalists in ethics is becoming ever more urgent. In Poland several dozen universities offer education in the field of journalism. Unfortunately, not all of them provide courses on ethics in journalism.

Almost one and a half centuries ago John Stuart Mill wrote about the freedom of press: "The peculiar evil of silencing the expression of an opinion is, that it is robbing the human race, posterity as well as the existing generation, those who dissent from the opinion even more than those who hold it [McQuail 2007: 182]." This message of Mill ought to be essential not only for journalists themselves but also for media pilots and media organization owners. The temptation to break the rules of ethics cannot be eliminated by legal regulations. Deontological codes are only of a postulating nature and breaking them should lead to ostracism in the industry. But do the unethical people of the media live in solitude? Is there anyone to give them a hand? It seems that as long as these are only rhetorical questions, there will be a strong temptation and tendency to manipulate on the part of all members of the media. The media manipulator has a lot to win and little to lose in the contemporary world.

Discussion questions:

1. Obeying ethical standards should be one of the most essential premises of media activity. How can this be achieved by media organizations?
2. Why does the freedom of media constitute an essential value in democratic societies?
3. Indicate examples of manipulation you have come across in media messages.

Chapter 10. Developmental Trends of Media Organizations. Indicators of the Future of the Media

Jacques Attali [2008: 9] forecasts that market forces take the planet in hand. The ultimate expression of unchecked individualism, this triumphant march of money explains the essence of history's most recent convulsions." He is convinced that history is governed by its own rules that make it possible to both forecast it and influence its course. The introduction to his monograph warned against the pernicious effects of forecasting the future. However, taking into consideration the words of J. Attali as well as past events and its governing rules, one may with some dose of probability try to anticipate future trends concerning the media, media markets, and media organizations within the coming years. A further forecasting would be like reading coffee grounds and would similarly make no sense. Therefore, main directions of media development and other factors that should be considered by the ones in charge of the media are as follows:

1. digitization and convergence;
2. global vs. local processes;
3. new realm of the Internet;
4. digital exclusion;
5. audience fragmentation;
6. competition between network and hierarchical organizations.

The process of media digitization has already come to an end in many developed countries. The process of convergence is pending and it is difficult to predict what will be its final outlook. The process of digitization in the electronic media was to have been completed by August 1, 2013. The printed media have been using the digitization process intensively as well. The number of articles placed in printed form is gradually decreasing while one notices an increase in online editions. This requires the continuous updating of the content, front page stories, photo galleries, audio and video files as well as blogs. This stream of one's own information has perpetually been enriched with contents provided by users in many possible forms (forum, blog, chat, photographs, movies, etc.).

Along with digitization, the convergence process is developing. Internet issues of newspapers provide us with a substitute for television. Radio includes short clips highlighting the events taking place on the Internet. Television features texts of presented information. In a word, the process of convergence is deepening. Differences among the individual media are becoming illusive the moment the basic media consumption takes place by means of the Internet. Whether customers will decide to consume the content of a given medium remains unknown. The only thing that is clear is that media consumption will take place by means of the Internet. It is not known what kind of global and local realm the web is going to have. Will globalization be a sufficient notion for the purpose of describing this phenomenon? – this is not known either.

Marshal McLuhan's notion [2004: 39–53] of the relay which became a relay itself was acknowledged right before our eyes. It was the said researcher who in the mid-20th century proclaimed the rising of a matrix:

> For the man in a literate and homogenized society ceases to be sensitive to the diverse and discontinuous life of forms. He acquires the illusion of the third dimension and the 'private point of view' as part of his Narcissus fixation, and is quite shut off from Blake's awareness or that of the Psalmist, that we become what we behold.

I. Fiut [2006: 12] notices that, following McLuhan's thinking, every technological explosion is preceded by an implosion. The new is born from the ashes of the old. It seems that in the technological sense we are currently dealing with such a state. The moment the Internet was born as a new means of communication its researchers usually adopted one of two approaches. Pursuant to the first one the Internet is a culmination of historical process of formation of public relations in the form of social interactions by means of virtual networks. According to the second one, the Internet leads to alienation and breaks off social communication and even familial bonds. It appears that it is a false antonym as research confirms that the network causes both phenomena. In the opinion of Manuel Castells [2003: 108, 135] there are two features which are decisive for the success of the "workforce" in the network: talent and ability for continuous learning. And this for the duration of their professional life. Such an individual is capable of "reprogramming" on one's own. The success of an organization depends on the ability to attract, keep and use talented employees. In conditions of such high demand for a workforce comprised of those capable of "reprogramming" themselves, the companies need to employ various incentives to keep their best employees. Chapter 3 discusses in detail a completely new issue in world history: gaining advantage by a network-type organization over hierarchical-type organizations. It has become possible thanks to information becoming the basic resource of the 21st century, whereas the "mine" to derive this resource is the network, with its properties that still have not been identified.

10.1. Language of the new media

Erich Fromm [1994: 208–214], the author of *The Forgotten Language*, would probably describe the Internet as an interpretation of the story of Aladdin's lamp. It would have been perceived by Fromm as a treasure house where the poor man can find the magic lamp with a genie fulfilling his wishes. But only those who currently are in possession of the lamp are capable of communicating with the genie. Would Fromm – who presented the Sabbath as a description of commands of peculiar balance between interference into the environment and its lack thereof – have seen a warning custom-made for the biblical tale of the tree of good and evil? One does not know. However, it seems that Fromm's legacy entitles us to such speculations. For the Internet is in fact something shaped in the form of a biblical tree. One may find recipes for making sour pickles as well as building homemade bombs. We refer to the Internet just as to a hypermarket for different products. The Internet has democratized the world in an incredible fashion. Previously there was no need for journalists to describe it. Journalists were some kind of social elites, this filter which strained information. Nowadays everyone can be a journalist, therefore the prestige of this profession is constantly declining (as delineated in Chapter 8). Being a press, radio or TV journalist used to be something close to unattainable. Journalists used to have a status similar to movie stars. The Internet crossed out everything. The process of media convergence has increasingly limited the role and significance of professional journalists in favor of consumers who edit things they read and watch on their own.

The language of the new media is not just, or first and foremost semantic issues, but primarily new means of expression, but also of belonging. Our ancestors used to meet at the campfire, on the market square or inside the church. New technical inventions mean that communication has become possible without leaving one's home. The author is not aiming to evaluate whether a phenomenon has positive or negative consequences from the social point of view. The contemporary world is simply like that. Howard Rheingold claims that virtual relationships are more direct than the ones in the real world as Internet users immediately go straight to topics of their interest, whereas in the "offline" world one's first interaction with another is merely that of acquaintance [Rheingold 1996: 2]. Other researchers say that society is more than just a group of people scattered all over the world tapping on a computer keyboard. Łucja Teszner has made a provocative comparison referring to the "online" society. When entering a room full of people we may stand by or start a conversation. One may talk to one person or join a discussion. In both cases one has to present oneself in a way that encourages others to a discussion, otherwise he or she becomes lost in the crowd. In the real world, we achieve this by the way we talk, behave, dress, and etc. In cyberspace the only feature which characterizes us is what we say [Teszner 1999: 89]. The real word and cyberspace do not have to exclude each other. Many groups have their beginnings in *real* life, and later on shift their contacts to the Internet. However, there are reverse cases when Internet users "band together" in order to conduct a common event, sometimes even just to conduct a one-time campaign.

Blogs, social networking sites, and hypertexts are notions without which communication in the contemporary world has become basically impossible. This statement leads to the conclusion that without getting to know and understand the language of new media it is impossible to function in the contemporary world. Researchers have called this phenomenon a digital exclusion [Lister, Dovey, Giddings, Grant, Kelly 2009: 10]. The first computer was created in the laboratories of IBM in the 1980s. The World Wide Web (WWW) emerged at the beginning of the 1990s. Its formation was proof that the concept of social forms refers not only to hardware, but also to forms of knowledge.

The appearance of HTML (Hyper Text Markup Language). Its creators decided in favor of a publicly available code which "told" various computer systems what to do with data [ibid., 266–268]. New media are interpreted as a "technical equivalent of post-modernistic thought" which is characterized by velocity, flexibility, digitization and hypertextuality. However, can the tools of political economy be applied to these innovative technical and social forms? Well, they can.

Chapter 5 describes Chris Anderson's concept of "a long tail" [2006: 53]. According to this research, the «long tail» simply stands for "culture which issue of economic scarcity does not concern." There are two factors that build such an approach [Lister 2009: 297]:

1. lowering production costs,
2. influence of new technologies on the way of recommendation and distribution.

Lowering of production costs became a fact by the means of digital media. Barriers of market entrance and exit have lowered considerably. Maintaining a blog costs significantly less than maintaining a newspaper (Chapter 7; the case of a blogger M. Lee, accredited by ONZ). A video clip posted on YouTube costs a fraction of the traditional TV advertisement.

New media technologies make it possible to reach the most unusual and non-standard products and verify their usefulness. The first of them are ensured by more and more efficient search engines. The latter ones are ensured by social networking sites, various forums and blogs that facilitate consumers' decisions concerning products that belong to the "long tail." The post-shopping discord becomes smaller whereas choice individualization increases. Anderson declares that as an effect the natural curve of demand has been formed, and that they deform narrow channels of distribution, shortage of information or limited space on shelves. The shape of this curve is much less dependent on various hits on media markets than it has ever been thought. In Anderson's opinion, this mixed demand is a reflection of societal diversification [Anderson 2006: 53].

Some authors warn against identifying the variety of consumers' choices with economic and political power. In their opinion economic freedom related to the "long tail" of making unlimited choices is by minority participation – even in the world of broadband connections. A non-liberal mantra which praises freedom omits the fact that the said free choice happens at the expense of economic, political and ecological selection taking place somewhere else. They add that while writing about the democratization of production means, Anderson did not claim that a whole army of users equipped with digital cameras would be able to endanger the power of Fox or Warner Bros [Lister et al. 2009: 298]. The author of this discussion indicates that the phenomenon of a "long tail" objectively exists and undoubtedly should be one of the conditions connected with decisions of media managers who are planning the future of media organizations under their management.

10.2. Challenges for managers

Factors described above will certainly be the basic conditions that should be taken into consideration by media managers of the 21st century. Dan Shaver and Mary Alice Shaver [2006: 639] add additional factors to the previously mentioned ones: new consumption factors and regulations on a global scale. In their opinion, the basic distinguishing feature that refers to media management shall be one word: change.

The pace of changes is becoming faster and shapes of transformations are poorly predictable. At the end of the 20th century, the "world wide web" (www) transformed from a curiosity into the main distribution channel of information. This is one of the most symptomatic examples of convergence being a reflection of social, technological and economy development: convergence that brought a completely new media and totally new ways of their consumption. Online games for example offer advantages which traditional games do not possess: an unlimited number of people participating in an illusion of real behaviors. For many young participants of such games the border between what is the matrix and what is real becomes obliterated. From an economic standpoint a developing auditorium fragmentation is an effect of convergence. For media managers it means that in order to sustain or gain new customers it is necessary to introduce a proceeding diversification of offered media contents. Moreover, it means that media content will take on an even more condensed form in order to keep the customer's attention. Media managers will be forced to look for vertical concentration and developing media conglomerates capable of shifting the content from one medium to another. This, in turn, poses a challenge before managers related to seeking new business models that are going to either increase revenues or decrease costs. It is going to extort a new approach to advertising and the issue of looking for new sources of financial backing of media organizations.

In the contemporary media world it is probably viewers' attention that constitutes the most valuable good. More and more media are competing for this rare good, as well as more and more titles, radio and TV channels, and even more websites. An effect of this increasing competition is the proceeding fragmentation of the audience. It appears that the era of mass media of multi-million customers is coming to an end. Such a new way of media consumption will require twofold actions from the managers: 1. looking for new sources of financial supply related to a declining auditorium and smaller earnings from advertising; 2. retaining consumers from other media bidders. A ready prescription as how to achieve it does not exist, yet providing a solution to this dilemma shall be a big if not the biggest challenge for media managers.

Regulations in the media market are another factor that ought to be considered by managers. On the one hand, the concentration of the market is regulated by state provisions which in general determine its borders; however, in relation to international institutions these regulations are less strict, or they do not exist at all. It fosters the concentration of properties on an international scale and the formation of even larger international media conglomerates. Activities of media enterprises inside the given country are appointed by regulations which impose many requirements regarding the content. Poland as well as other EU countries require a specific share of programs produced primarily in a given country or the EU. In Poland this concerns all media organizations broadcasting radio and TV programs apart from RTL7 which operates according to the rules of cross-border television and does not require a Polish concession.

For managers of international media corporations, it is essential to open new markets to media contents and services. The most lucrative markets include China. Markets of Africa and South America are potentially intriguing as well. For some investors provisions concerning human rights violations in China by the governing communist party were unimportant. It was profit that mattered. While entering in the Chinese market in 2006, the most popular Internet search engine – Google – agreed to censor content accessible by means of the website. In 2010, they announced that the years of censorship were over. Why barely after four years? – one may ask. Well, over the four years Google managed to win just a 17% share in the Chinese market. During the last year this share dropped by a few percentage points. Google failed to defeat or even come close to the level of the largest local competitor Baidu [http://antyweb. pl/google-konczy-z-cenzura-w-chinach-czy-to-koniec-google-cn/]. However, taking into consideration the scale of Chinese economy it may be noticed that as much as 17% on the local market constitutes amounts to much more than 100% of the market in quite a few European countries.

The fundamental and decisive assumption in many particular situations will be information. It is going to refer not only to the media managers but also to the so-called average people. Access to information and the ability to use it will be essential. The phenomenon of asymmetry which favors some companies (for example due to better access to information) is considered as unfavorable for the market, as proven by Nobel prize winner, Joseph E. Stiglitz [2004].

Information is the basic source in the modern world. In the initial period the Internet was simply a tool which enabled access to various websites. Web 2.0 brought social networking sites, blogs, and discussion forums where one is able to discuss diverse issues: beginning with advice on wedding gifts and plasma TVs, to the simulacrum of Jean Baudrillard. An Internet user could ask other users for advice on problematic issues. Currently, the www is entering the epoch of Web 3.0, the main attribute of which seems to be artificial intelligence. The Internet browser is going to look not only for connections with key words, but further analyze the sense of entire sentences. It is going to stand for an ability to differentiate the literal formulation from a metaphor or a joke. A step in this direction can be for instance services provided by a company called *Entelico* from Krakow which offers the configuration of various telecommunications tariffs depending on individual customer needs and habits. The service consists in analyzing customer accounts from the previous several months and selecting tariffs which make it possible to lower costs. As shown by practice, the lowering of costs was significant.

For the publishing industry, technological transformations will pose a great challenge. E-newspapers and e-books are completely modifying publishing markets. The publishing chain loses its existing connections. A new form of a book (electronic one) is distributed by means of the Internet. Traditional editions (paper versions) are offered in a conventional way by a chain of Internet bookstores. Placing orders online has become common. Only the older generation who have difficulties using their computers and understanding the net remain reserved. Nevertheless, from the economic point of view electronic versions are rather likely to displace traditional ones. One may imagine printing a newspaper or a book *on demand*, similarly to individual TV programs offered by television platforms or cable networks, yet due to costs such a service would be available only at a very high price. Another problem which managers in the publishing industry still will have to cope with is the debilitation of traditional bonds between publishers and distributors. Beginners are going to avoid publishing houses and are going to try to reach their customers directly with their offer. Due to the low costs connected with production and distribution on the web, even a small circle of customers is able to provide the supplier with satisfactory earnings [Shaver, Shaver 2006: 644–645]. Additionally, this phenomenon will overlap with copyright issues. At present publishers, especially in music but also film, are trying to control the phenomenon of illegal content use (so-called media bootlegging) without relevant charges. This involves searching for new ways of sharing the work with its audience. An example of such an activity is *Creative Commons*, a non-profit organization which tries to find a compromise between full protection of the work and its free enjoyment. It pertains not only to artistic but also to scientific creativity. Alternative technologies that have been offered by the web to publishing industries mean that high barriers of entering and exiting have been lowered drastically. This has led to an inflow of new entities that even intensified competition in this market. Completely new ways of applying traditional marketing tools have appeared, such as merchandising. Magazine publishers used the phenomenon of convergence in order to create online versions along with traditional paper ones. However, the basic dilemma of managers who administer these media is to decide when exactly to get rid of traditional paper versions. Perhaps the time is approaching but maintaining profitable magazines requires an adequate number of recipients who are likely to approve of the cost of this new media use. While creating online versions, newspaper publishers offered them for free. It is hard to convince the audience that they have to pay for something which up until now they were using for free. In March 2011 the New York Times, the third largest American newspaper, introduced charges for using its Internet version. The monthly fee for full access to the title amounts to USD 15. The fee does not include a subscription to the paper version or its smart phone version. A reader who has used fewer than twenty articles will not have to pay. However, one does not know whether this step is going to bring expected revenues to the publisher. This is because David Hayes, a Canadian programmer, broke safeguards and publicized the coded access to the NYT. All articles offered on the Internet by the newspaper became accessible without limits.

10.3. Public media

The public media are a declining, yet still strong player in the media market. From the standpoint of public media institutions' management the most essential are financing and power sources. In the case of public institutions in the narrow sense, financial resources are constituted by public funds and a mandate of the political formation which has won the election. In the event of public institutions in the wide sense, the makeup might be mixed: public and/or private, whereas the source of power is property: public and/or private. Apparently, the latter category refers to public media enterprises. It is essential to define the notion of "enterprise," and in particular the "media enterprise." It has been accepted in the European Union Law that an enterprise stands for: an "entity (unit) that leads an activity for the market needs" [Emmerich 1999: 666]. And it is of no importance whether a given entity is subject to public or private law. According to EU Regulations the assumption of dominating influence on the enterprise has been considered the cardinal principle. This rule is realized in one, two or three cases, separately or jointly [Dudzik 2002: 137]:

- public authorities possess a greater share of initial capital of an enterprise,
- public authorities control the majority of votes per share (shares) emitted by an enterprise,
- public authorities might appoint over half of all members of administrative, management and supervisory organs of an enterprise.

In the context of these regulations that manage the Polish public media, Articles 23–28 of the Broadcasting Act fulfil requirements of public enterprises. Public organizations (enterprises) are created in order to realize public interest. Organizations of this type are not always profit-oriented. Their tasks are appointed by the owner, i.e., society, whereas state organs appointed by voting should speak for it, devoting public funds for the implementation of these tasks. At this point one comes across difficulties as public money ought to be disbursed on public tasks. Such assignments tend to be referred to as 'mission,' and there is difficulty with its formulation. A highly symptomatic example is that of the commission appointed by the British Government meant to elaborate on the concept of the BBC's digitization, including redefining the essence of Public British Radio Broadcasting. As written by the commission in the final report:

> we have not managed anything so ambitious in the six months we have had at our disposal. When we each tried to define public service broadcasting, some very familiar words started to appear – information, education, extension of horizons, impartiality, independence, universal access, inclusivity, service of minorities, lack

of commercial motivation, etc. We decided that we may not be able to offer a tight new definition of public service broadcasting, but we nevertheless each felt that we knew it when we saw it [Report of the Independent Review Panel].

Karol Jakubowicz [2007: 96] denotes three main orientations concerning the level of state intervention in the media:

- Minimalistic – occurs in countries where the commercial content media is not regulated, and the public funding does not exceed USD 30 per capita (Italy, New Zealand, Portugal, Spain, the USA);
- Media as a "cultural exception" – commercial broadcasters are imposed with an obligation to produce programs enhancing national identity, and public financing will not exceed USD 30 per capita;
- A large level of intervention – intervention in the program is justified by public interest, and public financing does not exceed USD 50 per capita (Germany, Holland, Sweden, Great Britain).

It seems that in the case of public media management one of the most substantial elements is the lack of commercial motivation. It is possible only when the public media is not forced to seek for resources in commercial market. In countries like: Great Britain, Denmark, Norway, Sweden or Japan, the share of public money in the revenues of public media institutions amounts to almost 100% [Jędrzejewski 2003: 39]. In Poland, public media enterprises are forced to look for sources of financing in the commercial market. The contribution of public resources in the implementation of public tasks (so-called mission) amounts yearly to about 27–28% (public TV) to about 72–73% (public radio).

Therefore, with the current legal status, managing Polish public media must make up a combination of two aims: commercial and public interests. Polish public media were formed as profit-oriented companies. Such are the expectations of the Minister of the Treasury who performs proprietary functions in relation to media companies. On the other hand, the Polish public media have been subject to the Broadcasting Act, in which is included a description of the public interest (mission). For many years, successive governments have been trying to solve this puzzle yet generally they end up on announcements and have an overtaking influence over the public media. K. Jakubowicz [2007: 252] writes frankly about the validity crisis of the public media's existence. According to research, customers declare the necessity of their being, whereas on the other hand they are disappointed by their practices. It appears that the public media can constitute an essential element of constructing a public society. Nevertheless, it requires redefining them, assuring firm sources of financing and utilizing professional managerial staff, free from direct political pressures. An amended in 2010, the Broadcasting Act includes pioneering provisions regarding the appointment of media managers. Article 27 of the same act states that: "Among candidates selected in the competition carried out by a supervisory board, only a person competent in management and broadcasting may be appointed a member of the board." The National Broadcasting Council ordered by means of an ordinance to record the course of interviews with candidates by means of devices that record picture and sound. The Board of Supervisors may also allow for the presence of journalists during talks with candidates for the management positions in the public media. These records can be made available after the termination of the competition and undoubtedly the aim should be the elimination of candidates benefiting from political opportunism in favor of professionals and media managers.

Discussion questions:

1. Indicate future challenges for the managers of media organizations.
2. New media have been making use of a new language. What are its most substantial defining features?
3. Point to similarities and differences between the public media in your country and the Polish media.
4. Weigh the following problem: are public (educational) media necessary? Perhaps commercial media are enough?

Summary

The aim of this work was to introduce the most crucial academic achievements of the scholars who deal with media management all over the world into Polish scientific knowledge and usage. Their most important elements were created by the scholars working in the United States and the Scandinavian countries, especially in Sweden and Finland. Many achievements in the field of media management are inseparably linked to the media economy. This work, therefore, is based on this assumption.

As previously mentioned, there are few scholars concerned with this issue in the Polish scientific community and even less, lest say: if any, dissertations devoted to it. Thus, in this respect, the work is pioneering and the author is aware of the fact that it might not be flawless, as it is often the case with pioneering research. The author also expects to hear not only from the scientific community but also from media practitioners, since management in general, while media management in particular, is both a theoretical and a practical field. It requires media managers to possess a range of managerial, economic, psychological and even artistic skills. As it was highlighted in the introduction, one of the most necessary skills a media manager should possess is the ability to forecast future trends and the media industry development. Certainly, every prognosis is encumbered with some mistake and in the case of the branch of economy which develops as rapidly as media industry and the turbulent environment the mistake may turn out to be so big that it may subject the forecaster to ridicule.

Dennis McQuail justly points out that "history of previous technical evolutions in communication (…) says that one needs to remain careful when forecasting the future events based on technical options."

Having made this reservation, it seems that the coming years of the media's operation and consequently media management will be defined by several processes and factors:

1. Dual nature of the media businesses,
2. Information as goods independent of any classical rules of economics,

3. A shift from hierarchical to network structures as they are more efficient at using a resource such as information, as well as reaching goals of media organizations,
4. Digitization and convergence as indicators of new structuring of the media market.

In the nearest future these determinants should become indicators of molding the method and tools of media management. Understanding these dependencies not only will require a talent but also an extensive knowledge, which is and will be a challenging task. In this case, media organizations should provide universities with support, producing competent students equipped with knowledge and skills in this scope. Jagiellonian University was the first university in Poland which offered such support. Other universities will probably follow in its footsteps since what seems to be a pioneering action today, tomorrow may soon become a daily necessity, an indispensable condition of media organizations' operation.

In this monograph an endeavor was taken to incorporate widely used notions and terms from media management into the Polish media discussion. Nonetheless, the author does not claim to be infallible. At present and with the current state of knowledge, the proposals made in the monograph appear to be adequate for Polish research and tradition in this branch. Case in point, the style of management by objectives, for instance, is commonly applied by societies of various media organizations not only worldwide but in Poland as well, which was proven in Chapter 7.

Additionally, the author intended to prove that Peter Drucker's statement about information becoming the most fundamental resource of the 21st century is not only right (proving it would be a trivial and a rather arid endeavor in reference to academic output), but it has far-reaching consequences in the form of new paradigms. Say, the larger the scope of information is the more valuable it gets, which contradicts the fundamental economic rules concerning traditional goods. One of the goals of this work was to verify Peter Drucker's claim basing on own and other scholars' data, especially R. Picard, whose indisputable contribution was the introduction of the term of media businesses dualism into science. It enabled to scientifically prove a seemingly trivial point, that media organizations are different from any other companies.

The author tried to achieve these aims and scientific assumptions in ten chapters within the work. Starting with Chapter 1, in which the author outlined the genesis of management studies and specialized studies referring to management, including media management.

Chapter 2 researched the usability of system methodology for describing media management. In the chapter, various system concepts were presented along with various media systems. The starting point of those considerations was the mid-twenty-century *Four Theories of the Press* by Fred Siebert, Theodore Peterson and Wilbur Schramm. Own research in this respect (Media Power Triangle concept) was confronted with achievements of Polish (among others: Janusz Adamowski, Boguslawa Dobek-Ostrowska, Marian Gierula, Bartlomiej Golka, Beata Ociepka or Zbigniew Oniszczuk) and foreign scholars (especially Daniel Hallin and Paolo Mancini). As a result, it was proved that system methodology is a useful tool for studying various fields relating to media management research.

Chapter 3 presented the study of system and economic aspects of information, which Peter Drucker indicated as the basic resource of the 21st century. It underlines the consequences of this situation, both positive and negative. One of the negative results of the information revolution is the exclusion phenomenon. What is more important, it is a permanent danger, because neglecting the request for ceaseless education results in exclusion almost instantly.

Chapter 4 continued the debate from Chapter 3. Chapter 4 (the most important one, considering thoughts within the monograph) presented the proof validating Peter Drucker's paradox, that information gains value along with its popularity. Execution of the proof would be impossible without the research by Robert Picard, who showed that media businesses (in contrast to other economic organizations) are of a dual nature: they provide media content and simultaneously have the ability to draw attention to them. The chapter also showed that information may and should be managed. A singular case of Polish public media was quoted – according to the law in force, they should be managed in such a way that they combine two purposes: the commercial and the public interest. On the one hand Polish public media have been given the form of commercial companies, which are focused on profit by nature. On the other hand, they have been subjected to the requirements of the Broadcasting Act, which describes their tasks (mission).

Chapter 5 was a consequence of thoughts within Chapter 4. It describes the economic aspects of media management, quoting after Denis McQuail that media is "business like no other". To verify this description, R. Picard's and other scholars' research was used. Some of the "media economics" definitions were quoted, which Alan B. Albarran defined as a discipline studying the way media industries use rare goods to create and distribute media content among customers, which satisfy different needs and demands on an acceptable level. This chapter included the study of consequences that have and will have new media for economic aspects of media organizations' operation. For example, Chris Anderson's Long Tail economics is mentioned here. In reference to public media, various methods of financing were presented, especially subscription.

Advertisement is the basic upkeep for commercial media. For public media it may play a supportive role for funds from other sources (unfortunately, it is the fundamental source, which easily leads to commercialization of these media). These issues were included in Chapter 6. It briefly characterized the development, most crucial purposes and functions of advertising. It also points out methods of audience research, out of which the so called mini-market is the most efficient. There are only three such research projects: two in the US and one in Europe, in Germany. Since 1986, in Haßloch, studies have been carried out, which evaluate the efficiency of the studied advertisement campaigns with almost 100% accuracy.

Chapter 7 presented human resources in the media. It was shown that for decades journalism was a kind of social service, and nowadays it is simply becoming an occupation in the media. It was established that the style preferred by media managers in Poland (similarly to the rest of the world) is management by goals. It was also shown, that one of the most essential skills media managers should be equipped with is the ability to forecast future trends and courses of development of the media industry.

Strategies of media businesses and the creation of values were covered in Chapter 8. It presents the basics of creating a chain of values in media organizations and describes the creation of a media value chain. A crucial issue is to identify particular stakeholders' needs, which are basically different. Changes in this scope were illustrated by R. Picard's research.

Chapter 9 discussed the limits of media freedom, including cases of disregarding morality, which for libeled people or institutions are often treated as personal tragedies. The chapter also points out what a big challenge for media managers is to meet ethical requirements, because in the contemporary media world, morality and good taste is often violated. It is mainly because of the race for profit. This chapter also underlines the fact that sensationalism is the domain not only for tabloids, but increasingly for "respectable" media. "Infotainment" is becoming a common rule – a particular fusion of information and entertainment or information and sensation.

The book is closed by the chapter devoted to potential trends and ways of development of the media industry. Emphasizing those challenges is not only an attempt to determine areas of research in media management, but also to illustrate potential opportunities and threats to media managers, who may encounter them in businesses they manage. They are the aforementioned five main factors: media businesses' dualism, properties of information as a resource which does not abide by traditional rules of economics, transition from hierarchy to system structures, digitization and convergence. These are the factors which may determine near future (maybe also distant future) of media organizations and will shape the ways they are managed.

Media management is a new field of research, having a rather small scholarly output. It requires a new research apparatus, creative adaptation of the existing terms for research needs, and determination of the scope of research for the new discipline, which media management may become. The author of the monograph hopes that their work is a step in this direction.

It seems that next years will increase interest in media management – both the academic world of current and prospective researchers and students, and political and business societies. It does and will have its source in the increasing importance of media industries. Issues outlined in the monograph seem to be an interesting field of research in reference to commercial and public media. It seems that public media will divert from politics in the near future. It will be replaced by culture understood as the sense and the substance of basic tasks attributed to public media. Many cultural and even artistic endeavors have their media dimension. For instance, virtual museums or libraries. This reciprocal overlap of culture and media will result in new areas of research. Tomasz Goban-Klas pointed out, however, that electronic media were born as mass media to "massage mass audience's brains," but the technological development proved the one-way communication little effective. The audience is looking for new ways of mediatized interaction. This consequently points out the direction in which the aforementioned processes related to management shall proceed.

Media are becoming a kind of a net, which means that media helmsmen may lose their monopoly for management. Manuel Castellas emphasized the advantages of social net organizations: "For the bigger part of human history, in contrast to the biological evolution, nets have been losing as management tools against organizations, which could focus resources on most valid tasks..." Sometimes, management is compared to some sort of journey through chaos. This monograph does not claim the right to adjust the entire chaos. The author hopes achieved the superior goal, which guided the long-term research: to arrange the basic issues referring to media management in Poland, which the author carried out basing on own studies and research of scholars from around the world.

Bibliography

1. Documents and materials

Bughin, J. (2000), *Broadband Internet: Changes and opportunities for the European radio industry*, EBU SIS Briefings Feb., nr 37.

Communication from the Commission to the Council, the European Parliament, the Economic and Social Committee and the Committee of the Regions on certain legal aspects relating to cinematographic and other audiovisual works, Brussels 2001, COM (2001) 534 final.

European Commission, *XXIX Report on Competition Policy*, Brussels-Luxembourg 2000, Box 11.

Komunikat Komisji Europejskiej „Electronic Communications: the Road to the Knowledge Economy" (COM (3003) 65 final).

Konstytucja Rzeczypospolitej Polskiej z dnia 2 kwietnia 1997 r. (Dz. U. z 16 lipca 1997 r.).

Porozumienie Polskich Nadawców Telewizyjnych „Przyjazne Media".

Radio i Telewizja w Polsce: Raport o stanie rynku w chwili przystępowania do Unii Europejskiej, (2004), KRRiT, Warszawa.

Raport Departamentu Kultury, Mediów i Sportu rządu Wielkiej Brytanii, 2001 r.

Review of Public Broadcasting Around the World (2004), McKinsey Company, London.

The Future Funding of the BBC. Report of the Independent Review Panel, (1999), Department for Culture, Media and Sport, London.

Ustawa z dnia 15 IX 2000 r. Kodeks spółek handlowych.

Ustawa z dnia 15 XII 2000 r. o ochronie konkurencji i konsumentów.

Ustawa z dnia 5 czerwca 1998 r. o samorządzie województwa.

Ustawa o opłatach abonamentowych z dnia 21 kwietnia 2005 r.

Ustawa z dnia 29 XII 1992 r. o radiofonii i telewizji.

2. Books

Ackoff, R.L. (1974), *Redesigning the Future. A System Approach to Societal Problems*, John Wiley & Sons, New York.

Adamowski, J., Golka, B., Stasiak-Jazukiewicz, E. (1996), *Wybrane zagraniczne systemy informacji masowej*, Dom Wydawniczy Elipsa, Warszawa.

Adorno, T.W., Horkheimer, M. (2002), *Dialektika razsvetljenstva. Filozofski fragmenti*, Ljubljana, Slovenia: ISH.

Albarran, A.B. (2010), *The Transformation of the Media and Communication Industries, Media Markets Monographs*, issue 11, Universidad de Navarra, Pamplona.

Albarran, A.B., Chan-Olmsted S.M., Wirth M.O., eds. (2006), *Handbook of Media Management and Economics*, Routledge, New York.

Albarran, A.B. (1996), *Media economics: Understanding markets, industries and concepts*, Iowa State University Press, Ames.

Albarran, A.B. (2010), *Media economics*, Routledge, New York.

Albarran, A.B. (2010), *The Transformation of the Media and Communication Industries*, Media Markets Monographs, issue 11, Univesidad de Navarra, Pamplona.

Albarran, A.B., Chan-Olmsted, S. (1998), *Global media economics: Commercialization, concentration and integration of world media markets*, Iowa State University Press, Ames.

Anderson, P.J., Ward G. (2010), *Przyszłość dziennikarstwa w dojrzałych demokracjach*, Wyd. Akademickie i Profesjonalne, Warszawa.

Aljas (1907), *Jak należy się reklamować?*, Kraków.

Anderson, B. (1983), *Imagined communities*, London: New Left Books.

Anderson, Ch. (2006), *The Long Tail. Why the Future of Business is Selling Less of More*, Hyperion, London.

Ansoff, I., McDonnell, E. (1990), *Implanting Strategic Management*, Prentice Hill, New York.

Arche, G.L. (1939) *Big Business and Radio*, The American Historical Company, New York.

Arendt, H. (1958), *The human condition*, Chicago University Press, Chicago.

Arystoteles (2002), *Polityka*, transl. L. Piotrowicz, Wyd. DeAgostini Polska, Warszawa.

Arystoteles, (2003), *Metafizyka*, Wydawnictwo De Agostini Polska, Warszawa.

Atalli, J. (2008), *Krótka historia przyszłości*, Wyd. Prószyński i S-ka, Warszawa.

Avritzer, L. (2002), *Democracy and the public space in Latin America*, Princeton, NJ: Princeton University Press.

Bajka, Z. (2008), *Historia mediów*, Wyd. Rebis, Kraków.

Barney, J. (1991), *Firm Resources and Sustained Competitive Advantage*, „Journal of Management" 17.

Barta, J., Markiewicz, R., Matlak, A. (2001), *Prawo mediów*, Wydawnictwo Lexis, Kraków.

Barta, J., Markiewicz, R., Matlak, A. (2005), *Prawo mediów*, Warszawa.

Benjamin, W. (1968), *Illuminations*, Harcourt, New York.

Bertalanffy, L. von (1950), *The Theory of Open Systems in Phisics and Biology*, „Science", 111.

Bertalanffy, L. von (1984), *Ogólna teoria systemów*, Wydawnictwo Naukowe PWN, Warszawa.

Bielski, M. (1997), *Organizacje: istota, struktury, procesy*, Wyd. Uniwersytetu Łódzkiego, Łódź.

Bishop, B., (2001), *Marketing globalnej ery cyfrowej*, PWE, Warszawa.

Bochenek, J. (2006), *Przyszłość mediów elektronicznych w Polsce. Wartość za pieniądze – czyli jak mierzyć realizację misji i efektywność funkcjonowania mediów publicznych*, Andersen Business Consulting.

Bowman, C., Ambrosini, V. (2000), *Value Creation Versus Value Capture. Towards a Coherent Definition of Value in Strategy*, „British Academy of Management".

Brecht, B. (1954), *Wiersze wybrane*, przekł. J.S. Lec, Wyd. Nasza Księgarnia, Warszawa.

Budzyński, W. (1999), *Reklama – techniki skutecznej perswazji*, Poltext, Warszawa.

Carey, J. (1989), *Communication as Culture: Essays on Media and Society*, Routledge, London.

Carlisle, H.M. (1987), *Management Essential: Concept for Productivity and Innovation*, Science Research Associates, Chicago.

Carter, T.B., Franklin, M.A., Wright, J.B. (1994), *The First Amendment and the Fifth Estate: Regulation of Electronic Mass Media*, 3rd ed.

Castells, M. (1996), *The Rise of Network Society*, Blackwell, Oxford.

Castells, M. (2003), *Galaktyka Internetu*, Dom Wydawniczy Rebis, Poznań.

Chandler, A.D. (1978), *Strategy and Structure. Chapter in the History of the American Industrial Enterprise*, MIT Press, Cambridge.

Chyliński, M., Russ-Mohl, S. (2007), *Dziennikarstwo*, Grupa Wydawnicza Polskapresse, Warszawa.

Chyliński, M., Russ-Mohl, S. (2007), *Dziennikarstwo*, Grupa Wydawnicza Polskapresse, Warszawa.

Clausewitz, von C. (1958), *O wojnie*, Wydawnictwo Ministerstwa Obrony Narodowej, Warszawa.

Cobo, C., Shaughnessy, H. (1990), *The Cultural Obligation of Broadcasting*, Manchester.

Cohen, B. (1963), *The Press and Foreign Policy*, Princeton University Press, New York.

Compaine, B.M. (1978), *The book industry in transition: An economic study of book distribution and marketing*, Knowledge Industry Publications, New York.

Compaine, B.M. (1979), *Who owns the media?*, Knowledge Industry Publications, New York.

Connected Marketing, the viral, buzz and word of mouth resolution (2005), eds. J. Kirby, P. Mardsen, Butterworth-Heinemann, Oxford.

Czarnecki, P. (2008), *Etyka mediów*, Difin, Warszawa.

Dahlgren, P. (1991), *Introduction*, [in:] *Communication and citizenship*, eds. P. Dahlgren, C. Sparks, Sage, London.

Derrick, D.F. (2003), *Media Management. In the Age of Giants*, Iwoa State Press, Ames.

Dobek-Ostrowska, B. (2004), *Podstawy komunikowania społecznego*, Wydawnictwo Astrum, Wrocław.

Doktorowicz, K. (1995), *Europejska telewizja publiczna. Zmiana modelu w Europie Zachodniej*, Wydawnictwo Uniwersytetu Śląskiego, Katowice.

Doliński, D. (2001), *Psychologia reklamy*, Aida, Wrocław.

Dominiak, T. (2006), *48 godzin* (rozmowa z Gregiem Dykiem, byłym dyrektorem generalnym BBC), Press, kwiecień.

Doyle, P. (2003), *Marketing wartości*, Wyd. Felberg SJA, Warszawa.

Drucker, P.F. (1942), *The Future of Industrial Man*, John Day, New York.

Drucker, P.F. (1954), *The Practice of Management*, Harper and Row, New York.

Drucker, P.F. (1992a), *Innowacja i przedsiębiorczość. Praktyka i zasady*, PWE, Warszawa.

Drucker, P.F. (1992b), *Praktyka zarządzania*, „Nowoczesność" sp. z o.o., Warszawa.

Drucker, P.F. (1999), *Społeczeństwo prokapitalistyczne*, Wydawnictwo Naukowe PWN, Warszawa.

Drucker, P.F. (2000), *Zarządzanie w XXI wieku*, Wydawnictwo Muza, Warszawa.

Drucker, P.F. (2001), *Myśli przewodnie Druckera*, Wyd. MT Biznes, Warszawa.

Dudzik, S. (2002), *Pomoc państwa dla przedsiębiorstw publicznych w prawie Wspólnoty Europejskiej. Między neutralnością a zaangażowaniem*, Kantor Wydawniczy Zakamycze, Kraków

Durkheim, É. (2000), *Zasady metody socjologicznej*, Wydawnictwo Naukowe PWN, Warszawa.

Dyke, G. (2004), *Inside Story*, Harper Perennial, London.

Eley, G. (1992), *Nations, publics, and political cultures: Placing Habermas in the nineteenth century*, [in:] *Habermas and the public sphere*, ed. C. Calhoun, MIT Press, Cambridge.

Fauconnier, G. (1975), *Mass Media and Society*, Leuven University Press, Leuven.

Fill, Ch. (1999), *Marketing Communications*, Prentice Hill, London.

Fiut, I.S. (2006), *Media, kobieta i śmiech*, Uczelniane Wyd. Naukowo-Dydaktyczne AGH w Krakowie, Kraków.

Flaherty, J.E. (1999), *Peter Drucker: Shaping Managerial Mind*, Jossey-Bass, New York.

Fraser, N. (1992), *Rethinking the public sphere*, [in:] *Habermas and the public sphere*, ed. C. Calhoun, MIT Press, Cambridge.

Fromm, E. (1994), *Zapomniany język*, PIW, Warszawa.

Giles, R.H. (1988), *Newsroom management: A Guide to Theory and Practice*, Media Management Books, Detroit.

Goban-Klas, T. (2000), *Media i komunikowanie masowe. Teorie i analizy prasy, radia, telewizji i Internetu*, Wydawnictwo PWN, Warszawa–Kraków.

Godzic, W. (1996), *Oglądanie i inne przyjemności kultury popularnej*, Universitas, Kraków.

Golka, B. (1996), *Wstęp*, [in:] *Wybrane zagraniczne systemy informacji masowej*, eds. J. Adamowski, B. Golka, E. Stasiuk-Jazukiewicz, Wyd. Elipsa, Warszawa.

Golka, B. (2001), *System medialny Francji*, Wyd. Elipsa, Warszawa.

Golka, B. (2004), *System medialny Stanów Zjednoczonych*, Wyd. Szkolne i Pedagogiczne, Warszawa.

Graham, N., Collins, R., Locksley, G., Davis, J., Hayward, P., Reem, D. (1986), *The Economics of UK Television*, London Centre for Information and Communication Studies, London.

Griffin, R.W. (1999), *Podstawy zarządzania organizacjami*, Wydawnictwo Naukowe PWN, Warszawa.

Grudzewski, W.M., Hejduk, I.K., Sankowska, A., Wańtuchowicz, M. (2010), *Sustainability w biznesie, czyli przedsiębiorstwo przyszłości. Zmiana paradygmatów i koncepcji zarządzania*, Wyd. Poltext, Warszawa.

Grzelewska, D. (2001), *Historia polskiej radiofonii w latach 1926–1989*, [in:] *Prasa, radio i telewizja w Polsce. Zarys dziejów*, Wyd. Elipsa, Warszawa.

Grzelewska D., Habielski R., Kozieł A., Osica J., Piwońska-Pykało L. (2001), *Prasa, radio i telewizja w Polsce. Zarys dziejów*, Wyd. Elipsa, Warszawa.

Habermas, J. (1989), *The Stuctural Transformation of the Public Sphere: An Inquiry into a Category of Bourgeois Society*, Polity Press, Cambridge.

Habermas, J. (1999), *Teoria działania komunikacyjnego*, Wydawnictwo Naukowe PWN, Warszawa

Hahn, Ch., Dunn, E., eds. (1996), *Civil society: Challenging western models*, Routledge, London.

Hallin, D.C., Mancini, P. (2007), *Systemy medialne. Trzy modele mediów i polityki w ujęciu porównawczym*, Wydawnictwo Uniwersytetu Jagiellońskiego, Kraków.

Handbook of Media Management and Economics, (2006), eds. A.B. Albarran, S.M. Chan-Olmsted, M.O. Wirth, Routledge, New York.

Handy, Ch. (1996), *Wiek paradoksów*, Dom Wydawniczy ABC, Warszawa.

Hardt, H. (1979), *Social theories of the press*, Beverly Hills, CA: Sage.

Herrick, D.F. (2003), *Media Management. In the Age of Giants*, Iowa State Press, Ames.

Hofstede, G., Hofstede, G.J. (2007), *Kultury i organizacje*, Polskie Wydawnictwo Ekonomiczne, Warszawa.

Huntington, S. (1995), *Trzecia fala demokratyzacji*, Wydawnictwo Naukowe PWN, Warszawa.

Huxley, A. (2006), *Nowy wspaniały świat*, Wyd. Muza, Warszawa.

Iłowiecki, M. (2009), *Krzywe zwierciadło. O manipulacji w mediach*, Wyd. Archidiecezji Lubelskiej „Gaudium", Lublin.

Ind, N., (2001), *Wielkie kampanie reklamowe*, Wyd. Prószyński i S-ka, Warszawa.

Jakubowicz, K. (2007), *Media publiczne. Początek końca czy nowy początek*, Wydawnictwa Akademickie i Profesjonalne, Warszawa.

Jay, M. (1985), *Habermas and modernism*, [in:] *Habermas and modernity*, ed. R. Bernstein, UK: Polity, Oxford.

Jędrzejewski, S. (2003), *Radio w komunikacji społecznej. Rola i tendencje rozwojowe*, Profi-Press, Warszawa.

Jędrzejewski, S. (2010), *Radiofonia publiczna w Europie w erze cyfrowej*, Universitas, Kraków.

Jovanocic, B. (1982), *Selection and Evolution of Industry*, „Econometrica".

Kall, J. (1999), *Reklama*, PWE, Warszawa.

Kapuściński, R. (2003), *Autoportret reportera*, Wyd. Znak, Kraków.

Kapuściński, R. (2000), *Lapidarium IV*, Czytelnik, Warszawa.

Kapuściński, R. (2003), *Autoportret reportera*, Wyd. Znak, Kraków.

Kartezjusz, (1989), *Rozprawa o metodzie*, Wyd. PAX, Warszawa.

Kast, F.E., Rosenzweig, J.E. (1972), *Organization and Management. Environment and Perceived Environmental Uncertainty*, „Administrative Science Quarterly".

Kaye, J., Quinn, S. (2010), *Funding Journalism in the Digital Age. Business Models, Strategies, Issues and Trends*, Peter Lang, New York.

Keane, J. (1991), *The media and democracy*, Polity, Oxford.

Kepplinger, H.M. (1992), *Ereignismanagement. Wirklichkeit und Massenmedien*, Edition Interform, Zurich.

Kieżun, W. (1997), *Sprawne zarządzanie organizacją*, Wydawnictwo Szkoły Głównej Handlowej, Warszawa.

Kindler-Jaworska, E. (2000), *Przewodnik po telewizji cyfrowej*, Wyd. TVP SA Ośrodek Szkolenia – Akademia Telewizyjna, Warszawa.

Kirby, J., Mardsen, P., eds. (2005), *Connected Marketing, the Viral, Buzz and Word of Mouth Resolution*, Butterworth-Heinemann, Oxford.

Komunikowanie w perspektywie ekonomicznej i społecznej, (2001), ed. B. Jung, Oficyna Wydawnicza Szkoły Głównej Handlowej, Warszawa.

Kopaliński, W. (1983), *Słownik wyrazów obcych i zwrotów obcojęzycznych*, Wiedza Powszechna, Warszawa.

Kopaliński, W. (1994), *Słownik wyrazów obcych i zwrotów obcojęzycznych*, Wiedza Powszechna, Warszawa

Kostera, M. (2010), *Zarządzanie w XXI w. Jakość. Twórczość. Kultura*, Wydawnictwa Profesjonalne i Akademickie, Warszawa.

Kotarbiński, T. (1965), *Traktat o dobrej robocie*, Wyd. Ossolineum, Wrocław–Warszawa–Kraków.

Kotler, Ph. (1999), *Marketing. Analiza, planowanie, wdrażanie, kontrola*, Wyd. Felberg SJA, Warszawa.

Kowal, W. (1997), *Analiza sytuacji*, [in:] R. Kłeczek, W. Kowal, J. Woźniczka, *Strategiczne planowanie marketingowe*, ed. A. Styś, PWE, Warszawa.

Kowalczyk, J. (2005), *Szef firmy w systemie zarządzania przez jakość*, Wyd. CeDeWu, Warszawa.

Kowalski, T., Jung, B. (2006), *Media na rynku. Wprowadzenie do ekonomiki mediów*, Wyd. Akademickie i Profesjonalne, Warszawa.

Koźmiński, A.K. (1979), *Analiza systemowa organizacji*, Wydawnictwo Naukowe PWN, Warszawa.

Koźmiński, A.K. (2004), *Zarządzanie w czasach niepewności*, Wydawnictwo Naukowe PWN, Warszawa.

Koźmiński, A.K. (2004), *Zarządzanie*, Wydawnictwo Naukowe PWN, Warszawa.

Koźmiński, A.K., Obłój, K. (1989), *Zarys teorii równowagi organizacyjnej*, Wydawnictwo Naukowe PWN, Warszawa.

Krzyżanowski, L. (1992), *Podstawy nauk o organizacji i zarządzaniu*, Wydawnictwo Naukowe PWN, Warszawa.

Kunczik, M., Zipfel, A. (2000), *Wprowadzenie do nauki o dziennikarstwie i komunikowaniu*, Wydawnictwo Naukowe Scholar, Warszawa.

Küng, L. (2010), *Strategie zarządzania na rynku mediów*, Oficyna Wolters Kulwer, Warszawa.

Kurnal, J. ed. (1979), *Teoria organizacji i zarzadzania*, Wyd. PWE, Warszawa.

Kwarciak, B. (1997), *Co trzeba wiedzieć o reklamie*, Wyd. Profesjonalnej Szkoły Biznesu, Kraków.

Lane, J.E. (1993), *The Public Sector. Concepts, Models, Approaches*, Sage Publications, London.

Lange, A. (2000), *Economic Performance of the Public Radio-Television Systems in the European Union (1994–1999)*, Europejskie Obserwatorium Audiowizualne, Strasbourg.

Laszlo, E. (1978), *Systemowy obraz świata*, Państwowy Instytut Wydawniczy, Warszawa.

Lavine, J.M., Wackman, D.B. (1988), *Managing Media Organizations*, Longman, New York.

Leiss, W. (1990), *Social Communication in Advertising*, Routledge, London.

Lister, M., Dovey, J., Giddings, S., Grant, I., Kelly, K., (2009), *Nowe media. Wprowadzenie*, Wyd. Uniwersytetu Jagiellońskiego, Kraków.

Loska, K. (2001), *Dziedzictwo McLuhana – między nowoczesnością a ponowoczesnością*, Wyd. Rabid, Kraków.

Lytton, E.G. (1988), *Ostatnie dni Pompejów*, transl. L. Belmont, Wyd. Novum, Warszawa.

Łodziana-Grabowska, J. (1996), *Efektywność reklamy*, PWE, Warszawa.

Mackay, H. (1988), *Swim with the Sharks without Being Eaten Alive*, Fawcett Columbine Book, New York.

Malinowski B. (1958), *Szkice z teorii kultury*, Wyd. Książka i Wiedza, Warszawa.

Mallette, M.F., ed. (1996), *Zasady i tajniki dziennikarstwa. Podręcznik dla dziennikarzy Europy Środkowej i Wschodniej*, Warszawa.

Maslow, A.H. (1954), *Motivation and Personality*, Harper & Bros., New York.

Mattelart A., Siegelaub S. (1973), *Communication and Class Struggle*, International General, New York.

Mattelart A., Siegelaub S. (1979), *Communication and Class Struggle*, International General, New York.

Mattelart, A., Mattelart, M. (2001), *Teorie komunikacji*, Wydawnictwo PWN, Warszawa–Kraków.

McLuhan, M. (2001), *Wybór tekstów*, Wyd. Zysk i S-ka, Poznań.

McLuhan, M. (2004), *Zrozumieć media. Przedłużenie człowieka*, Wyd. Naukowo-Techniczne, Warszawa.

McQuail, D. (2007), *Teoria komunikowania masowego*, Wydawnictwo Naukowe PWN, Warszawa.

McQuail, D. (1992), *Media Performance: Mass Communication and the Public Interest*, Sage Publications, London.

McQuail, D. (1994), *Mass Communication Theory. An Introduction*, Sage Publications, London.

McQuail, D., Windahl, S. (1993), *Communications models for the study of mass communication*, Longman, London.

Measuring Media Content, Quality and Diversity, (2000), ed. R.G. Picard, Suomen Akademia, Turku.

Media i dziennikarstwo na przełomie wieków (1998), ed. J. Adamowski, Dom Wydawniczy Elipsa, Warszawa.

Media, komunikacja, biznes elektroniczny, (2001), ed. B. Jung, Wydawnictwo Difin, Warszawa.

Media, reklama i public relations w Polsce, (2005), ed. J. Olędzki, Oficyna Wydawnicza Aspra-Jr, Warszawa.

Merriles, W.J. (1983), *Anatomy of Price Leadership Challenge: An Evaluation of Pricing Strategies in the Australian Newspaper Industry*, „Journal of Industrial Economics", 31.

Michalczyk, S. (2000), *Media lokalne w systemie komunikowania*, Wydawnictwo Uniwersytetu Śląskiego, Katowice.

Mik, C. (1999), *Media masowe w europejskim prawie wspólnotowym*, Wyd. TNOiK, Toruń.

Mikułowski-Pomorski, J. (1980), *Badanie masowego komunikowania*, Państwowe Wydawnictwo Naukowe, Warszawa.

Molier (1951), *Mieszczanin szlachcicem*, transl. C. Jastrzębiec-Kozłowski, Wyd. M. Kot, Kraków.

Mondy, R.W., Holmes, R.E., Flippo, E.B. (1983), *Management: Concepts and Practices*, Allyn and Bacon, Boston.

Mrozowski, M. (2001), *Media masowe: władza, rozrywka i biznes*, Aspra-Jr, Warszawa.

Munk, N. (2004), *Fools rush*, [in:] *Steve Case, Jerry Levin and the unmaking of AOL Time Warner*, Harper Business, New York.

Negrine, R. (1994), *Politics and the Mass Media In Britain*, Routledge, London.

Nęcki, Z. (2005), *Negocjacje w biznesie*, Wydawnictwo Antykwa, Kraków.

Nierenberg, B. (2009), *Terroryści – mistrzowie zarządzania informacją*, [in:] *Media masowe wobec przemocy i terroryzmu*, eds. A. Kozieł, K. Gajlewicz, Wyd. Aspra-Jr, Warszawa.

Nierenberg, B. (2004), *Reklama jako element procesu komunikacji rynkowej*, Wyd. PAN Oddział w Katowicach i Wyższa Szkoła Zarządzania i Administracji w Opolu, Opole.

Nierenberg, B. (2007), *Publiczne przedsiębiorstwo medialne. Determinanty, systemy, modele*, Wydawnictwo Uniwersytetu Jagiellońskiego, Kraków.

Nierenberg, B. (2011), *Zarzadzanie mediami. Ujęcie systemowe*, Wyd. Uniwersytetu Jagiellońskiego, Kraków.

Nierenberg, B. et al. (2009), *Wiedza o reklamie*, Wydawnictwo Szkolne PWN, Bielsko-Biała.

Nieto Tamarago, A. (1968), *El concepto de empresa periodística*, Eunsa, Pamplona.

Nieto Tamarago, A. (1973), *La empresa periodística en España*, Eunsa, Pamplona.

Norberg, E.G. (1996), *Radio Programming: Tactics and Strategy*, Focal Press, Newton.

Nowińska, E. (2002), *Zwalczanie nieuczciwej reklamy*, Universitatis, Kraków.

Nowińska, E., Traple, E. (1994), *Prawo reklamy*, Wyd. Międzyuczelniany Instytut Wynalazczości i Ochrony Własności Intelektualnej Uniwersytetu Jagiellońskiego, Kraków.

Obłój, K. (1993), *Strategia sukcesu firmy*, PWE, Warszawa.

Ociepka, B. (2003), *Dla kogo telewizja? Model Publiczny w postkomunistycznej Europie środkowej*, Wydawnictwo Uniwersytetu Wrocławskiego, Wrocław.

Oleński, J. (2003), *Ekonomika informacji. Metody*, PWE, Warszawa.

Orwell, G. (2007), *1984*, Wyd. Propaganda, Poznań.

Orzechowski, E. (2009), *Dziś nawet żebrak musi być sprawnym menedżerem. O zarządzaniu kulturą i szkolnictwem wyższym*, Wyd. Attyka, Kraków.

Ouchie, W.G. (1981) *Theory Z. How American Business Can Meet the Japanese Challenge*, Addison-Wesley, Reading.

Owen, B.M. Wildman, S.S. (1992), *Video economics*, Harvard University Press, Cambridge.

Parsons, T. (2009), *System społeczny*, Nomos, Kraków.

Pember, D. (1974), *Mass Media in America*, Science Research Associates, New York.

Penc, J. (1996), *Decyzje w zarządzaniu*, Wyd. Profesjonalnej Szkoły Biznesu, Kraków.

Picard, R.G. (2010), *Value Creation and Future of News Organizations (Why and How Journalism Must Change to Remain Relevant in the Twenty-first Century)*, Media XXI, Barcelona/Sevilla.

Picard, R.G. (1989), *Media economics: Concepts and issues*, Sage, Newbury Park.

Picard, R.G. (2006), *Historical Trends and Patterns in Media Economics*, [in:] *Handbook of Media Management and Economics*, eds. A.B. Albarran, S.M. Chan-Olmsted, M.O. Wirth, Routledge, New York.

Platon (2002), *Państwo*, Wyd. DeAgostini Polska, Warszawa.

Postman, N. (1985), *Amusing Ourselves to Death. Public Discourse in the Age of Show Business*, Penguin, New York.

Powell, C.L., Persico, J.E. (1995), *My American Journey*, Random House, New York.

Prawelska-Skrzypek, G. (2003), *Polityka kulturalna polskich samorządów. Wybrane zagadnienia*, Wyd. Uniwersytetu Jagiellońskiego, Kraków.

Pringle, Ch.D., Jennings, D.F., Longenecker, J.G. (1988), *Managing Organizations: Functions and Behavior*, OH: Merrill, Columbus.

Pringle, P.K., Starr, M.F. (2006), *Electronic media management*, Focal Press, Burlington.

Problemy współczesnego zarządzania, (2003), ed. A. Matczewski, Wyd. Uniwersytetu Jagiellońskiego, Kraków.

Przybyłowski, K., Hartley, S.W., Kerin, R.A., Rudelius, W. (1998), *Marketing*, Wyd. ABC, Poznań.

Pszczołowski, T. (1978), *Mała encyklopedia prakseologii i teorii organizacji*, Wyd. Ossolineum, Wrocław.

Rheingold, H. (1996), *The Virtual Community. Homesteading on Electronic Frontier*, Addison-Wesley, Reading.

Rizutto, R.J. (2006), *Issues in Financial Management*, [in:] *Handbook of Media Management and Economics*, eds. A.B. Albarran, S.M. Chan-Olmsted, M.O. Wirth, Routledge, New York.

Russell, J.T., Lane, W.R. (2000), *Reklama według Ottona Kleppera*, Felberg SJA, Warszawa.

Rutkiewicz, I. (2003), *Jak być przyzwoitym w mediach*, Wyd. Ośrodek Szkolenia TVP SA, Warszawa.

Rynek audiowizualny w Polsce. Ocena i perspektywy, (2003), ed. J. Adamowski, Wyd. Aspra-Jr, Warszawa

Scherer, F.M. (1992), *Industrial Market Structure and Economic Performance*, Rand Mc Nally, Chicago 1980.

Schiller, H.I. (1969), *Mass Communications and American Empire*, Augustus Kelly, New York.

Schoderbek, P.P., Cosier, R.A., Aplin, J.C. (1988), *Management*, Harcourt Brace Jovanovich, San Diego.

Schretter, D. (2000), *Kształcenie w zakresie środków masowego przekazu w krajach Europy Zachodniej*, referat przewodniczącego Europejskiego Stowarzyszenia Edukacji Medialnej (AEEMA) wygłoszony 18 października 2000 r. w Warszawie podczas konferencji „Edukacja Medialna – potrzeba i wyzwanie przyszłości".

Sepstrup, P. (1994), *Transnationalization of Television in Western Europe*, London.

Shani, D., Chalasani, S. (1992), *Expoliting Niches Using Relationship Marketing*, „Journal of Consumer Marketing".

Shapiro, D.S. (2004), *Hey Big Media: The Jig Is up on Big Media Mergers*, „Banc of America Equity Research", July.

Shimbungaku, (1995), eds. N. Arai, M. Inaba, K. Katsura, Nihon Hyoronsha, Tokyo.

Siebert, F.S., Peterson, T., Schramm, W. (1956), *Four Theories of the Press*, University of Illinois Press, Urbana.

Simmons, G.F., Vazquez, C., Harris, Ph.R. (1996), *Komunikacja między kulturowa, zderzenia i spotkania*, Instytut Kultury, Warszawa.

Sklair, L. (2002), *Globalization: Capitalism and its alternatives*, Oxford University Press, Oxford.

Skoczek, T. (2004), *Telewizja publiczna*, Wydawnictwo Plus, Kraków.

Skrzypek, E. (2000), *Jakość i efektywność*, Wydawnictwo Uniwersytetu Marii Curie-Skłodowskiej w Lublinie, Lublin.

Smith, A. (1989), *Teoria uczuć moralnych*, Wydawnictwo PWN. Warszawa.

Smith, A.D. (1990), *Towards a Global Cuture*, „Theory Culture and Society" 7 (2/3).

Smith, A. (2003), *Badania nad naturą i przyczynami bogactwa narodów*, Wyd. DeAgostini, Warszawa.

Smythe, D.W. (1969), *On the political economy of communications*, „Journal Quarterly" 69 (3).

Sobczak, J. (2001), *Ustawa o radiofonii i telewizji: komentarz*, Oficyna Wydawnicza Ab initio, Kraków.

Sobczak, J. (2003), wypowiedź podczas konferencji „Rynek audiowizualny w Polsce – ocena i perspektywy", [in:] *Rynek audiowizualny w Polsce – ocena i perspektywy*, ed. J. Adamowski, Wyd. Oficyna Wydawnicza Aspra-Jr, Warszawa.

Sohn, A., LeBlanc Wicks, J., Lacy, S., Sylvie, G. (1999), *Media Management. A Case Approach*, Lawrence Erlbaum Associates, New York.

Sokołowska, S. (2009), *Organizacja i zarządzanie. Ujęcie teoretyczne*, Wydawnictwo Uniwersytetu Opolskiego, Opole.

Sorlin, P. (2001), *Mass media*, Wyd. Astrum, Wrocław.

Spannagel, J., Dworzecki, Z., Kisiel, J. (1994), *Zasady efektywnej reklamy*, Warszawa.

Sperber, A.M. (1986), *Murrow, his life and times*, Ferundlich, New York.

Splichal, S. (2003), *Principles of publicity and press freedom*, Rowman & Littlefield, Lanham.

Stiglitz, J.E. (2004), *Ekonomia sektora publicznego*, Wydawnictwo Naukowe PWN, Warszawa.

Strategia publicznego przedsiębiorstwa medialnego, ed. B. Nierenberg, (2006), Wyd. Radio Opole S.A., Opole.

Strategia rozwoju spółki Telewizja Polska SA 2002–2006, wstęp i opracowanie T. Skoczek, Prowincjonalna Oficyna Wydawnicza, Bochnia 2003.

Sznajder, A. (1993), *Sztuka promocji, czyli jak najlepiej zaprezentować siebie i swoją firmę*, Wyd. Businessman Book, Warszawa.

Sznajder, A. (1991), *Sztuka promocji*, Międzynarodowa Szkoła Menedżerów, Warszawa.

Sztucki, T. (1997), *Promocja, sztuka pozyskiwania nabywców*, Wyd. Placet, Warszawa.

Środki masowej informacji w Polsce po likwidacji cenzury (1990–2000), ed. J. Adamowski, Oficyna Wydawnicza Aspra, Warszawa 2000.

Tetelowska, I. (1972), *Informacja – odrębny gatunek dziennikarski*, [in:] *Szkice prasoznawcze*, eds. P. Dubiel, W. Pisarek, Kraków.

Thompson, B.J. (2001), *Media i nowoczesność. Społeczna teoria mediów*, Wydawnictwo Astrum, Wrocław.

Tirole, J. (1990), *The Theory of Industrial Organization*, MIT Press, Cambridge.

Transformacja systemów medialnych w krajach Europy Środkowo-Wschodniej po 1989 roku (2002), ed. B. Dobek-Ostrowska, Wyd. Uniwersytetu Wrocławskiego, Wrocław.

Trotta, R.J. (2003), *Translating Strategy into Shareholder Value. A Company-Wide Approach to Value Creation*, American Management Association, New York.

Weinberg, G.M. (1979), *Myślenie systemowe*, Wyd. Naukowo-Techniczne, Warszawa.

Weinberg, G.M., Weinberg, D. (1988), *General Principles of System Design*, Dorset House Publishing, New York.

Węglarczyk, B. (2010), *Stuxnęli Iran*, „Gazeta Wyborcza", nr 231.

White, R. (1997), *Reklama, czyli co to jest i jak się ją robi*, Business Press, Warszawa.

Woodruff, R.B., Gardial, S. (1996), *Know Your Customer. New Approaches to Understanding Customer Value and Satisfaction*, Blackwell Publisher, Malden.

Wren, D. (1987), *The Evolution of Management Theory*, Wiley, New York.

Wybrane systemy medialne (2008), ed. J. Adamowski, Wyd. Akademickie i Profesjonalne, Warszawa.

Zarządzanie. Teoria i Praktyka (2004), eds. A.K. Koźmiński, W. Piotrowski, Wydawnictwo Naukowe PWN, Warszawa.

Zieleniewski, J. (1969), *Organizacja i zarządzanie*, Wydawnictwo Naukowe PWN, Warszawa.

Zymonik, Z. (2002), *Koszty jakości w zarządzaniu przedsiębiorstwem*, Oficyna Wydawnicza Politechniki Wrocławskiej, Wrocław.

3. Articles

Ackoff, R.L. (1973), *O system pojęć systemowych*, „Prakseologia" 2.

Adamowski, J. (2002), *Transformacja rosyjskich środków masowej informacji*, [in:] *Transformacja systemów medialnych w krajach Europy Środkowo-Wschodniej po 1989 roku*, ed. B. Dobek-Ostrowska, Wyd. Uniwersytetu Wrocławskiego, Wrocław.

Albarran, A.B. (2006), *Historical Trends and Patterns in Media Management Research*, [in:] *Handbook of Media Management and Economics*, eds. A.B. Albarran, S.M. Chan-Olmsted, M.O. Wirth, Lawrence Erlbaum Associates, New York.

Amit, R., Zott, Ch. (2001), *Creation in E-business*, „Strategic Management Journal" 22.

Bajka, Z. (1994), *Krótka historia reklamy na świecie i w Polsce (I)*, „Aida Media", 6.

Bajomi-Lazar, P. (2002), *Transformacja mediów elektronicznych na Węgrzech*, [in:] *Transformacja systemów medialnych w krajach Europy Środkowo-Wschodniej po 1989 roku*, ed. B. Dobek-Ostrowska, Wyd. Uniwersytetu Wrocławskiego, Wrocław.

Bajomi-Lazar, P. (2002), *Wojna o media*, [in:] *Transformacja systemów medialnych w krajach Europy Środkowo-Wschodniej po 1989 roku*, ed. B. Dobek-Ostrowska, Wyd. Uniwersytetu Wrocławskiego, Wrocław.

Barry, J. (1995), *A historical postscript*, [in:] *Shifting the boundaries*, eds. D. Castiglione, L. Sharpe, University of Exeter Press, Exeter.

Beaud, P., Kaufmann, L. (2001), *Policing opinion: Elites, science, and popular opinion*, [in:] *Public opinion and democracy*, ed. S. Splichal, Hampton Press, Cresskill, New York.

Bertalanffy, L. von (1950) *The Theory of Open Systems in Physics and Biology*, „Science", nr 111.

Besanko, D., Dranove, D., Shanley, M. (2001), *Exploiting a Cost Advantage and Coping with a Cost Disadvantage*, „Management Sience" nr 2.

Chan-Olmsted, S.M., Chang, B.H. (2003), *Diversification strategy of global media conglomerates: Examining its patterns and determinants*, „Journal of Media Economics", 16.

Christensen, C.M., Raynor, M.E. (2003), *Why hard-nosed executives should care about management theory*, „Harvard Business Review".

Cuilenburg, J. von (2000), *On Measuring Media Competion and Media Diversity: Concepts, Theories and Methods*, [in:] *Measuring Media Content, Quality and Diversity*, ed. R.G. Piccard, Suomen Akademia, Turku.

Czarnecki, A. (1996), *Skuteczność reklamy*, cz. 1, „Marketing i rynek", nr 3.

Doliński, D. (1996), *Wojna na słowa*, „Aida", 9.

Donaldson, L. (1988), *The Ethereal Hand. Governance Theories of Justice and Liberty*, „Journal of Management".

Emmerich, V. (1999), *Prawo antymonopolowe*, [in:] *Prawo gospodarcze Unii Europejskiej*, ed. M.A. Dauses, red. wyd. polskiego R. Skubisz, Warszawa.

Freeman, R.E. Reed, D.L. (1983), *Stockholders and stakeholders: A new perspective on corporate governance*, „California Management Review", 25/3.

Hrvatin, S.B., Petkovič, B. (2005), *Własność medialna i jej oddziaływanie na niezależność oraz pluralizm mediów w Europie Południowo-Wschodniej i nowych krajach członkowskich Unii Europejskiej*, [in:] *Własność medialna i jej wpływ na pluralizm oraz niezależność mediów*, ed. B. Klimkiewicz, Wyd. Uniwersytetu Jagiellońskiego, Kraków.

Hunek, J.K. (1989), *Systemy wczesnego ostrzegania*, „Przegląd Organizacji", nr 5.

I.B. *Ach, zrobić to jeszcze raz*, „Aida Media" 1997, 4/35, s. 16, „Advertising Age" 1/1996.

Ingham, A.G. (1974), *The Ringelmann effect: Studies of group size and group performance*, „Journal of Experimental Social Psychology", 10.

Jovanocic, B. (1982), *Selection and Evolution of Industry*, „Econometrica", 50.

Kaplan, R.S., Norton, D.P. (2008), *Mastering the Management System*, „Harvard Business Review", 8(1).

Kostera, M. (2004), *Zarządzanie międzynarodowe i międzykulturowe*, [in:] *Zarządzanie: Teoria i praktyka*, eds. A.K. Koźmiński, W. Piotrowski, Wydawnictwo Naukowe PWN, Warszawa.

Kostera, M., Kownacki, S. (2004), *Kierowanie zachowaniami organizacyjnymi*, [in:] *Zarządzanie: Teoria i praktyka*, eds. A.K. Koźmiński, W. Piotrowski, Wydawnictwo Naukowe PWN, Warszawa.

Koźmiński, A.K. (2004), *Organizacja*, [in:] *Zarządzanie. Teoria i praktyka*, eds. A.K. Koźmiński, W. Piotrowski, Wydawnictwo Naukowe PWN, Warszawa

Kranenburg, H.L. van, Hogenbirk, A. (2006), *Issues in Market Structure* [in:] *Handbook of Media Management and Economics*, eds. A.B. Albarran, S.M. Chan-Olmsted, M.O. Wirth, Routledge, New York.

Lasswell, H. (1948), *The Structure and Function of Communication In Society*, [in:] ed. L. Bryson, *The Communication of Ideas*, Harper, New York.

Lawson-Borders, G. (2003), *Integrating new media and old media: Seven observations of convergence as a strategy for best practices in media organizations*, „International Journal of Media Management" 5(2).

Lazarsfeld, P., Merton, R. (1948), *Mass Communication. Popular Taste and Organized Social Action*, [in:] ed. L. Byrson, *The Communication of Ideas*, New York.

Levin, H.J. (1958), *Economic structure and the regulation of television*, „Quarterly Journal of Economics".

Lewin, K. (1947), *Channels of Group Life*, „Human Relations", vol. 1, 2.

Magretta, J. (1998), *The Power of Virtual Integration (an interview with Michael Dell)*, „Harvard Business Review", March/April.

Merklejn, I. (2008), *System medialny Japonii*, [in:] *Wybrane zagraniczne systemy medialne*, ed. J. Adamowski, Wyd. Akademickie i Profesjonalne, Warszawa.

Merriles, W.J. (1983), *Anatomy of Price Leadership Challenge: An Evaluation of Pricing Strategies in the Australian Newspaper Industry*, „Journal of Industrial Economics", 31.

Mierzejewska, B. (2001), *Metody badania mediów*, [in:] *Media, komunikacja, biznes elektroniczny*, red. B. Jung, Wyd. Difin, Warszawa.

Mierzejewska, B. (2001), *Polityka medialna*, [in:] *Media, komunikacja, biznes elektroniczny*, ed. B. Jung, Wyd. Difin, Warszawa.

Mierzejewska, B., Hollifeild, A. (2006), *Theoretical Approaches in Media Management Research* [in:] *Handbook of Media Management and Economics*, eds. A.B. Albarran, S.M. Chan-Olmsted, M.O. Wirth, Lawrence Erlbaum Associates, New York.

Misiak, E. (2003), *Pisk mrówki*, „Rzeczpospolita", 13.

Noelle-Neumann, E. (1974), The Spiral of Silence. A Theory of Public Opinion, „Journal of Communication", 24.

Nossiter, T. (1986), *British Television: A Mixed Economy*, „Journal of Communication".

Nowińska, E. (1996), *Reklama radiowa w świetle prawa*, Aida, 9.

Obłój, K., Trybuchowski, M. (2004), *Zarządzanie strategiczne*, [in:] *Zarządzanie. Teoria i Praktyka*, eds. A. K. Koźmiński, W. Piotrowski, Wydawnictwo Naukowe PWN, Warszawa.

Ociepka, B. (2002), *Czeskie media po rozpadzie Czechosłowacji*, [in:] *Transformacja systemów medialnych w krajach Europy Środkowo-Wschodniej po 1989 roku*, ed. B. Dobek--Ostrowska, Wyd. Uniwersytetu Wrocławskiego, Wrocław.

Ossowski, S. (1983), *Wzory nauk przyrodniczych w empirycznej socjologii*, [in:] *O osobliwościach nauk społecznych*, Wydawnictwo Naukowe PWN, Warszawa.

Otheguy, P. (1998), *Ramy prawne europejskiej polityki audiowizualnej: swobodny przepływ i wyzwania kulturowe*, [in:] *Telekomunikacja i media audiowizualne w Unii Europejskiej*, eds. M. Pelski, M.K. Szewczyk, Wyd. Instytut Europejski, Łódź.

Puppis, M. (2010), *Media Governance: A New Concept for the Analysis of Media Policy and Regulation*, „Communication, Culture & Critique" (3), International Communication Association.

Ravald, A., Grönross, C. (1996), *The Value Concept and Relationship Marketing*, „European Journal of Marketing" 30(2).

Ray, R.H. (1951), *Competition in the Newspaper Industry*, „Journal of Marketing".

Reddaway, W.B. (1963), *The economics of newspapers*, „Economic Journal".

Redmond, J.W. (2006), *Issues in Human Realtions Management*, [in:] *Handbook of Media Management and Economics*, eds. A.B. Albarran, S.M. Chan-Olmsted, M.O. Wirth, Routledge, New York.

Ringelmann, M. (1913), *Recherches sur les Moteurs Animé Travalis de l'Homme*, „Annales de l'Institut National Agronomique", 2 (12).

Rizutto, R.J. (2006,) *Issues in Financial Management*, [in:] *Handbook of Media Management and Economics*, ed. A.B. Albarran, S.M. Chan-Olmsted, M. O. Wirth, Routledge, New York.

Roventa-Frumusani, D. (2002), *System medialny w postkomunistycznej Rumunii*, [in:] *Transformacja systemów medialnych w krajach Europy Środkowo-Wschodniej po 1989 roku*, ed. B. Dobek-Ostrowska, Wyd. Uniwersytetu Wrocławskiego, Wrocław.

Rumelt, R. (1984), *Toward a Strategic Theory of the Firm*, [in:] *Competitive Strategic Management*, ed. R. Lamb, Prentice-Hall, New York.

Schlapp, H. (2002), *Etos współczesnego dziennikarstwa*, [in:] *Kultura i prawo. Materiały z II Międzynarodowej Konferencji na temat: Wolność mediów, Lublin, 18–19 maja 2000*, eds. J. Krukowski, O. Theisen, Wyd. Towarzystwo Naukowe KUL, Lublin.

Shani, D., Chalasani, S. (1992), *Expoliting Niches Using Relationship Marketing*, „Journal of Consumer Marketing".

Shapiro, D.S. (2004), *Hey Big Media: The Jig is up on Big Media Mergers*, „Banc of America Equity Research", July.

Shaver, D., Shaver, M.A. (2006), *Directions for Media Management Research in the 21st Century*, [in:] *Handbook of Media Management and Economics*, eds. A.B. Albarran, S. M. Chan-Olmsted, M. O. Wirth, Lawrence Erlbaum Associates, New York.

Smith, D. (1990), *Towards a Global Culture*, „Theory Culture and Society", vol. 7, 2–3.

Smythe, D.W. (1969), *On the political economy of communications*, „Journal Quarterly" 69(3).

Starck, K. (1998), *Groping towards ethics in transitioning press system. The case of Romania*, „Journal of Mass Media Ethics", 14.

Steiner, P.O. (1952, May), *Program patterns and preferences, and the workability of competition in radio broadcasting*, „Quarterly Journal of Economics".

Stiglitz, J.E. (1987), *Technological change, sunk costs and competition*, „Brookings Papers on Economic Activity", 3.

Sznajder, A. (2001), *Promocja w intrenecie*, [in:] *Media, komunikacja, biznes elektroniczny*, ed. B. Jung, Wyd. Difin, Warszawa.

Szulczewski, G. (2002), *Racjonalizm, etyka dyskursu i komunikacji jako nowa podstawa współczesnych postaci etyki biznesu*, raport z badań, SGH, Warszawa.

Świderski, J. (2002), *Radio i telewizja w Polsce po 1989 roku*, [in:] *Transformacja systemów medialnych w krajach Europy Środkowo-Wschodniej po 1989 roku*, ed. B. Dobek-Ostrowska, Wyd. Uniwersytetu Wrocławskiego, Wrocław.

Tsetsura, K. (2005), *Międzynarodowe doświadczenia z zakresu przejrzystości mediów*, [in:] *Media, reklama, public relations*, ed. J. Olędzki, Oficyna Wydawnicza Aspra Jr., Warszawa.

Turow, J. (1991), *The Challenge of Inference in Interinstitutional Research on Mass Communication*, „Communication Research", 18.

Wernerfelt, B. (1985), *A Resource-based View of the Firm*, „Strategic Management Journal" 5.

Węglarczyk, B. (2010), *Stuxnęli Iran*, „Gazeta Wyborcza", nr 231 z 2–3 października.

Williamson, O.E. (1979), *Transaction Cost Economies. The Governance of Contractual Relations*, „Journal of Law and Economics" 22.

Williamson, O.E. (1994), *Strategizing, Economizing and Economic Organization* [in:] *Fundamental Issues in Strategy*, eds. R.P. Rumelt, D.E. Schnedel, D.J. Teece, Harvard Business School, Boston.

Wren, D. (1987), *Management History: Issues and Ideas for Teaching and Research*, „Journal of Management".

Wright, P. (1987), *A Refinement of Porter's Strategies*, „Strategic Management Journal", 8(1).

4. Internet resources

http://www.press.pl/newsy/pokaz.php?id=24491
http://www.washingtonpost.com
http://www.fee.gov
http//www.pbs.org
http://www.cpb.org
http://www.bbcgovernors.co.uk/
http://news.bbc.co.uk/2/hi/uk_news/politics/3441181.stm
http://www.krrit.gov.pl/
http://www. cogweb.ucla.edu/Abstracts/Fauconnier
http://www.newsguild.org/mission/today.php
http://www.nytimes.com/2007/04/30/business/media/30blog.html?_r=3&hp&oref=slogin
    &oref=slogin
http://www.stat.gov.pl/opracowania_zbiorcze/maly_rocznik_stat/2005/
http://www.krrit.gov.pl/ (*Informacja o podstawowych problemach radiofonii i telewizji
    w 2005 roku*, KRRiT, marzec 2006)
http://www.krrit.gov.pl/bip/Portals/0/publikacje/analizy/Analiza2009_04.pdf
http://www.press.pl/newsy/pokaz.php?id=25463/
http://www.krrit.gov.pl/bip/Portals/0/sprawozdania/spr2008/inf2008.pdf
http://www.radio.opole.pl/
http://pl.ejo-online.eu/
http://www.prsa.com.pl/
http://www.mediaregionalne.pl/news.
http://www.pardon.pl/artykul/1496/ciezkie_zycie_nadwornego_blogera_onz
http://www.serwis.ro.com.pl/
http://www.sagepub.com/mcquail6/PDF/Chapter14.pdf
http://www.asahi.com/shimbun/honsya/j/sales.html
http://www.radiomerkury.pl/
http://info.youmiuri.co.jp/company/data/
http://www.wirtualnemedia.pl/article/2334894_Gazeta_Wyborcza_zapewnila_Ago-
    rze_54_przychodow_w_I_kw._2008.htm
http://antyweb.pl/google-konczy-z-cenzura-w-chinach-czy-to-koniec-google-cn/
http://www.polskatimes.pl/pap/385768,new-york-times-wprowadza-oplaty-za-pelny-do-
    step-do-wydania,id,t.html?cookie=1
http://archiwum.rp.pl/artykul/510110_Misja_czy_eksmisja.html

Lists of Tables, Figures and Charts

List of Tables

List of Figures

List of Charts

Technical editor
Anna Poinc-Chrabąszcz

Proofreader
Małgorzata Szul

Typesetter
Katarzyna Mróz-Jaskuła

Wydawnictwo Uniwersytetu Jagiellońskiego
Redakcja: ul. Michałowskiego 9/2, 31-126 Kraków
tel. 12-663-23-80, 12-663-23-82, fax 12-663-23-83